History Elided

THE MAVERICK BARRISTER

Surjya Kumar Misra

pencil

ISBN 978-93-5667-223-9
© Surjya Kumar Misra 2022
Published in India 2022 by Pencil

A brand of
One Point Six Technologies Pvt. Ltd.
123, Building J2, Shram Seva Premises,
Wadala Truck Terminal, Wadala (E)
Mumbai 400037, Maharashtra, INDIA
E connect@thepencilapp.com
W www.thepencilapp.com

All rights reserved worldwide

No part of this publication may be reproduced, stored in or introduced into a retrieval system, or transmitted, in any form, or by any means (electronic, mechanical, photocopying, recording or otherwise), without the prior written permission of the Publisher. Any person who commits an unauthorized act in relation to this publication can be liable to criminal prosecution and civil claims for damages.

DISCLAIMER: *The opinions expressed in this book are those of the authors and do not purport to reflect the views of the Publisher.*

Author biography

Prof (Dr.) SURJYA KUMAR MISRA is a Professor of Business Administration. He did his MBA from Frank Barton School of Business, USA, in 1977. Post MBA he has worked for various organizations in USA and India. In 1983 he started his career as a full-time Faculty of Business Administration and contributed in his own way to its development in the state of Odisha; which was at the nascent stage at the time. At a later time he joined the Sambalpur University MBA Department as a Professor and headed it subsequently. Thereafter, he became Professor and Principal of Institute of Management and Information Technology, Cuttack, a constituent College of BIju Pattnaik University of Technology. He went on to become the first Dean of the University afterwards. After superannuation from service, he still is involved with the development of management education in the state and the doctoral programs of various Universities.

Prof. Misra had started his research on Utkal Ratna Barrister Biswanath Misra from 1972 and had written many articles on him; which were published in various newspapers and magazines of the state. From 1977 different organizations started observing his birth and death anniversaries in big scale; which gave Prof. Misra the impetus to conduct further research on Barrister

Biswanath Misra and his activities on the unification movement of the estranged Oriya-speaking tracts and formation of Orissa as a separate state.

The present offer in the form of a book is only the reflection of Prof. Misra's tireless work to find out the humongous contributions of the maverick, peerless and fearless Barrister Biswanath Misra.

CONTENTS

Foreword

Utkal Sammilani (Utkal Conference) met for the sixteenth convention at Chakradharpur. It was an extremely disturbing and fiery assemblage of leaders of the conference. On one side was, Utkalmani Gopabandhu Das and his followers who wanted the Utkal Sammilani to be subsumed under Indian National Congress and fight for the freedom of the country under the leadership of Mr. Gandhi; and on the other side were Barrister Biswanath Misra, Bagmi Biswanath Kar, Brajasundar Das, Bichitrananda Das, etc., under the silent leadership of Utkal Gaurav Madhusudan Das who opposed the merger vehemently and stubbornly, as their main objective was to see the separate province of Orissa formed. The merger with Indian National Congress was not acceptable to the latter group, as it meant non-cooperation with the British Government. The basic objective for which Utkal Sammilani was formed was to have a separate province of Orissa; and it was not possible without the cooperation of the British Government. The great divide was created in Utkal Sammilani because of clash of objectives of the two groups. The clash got to such a level that it became irreversible and opposers like Barrister Biswanath and others left the Sammilani for good. Even Madhusudan Das quietly sequestered himself from the activities of it. As a matter of fact, the Utkal Sammilani was also pushed to the backseat and became almost inactive.

Biswanath had joined the Utkal Sammilani, as a student volunteer from Ravenshaw College in its inception year in 1903. However, from 1904 he continued with the Sammilani, as a regular member till he quit it in 1921 under unusual circumstances. He was extremely active and regular in the conventions of Utkal Sammilani. His proposals in it had massive impact on the ongoing situations of the segregated Oriya-speaking tracts of the time and the formation of a separate Orissa state. His efforts through the Utkal Sammilani later bore fruits in all aspects including the development of higher education, Law and Engineering education of Orissa, a division under Bengal then. He too was the pioneer of bringing M.A. and science education into the state.

He was elected to the Central Legislative Assembly as a Member for three times from 1922 to 1933. He was an exceedingly fructuous and a leading legislator because of his arguments on the floor of the House. His arguments on Salt Taxation, Indian Mines Bill, Indian Military Academy, Employment of Oriyas in Railways, and Acts 145 and 146 etc., were milestone events in the Assembly. All those apart, he was more popular and well known as "Mr. Orissa." The reason for it was absolutely apt. Any opportunity he got in the House, he unfailingly harped at the unification of segregated Oriya-speaking tracts and formation of a separate state for Orissa. In those contexts, his lectures always centered on Orissa's history, maritime activities and coastal defense system, etc. The fellow Members of the Assembly used to hear him with rapt attention and got mesmerized by his eloquence. No wonder, they termed him as "Mr. Orissa."

Barrister Biswanath proved his mettle as "Mr. Orissa" all along his active period through his deeds in all facades of life. On September 12, 1933 when the Shimla session of the Central Legislative Assembly was on, Barrister Misra suffered a serious cardiac infarction after delivering a hyperactive talk on the Indian Military Academy to reveal the ill intentions of the British Government. Six days later on 19th September he succumbed to it and passed away in distant Shimla, far away from his near and dear ones at his home in Cuttack.

His sudden and sad demise had brought the Central Legislative Assembly to a standstill and all the Members were in deep shock and grief. The very next day a special session was called for in the Assembly to mourn the passing away of Barrister Misra. The members, irrespective of affiliation, praised the departed soul with bountiful of eulogies. In all the flowing tributes, the key element highlighted was his untiring efforts for the formation of a separate Orissa state. All of them in unison regretted that a man who sacrificed all the comforts and luxuries of life and the pleasure of being a patriarch, just to see the fructification of his ultimate dream of Orissa being a separate state, sadly departed untimely and so suddenly, right before his dream was about to become a reality. They all openly vouched that nothing could be more painful and distressing than such remorseful news.

Of all the tributes that came out of the mouths of the Members, the one from Joseph Bhore, the Leader of the House, has been quoted below.

He had said, "Death has again removed with tragic suddenness yet another sitting Member of this Assembly. Mr. B. N. Misra was, I believe, a Member of the first Assembly and also of the third Assembly. I personally will remember him best for his ardent advocacy of the claims of Orissa, his own home. Unhappily he has not been spared to see what we hope will be the fruition of his desires. It will be unnecessary for me to say much about one who was in such recent touch with us all. I need only say that his quiet unassuming presence made him liked by everyone with whom he came in contact. May I ask you, Sir, to convey to his relatives our deep sympathy with them in their bereavement?"

Utkal Ratna Barrister Biswanath Misra was a man of such great glorious standing that he was revered by all and sundry of the time for his high-mindedness, wisdom and selflessness for the cause of Orissa, as well as the nation. His relentless efforts could bolster the movement for unification of the sequestered parts of Orissa; which ultimately resulted in the formation of a separate Orissa state. Unfortunately the present day Orissa historians have neither given him his due place in the history of the state nor have given him his due respect as a great Oriya. The greatest travesty is that some present stalwarts of the state shamelessly proclaim that they even don't know him. What could be more unfortunate and shocking than that? It is nothing but the lack of respect for superiors and consequent lackadaisical attitude towards the respectable.

Acknowledgements

I honestly confess from the bottom of my heart that it was not an easy task to attempt writing the biography of a luminary like Utkal Ratna Barrister Biswanath Misra. However, gathering courage and getting encouraged by friends and relatives from all around, I have ventured into the seemingly impossible task of making it possible. I am thankful to all those well-wishers who encouraged me to delve into the project.

My first and foremost supporting crutch in this humble attempt was Late Manmohan Misra's biographical opus "Jati Prana Sindhura Aadya Taranga." I cannot but thank Late Misra from the bottom of my heart and openly confess my indebtedness to him for being the guiding light to my attempt at writing this book.

Secondly, I am unfathomably indebted to Mr. Barnaby Bryan, Middle Temple Inn Archive, for helping me out with all the documents relating to Biswanath Misra's Middle Temple stay and Bar-at-Law education, without which a lot about Biswanath's background could not have been revealed.

Thirdly, and most importantly, my heartfelt gratitude to all my family members, peers, teachers and students who have helped me at different stages of writing the book.

I specially thank my wife, Smt. Annapurna Mishra, for having gone through the entire manuscript and giving her invaluable suggestions at every step.

Last but not least, bountiful thanks to my nephew, Er. Manmohan Dash for providing all the technical assistance in the production stage; which has made the book possible to see the light of the day.

HISTORY THAT IS LOST

What is history? The answer is, facts that have really taken place in the past. Events, characters involved in the events and their activities have been all real and have really happened. These are neither fictitious nor mental fabrications. If they are otherwise, they could be myths, fictions or part of novel writing. Historical subject is fact-based. Facts are made available for historical writings directly or indirectly. The indirectly available facts are also derived ultimately from directly available facts. Without facts and truth, history cannot be considered as history. At best, it can be treated as a story fabricated by a man's mind. In other words, mentally fabricated lies cannot be the foundation of history; and contents of such books can never be treated as history. Historical revelations thus obtained, are nothing but false propagandas in the name of history.

A lot of knowledgeable people these days seem to be getting worried about such travesty of history. And many of them feel that the history of Orissa has not been written properly. They feel that a lot of its contents have been based on hearsay and rumors. A deeper investigation into Orissa's historical representations reveals that a lot of greats who have contributed immensely to the protection of Oriya as a language and formation of Orissa as a separate state have not found their places in the written history of Orissa. Some of them have made mammoth exemplary contributions at the state and national levels; but they have unfortunately found no mention in the written history of Orissa, as if the historians had never heard of them, or even worse, did not know them. Such lackadaisical attitude of the historians is not only extremely hapless but also regrettable. Honestly history is the true reflection of the identity of a race or nation. If history is incomplete or not based on facts, then such history is crippled and unreliable. It is peremptory that such history be rewritten; and that again, based on intense research findings. Hearsay be abrogated altogether when it comes to recording historical events, historical persons or history itself.

In this context, an example from Orissa's history can be referred to. History of Orissa contains many anecdotes of persons who have struggled all their lives for unification of Orissa by raising the demands for amalgamation of the estranged Oriya-speaking tracts and making Orissa a separate state; but there are some others who have been ignored by the history writers despite their contributions in this regard being humongous; and sometimes even the persons mentioned in the books of history have been overly eulogized without any supporting facts or facts contrary to the claims made. Surprisingly the super contributors to the cause have vanished from Orissa's written history. Whether their disappearance was part of ignorance of the writer or a deliberate attempt, cannot be found out now. However, a probe into it is certainly justifiable. Interestingly, a lot of highly educated elites of today even do not recognize them when their names are mentioned. Such ignorance of these people cannot be ascribed to their lack of information, may be it is all purpose-full and deliberate. In fact, it indicates how elaborately our history has been written and how much content-based it is. Underneath, such a great person has been brought up for discussion whose contributions for formation of Orissa as a separate state have been gargantuan; but incidentally he has been lost from the pages of Orissa's history.

Utkal Ratna Barrister Biswanath Misra was the person. He was born to Kulamani Misra and Radhika Devi, who were almost in indigence, at Nua Someswarpur village near Sakshi Gopal adjacent to Jagannath Puri. Despite the hard-pressed struggle for livelihood, after completing his education in the village chatshali (village elementary school), he joined for his primary education in Beraboi, a place almost 12 kilometers away from his village; which he had to walk both ways daily. Thereafter, he was scheduled to join Puri Zilla School for his high school education. A big stumbling block came on his way at that point, as the Brahman Samaj vehemently objected to Biswanath's pursuance of English education. It was considered blasphemous at the time for a Sashan Brahman to pursue English education. However, Biswanath's insistence and father Kulamani's persistence could make it happen. With great difficulty Kulamani was able to arrange twenty rupees as penalty for the purpose; which was deposited with the Brahman Samaj to get a positive nod from it for the purpose. Biswanath was able to join Puri Zilla School. He passed his Entrance Examination (the school final) in 1902 from there winning a scholarship for his meritorious performance. That helped and prompted him to pursue his college education at Ravenshaw College, Cuttack. He passed his FA from there, again in flying colors, in the year 1904. Thereafter, under the guidance of Utkal Gaurav Madhusudan Das, he went to Rasolkonda (today's Bhanjanagar) in Ghumusar, and joined as an Oriya Teacher in Rasolkonda Training School to teach the Ubhay Bhasha Prabina (both language expert) teacher-students. His job was to give right knowledge of Oriya to these students. Need it be mentioned here that it was the time when Ganjam district, which included Rasolkonda, was in Madras presidency – hence an estranged Oriya-speaking tract of Orissa.

BISWANATH AND PLEADERSHIP

Biswanath, as a teacher, felt that teaching was not empowering him sufficiently to dispense justice to the Oriyas in matters of their rights in this estranged tract. He decided to go to Madras for his education in Pleadership. After its completion he joined the Aska Bar and started practicing law there in 1906. He could have done the same in a more prosperous manner at Cuttack by coming to the Orissa Division; but he chose Aska as his place of work since the pain of the Oriyas in the estranged Oriya-speaking tracts always caused serious mental agony in him. His first remarkable contribution there, was to obtain official permission to use Oriya language in the courts of Ganjam for carrying out arguments and filing petitions. Prior to that, they could be done only in English and Telugu. In this, Sri Harihara Panda helped him immensely. "Star of Utkal" eulogized Biswanath's efforts in superlatives. However, Telugu clients rejected Biswanath to begin with, who distanced themselves from him; but sooner than later they came back and flocked around him because of his humane behavior and amicability.

BISWANATH AND BAR-AT-LAW

Biswanath was quite excited with his success in Aska; but his inquisitive mind could not stay quiet. His quest for higher education made him restless. Those were the times when there was no Oriya barrister and no Oriya had ventured into it either. To be a barrister was the greatest aspiration and dream of any member of an educated elite family in India then. Biswanath by character was a knowledge hankering high-spirited person. No wonder, he started dreaming about Bar-at-Law education day in and day out. Not only had he dreamed about it, he also started putting his relentless efforts in that direction to accomplish his objective. As a stepping-stone, he passed his 'Public Examination' in October of 1908 from Calcutta University. By dint of his tireless efforts he got admission for Bar-at-Law in Gray's Inn, London; but he could not reach London in time. The reason for that was worth observing and exemplary. It was the epitome of a son's veneration for his father. Before leaving for London, Biswanath went to his father to obtain his permission for undertaking the voyage. However, like all traditional conservative Indian fathers, Kulamani also denied permission to Biswanath to go to a foreign soil so far away. He categorically said that Biswanath would not go abroad as long as he (Kulamani) was alive. An obedient son, Biswanath, made his journey back to Aska without offering a single word of dissension. Time rolled on and exactly after four months, father Kulamani passed away. The tireless Biswanath started his endeavors to pursue his Bar-at-Law again. He was successful in his efforts and got admitted in Middle Temple Inn in London in the following session. It was a great experience for him, as amongst many stalwarts of the time, Sri Vallabhai Patel also turned out to be his classmate in the same Inn and in the same session. After spending two years of successful academic life from 1910 to 1912, they both cleared the Bar-at-Law requirements and were called to the Bar on the same day on 27th January 1913. Biswanath Misra not only became the first Oriya Barrister, he became the only Barrister of Orissa of the time.

BISWANATH AND LONDON

In 1912 after completion of his Bar-at-Law, Biswanath came back to India. However, towards the fag end of 1912, he again went to London to go through the rituals of attending the "Call to the Bar" formalities. After formally declared as a Barrister, he was nominated as a King's Counsel and in that capacity met King George V shaking hands with him. Even at that occasion he did not spare the opportunity to make the King aware of Orissa's problems and why it needed to be a separate state. During his stay at London he had accomplished two more milestone achievements. He could impress upon Mr. Mac Callum Scott, MP, House of Commons, and Mr. E.S. Montague, the Under Secretary of State, about the dire needs of Orissa with regard to the problems of the estranged Oriya-speaking tracts and the formation of a separate state for Orissa. In those regards, he could also evince positive opinions from both. Another feather in his cap was his deep research undertaken in British museum to write "A Short History of Ancient Utkal," the manuscript of which got lost or purloined by some ambitious writers working for him due to his untimely sudden demise. No further information could be made available about it; and even today it is untraceable.

BARRISTER BISWANATH ON HIS WAY BACK TO INDIA

In the month of July 1912 Biswanath Misra returned to India from London after successful completion of his Bar-at-Law. It used to take almost a month to come to India from London by sea route, the only route available then. Before undertaking his return journey, he had written a letter to Gopabandhu Das stating that after reaching India, he would first go to Satyabadi and meet him; and thereafter he would go anywhere. The letter had created sensation all over the Satyabadi area, as a London-returned local person was coming back to his birthplace. All the people of the area had become genuinely curious to find a person returning from London. Their curiosity further got aggravated when Gopabandhu out of pun had told his students that a person from our area was returning from London turning into a foreigner, he would be wearing foreign clothings, talking like the Britishers, and eating with spoon and fork. Such remark from a person like Gopabandhu created even more curiosity in the people of Sakshigopal area.

Biswanath after returning to India took a passenger train from Howrah for his journey to Sakshigopal. His intention was to travel during daytime in Orissa so that he could meet all his old acquaintances at the different stations where the train was scheduled to stop. From Jaleswar, as soon as the train entered Orissa, all the stations were filled with hordes of people to get a glimpse of the first Barrister of Orissa. Everyone expected a suited and booted barrister to be travelling in the train; but they were amazed to see a person wearing dhoti and kurta with the simplest manners instead. A lot of his old friends from Utkal Sammilani met and greeted him at the stations of Jaleswar, Baleswar, Bhadrak, Jajpur, etc. When the train arrived at Cuttack, Madhusudan Das, Brajasundar Das, Biswanath Kar, and many new and old pleaders joined the bandwagon in welcoming and greeting Barrister Biswanath. After going through the welcoming sessions at different railway stations, finally, he reached Sakshigopal. On arrival at Sakshigopal, he was greeted and welcomed by Gopabandhu Das, Nilakantha Das and Acharya Harihar, etc. An interesting incident took place there. Some of the students of Satyabadi Bana Vidyalaya, who were deputed by Gopabandhu to receive Biswanath from the train, not finding the westernly clad Biswanath, as described by Gopabandhu, came back to him and said that Barrister Biswanath probably did not come by that train. They further said that they had looked for him in all the bogies of the train; but they could not find any person who was dressed like the Britishers, as had been said by Gopabandhu. Gopabandhu had a hearty laugh and pointed out at the dhoti and kurta clad Biswanath to the boys. The boys were flabbergasted at the sight of the London-returned pure native gentleman.

At lunchtime, following the tradition of Satyabadi, Biswanath sat on the floor along with all the others including the students and ate his lunch with them from plates made out of leaves. Afterwards he enlightened the students by delivering a speech on the British lifestyle and English manners. The speech was highly motivating; and later led to the eventual creation of a students' union (sammilani) in 1914, during the tenth session of Utkal Sammilani held at Puri. Even in that session a committee was constituted to evaluate the need of establishing a permanent students' union.

After visiting Satyabadi, Biswanath went to Aska to see his wife and children. The very next day he went to Berhampur to attend a welcome meet arranged in his honor. After completing the string of felicitation meets over the next few days, he started his hunt for professional engagement. He chose Calcutta High Court for pursuing his legal practice.

Vyasa Kavi Fakir Mohan Senapati on the occasion of Barrister Misra's joining the Calcutta High Court, wrote a poem in Oriya in his book "Utkal Bhramana"; a translation of which has been attempted below:

Well Mr. B.N.Misra good-bye, good-bye,
With a good example, you opened everyone's eyes.
The shrewd pilgrim-agent would go to London,
And achieve what has never been done.
Pray you earnestly, keep the Oriya flag aloft,
Through your deeds in the High Court,
I say Mr. Misra again good-bye
Never forget your motherland's pitiable cry,

Wishing you for all success in the High Court
Be a Barrister with the greatest forte.

Sri Padma Charan Pattnaik in the same manner wrote a
poem in "Utkal Sahitya" published in May 1913; the
translation of which again has been attempted underneath:

Welcome home O' jeweled son of the nation,
We all together welcome you in one tone.
You held your aim high with intrepidity and discipline,
You accomplished your goal as per your design.
O' national hero, you have returned home with grace,
A pronounced ordeal you passed with great finesse.
Worked like a great saint with an unyielding heart,
You fulfilled your dreams facing dourly life's test.
Being oblivious of the social torture and torments,
You could accomplish glory with valor and courage.
With accomplishments unparalleled in the state,
You could paint my Utkal in a new shade.
For ages to come, your dedication will be adored,
Sons and daughters of Utkal, in stupor, will get aroused.
Your name will stay alive forever in every Utkal home,

Hence, my obeisance again to your excellence, O' Utkal
icon.

UTKAL RATNA AND BISWANATH

To make the return of Orissa's First Barrister Mr. Biswanath Misra to India memorable, Pundit Sri Nilamani Vidyaratna wrote a book titled "Samudra Jatrara Bichara" (Thought on a Sea Voyage) in 1913. The main objective of the book was to bring reformation in the society. To express his thoughts in the book, he used the ideology of Barrister Biswanath Misra as his main doctrine. In 1914/15 Sri Vidyaratna called for a meeting of the Pundits at Chikiti and bestowed the title "Utkal Ratna" on Barrister Biswanath Misra to the cheer and happiness of all present there. All the people gathered there hailed it as one of the best things to happen in the segregated Orissa.

BISWANATH THE REFORMER

After coming back from London, Biswanath, along with his entire family, was banished by the Brahman society along with his entire family; and had to undergo a lot of social torture because of his journey to a foreign soil. However, despite being castigated from the society with family en masse, he never complained about the villagers or the brahman society. That was the kind of a person he was, who never said a word of loathing against his villagers. An apt example in this respect can be given here to vouch for this claim. It was the occasion of the marriage of his niece. The groom was from the eminent Brahma family of Kashipur (near Nirakarpur railway station). On the day of marriage, the groom's procession was coming to the village with a lot of pomp and ceremony, playing the bands and bursting firecrackers. It became an eyesore for the villagers who mobbed up with sticks and bamboos attacking the groom's party. Biswanath, however maintaining his cool, requested and prayed the groom's party not to indulge in any kind of retaliation or retaliatory activities in spite of the villagers' vandalism. The groom's party was mad with anger; but maintained its calm on the request of Barrister Biswanath. The villagers seized all the procession decorative materials from the groom's party and locked them in the temple premises. The village chowkidar reported the matter in the Satyabadi Police Station. The Police Officer-in-Charge had to come to Nua Someswarpur to maintain peace and started the process of arresting the vandals. He came to Biswanath and informed that he was arresting the vandal villagers and taking them to the police station. It hurt the generous hearted Biswanath badly. He told the Police Officer that it was the day of her niece's marriage and he would look forward to the blessings of all the villagers. If he would arrest some of the villagers, their families would be extremely sad and morose. He further added that there was no fault on their part. They had only tried to protect the basic traditions of the village. Instead of seeing them getting arrested, he would look forward to getting their blessings for her niece's happiness and the happiness of her family members, out of wedlock. Such an attitude of Biswanath surprised the elderly members of the village and their hearts were filled with penance and sympathy for him. They forgot the last twelve years' castigation of Biswanath's family; and on the contrary accepted his invitation to join the marriage feast. The police officer was also invited to the party who was reluctant to join it; but finding the happiness of the villagers and the others present there, he also did not mind to be a part of it. All the villagers out of gratification exulted "Hari Bol" (Hail God) in unison.

Such was the character of Biswanath. He never had any hatred for the village lifestyle nor had any opposition for the traditions. He was only a highly ambitious, highly educated Oriya and Orissa-loving saint.

The kind of severe and harsh treatment he was meted out at the hands of his own villagers bore no parallel in the history of any other London-returned Oriya. Despite the persecution, he never reacted at the villagers or said harsh words to them. In the heart of hearts he was a social reformer; but he never ill-treated or showed disrespect to the conservative society. He never made rasping puns of the orthodox in the society. He always believed in rooting out orthodoxy and conservatism; but never raised his swords against the orthodox. In his life he had exemplified the above statement on numerous occasions. A few in light of the above are laid down below borrowing instances from his illustrious life.

Pundit Gopabandhu who was only a year older than Biswanath, was an inhabitant of a village close by. Biswanath always respected Gopabandhu as his own elder brother and carried out his orders, at least, in the social sphere and activities. Gopabandhu brought in an alliance proposal for Biswanath's eldest daughter, Sati Devi. The proposed groom to be was Gobind Tripathy. Gobind was a sasani brahman and a brilliant student academically; but his only disqualification was that he was a widower. He had already married to Revati, the younger sister of Pundit Lingaraj Misra who was a great intellectual; and later became the Education Minister of Orissa. Not only was Gobind married to her, but also had fathered an infant son. Revati had passed away at the age of only fifteen while delivering the child. The baby had been gifted to Revati's elder sister Sevati who had just turned a widow. At the time Gobind's proposal was brought in, he was the best student of B.A.(Hons.) in English at Ravenshaw College, Cuttack. Later he passed

M.A. in English as the topper from Patna University. Biswanath himself was a knowledge seeker and a great admirer of brilliant students. He accepted the proposal of Gopabandhu despite Gobind being a widower. At that time accepting an alliance with a widower was an unacceptable practice in the society. It was a great foot forward on the part of Barrister Biswanath in his attempts to reform the society. Castigated by the bramhan society earlier for years, Biswanath again took a bold step. Mentally he was an out and out social reformer; but he never objected to the social practices in vogue or went against the people who practiced them. However, he himself, in conduct of his own lifestyle, was guided by logic, knowledge and intelligence.

He was highly independent-minded and consciously always put his efforts for social independence of the women folks. Interestingly, instead of trying out his ideas on the society, he always tried them out at home and on his family members. An example of it was seen in the thirteenth session of Utkal Sammilani held in 1918 at Idgah Field in Cuttack. This meeting was presided over by Fakir Mohan Senapati. During that period women's education had hardly spread in the country. Biswanath was the seconder of the first resolution in that session. However, the most exciting aspect of that meeting was Biswanath taking his seat alongside his wife, Kamala Devi, on the dais. That was an unheard happening of the time and obviously became a very controversial matter. The orthodox Brahmins of Puri after coming to know about it, made a big issue of it. They put their palms over their heads in disgust and commented in a vilified tone that Biswanath had committed a sin by going to London and as if that was not enough, he had put his wife, a daughter-in-law of the village, on the dais in the public. Nothing could be more heinous than that. But he was Biswanath, after twelve years of castigation from the society; he again resorted fearlessly to something that he believed in. The critical and vilifying comments of the brahman samaj did not bother him. He just blew them away with a puff of air; but he, as his nature was, never protested against it. He was a man of iron will and did whatever he felt was right, despite all the odds that were likely to come on his way. He strongly believed in the societal progress of the women and always wanted them to take the same strides as men. He always had faith in himself and never regretted for whatever steps he had taken. He was convinced that reforms in the social practices were bound to come and necessary steps towards those must be undertaken.

Another interesting reform also started at his home. At present a girl or woman driving a car or riding a bike has become such a common occurrence; but in 1970s not many girls were riding a bike (bicycle) to even their schools or colleges. Interestingly though, Biswanath's youngest daughter who passed away at the age of 93 years in 2020, rode a bicycle to her school in those days of Cuttack. These were only a few of the incidents that glaringly reflected Barrister Biswanath Misra's progressive thinking and broad-minded attitude.

BISWANATH AND UTKAL SAMMILANI

In 1903 'Utkal Sammilani,' the brainchild of Utkal Gaurav Madhusudan Das, was born in Cuttack. The main objective of the organization was to awaken Oriya pride and bring all the Oriya-speaking segregated tracts together under one administration. During that period Orissa was a Division, and only Cuttack, Puri and Balasore were under it. The Orissa Division was under the administrative control of Bengal province. In the same way the Oriya-speaking Ganjam, Ghumusar and Koraput were under the Madras Presidency and Sambalpur, Bolangir and other western Oriya-speaking tracts were under Central Province.

Biswanath was a student of FA in Ravenshaw College in 1903. He was strongly influenced by the call of Madhusudan Das and joined the Utkal Sammilani as a student volunteer. He proved himself as a very active worker in the inaugural session of Utkal Sammilani.

In 1904 after passing out FA in flying colors, he left for Rasolkonda (present Bhanjanagar) to join Rasolkonda Training School as an Oriya Teacher (Oriya Pundit) under the advice and encouragement of Madhusudan Das to protect Oriya language and its originality, saving it from the influence of Telugu. In the capacity of an Oriya Pundit, he was made responsible to teach the Ubhay Bhasha Pravin (Both Language Expert) teacher-students. In the same year, December 1904, the Second Session of Utkal Sammilani took place. In real terms, the Sammilani started functioning from that year. Interestingly, the session; which was held at Cuttack met with such an ego clash that it was about to fizzle out even before it had started. However, it was saved from a collapsing debacle because of Biswanath's emotional and brilliant intervention. Due to his efforts normalcy could be restored and the session could become functional. The incident, which led to the unwarranted situation, has been laid down below:

A proposal about bringing all the segregated Oriya-speaking tracts under one political administration was brought up in the Sammilani. Biswanath using his meager experience, as an Oriya pundit, supported the proposal and went on to narrate the painful situations and circumstances the Ganjam Oriyas were in. His speeches invariably touched the hearts of the people, as he always spoke from his inner core. Besides, his speeches were always based on research findings and facts. The proposal of putting all the Oriya-speaking segregated tracts under one political administration was accepted by all present in the convention; but another issue made the whole meet land up in a conflicting situation. Interestingly, the conflict came up due to the diverse views of the doyens, Madhusudan Das and Gopabandhu Das on the issue. Gopabandhu wanted that all the Oriya-speaking tracts including Sambalpur be merged and put under the

Central Province. However, Madhusudan Das did not subscribe to that view. He was of the opinion that Sambalpur, Ganjam and all other segregated Oriya-speaking tracts be put under Bengal. The conflict at one time became so intense that the convention was about to be dissolved even before it had taken a baby-step forward. At that point Biswanath saved the situation with his astute approach. He expressed himself in a blazing tone with great emotion based on research findings. His effective speech changed the course of the meeting and brought back members with diverse views belonging to the two camps to one platform successfully. Biswanath said that the Oriya-speaking large geographic expanse, which had spread at one time from Mahendragiri to Meghasan, did not entail the discussion whether the tracts would go under Bengal or Central Province at that juncture. It could be discussed later. The entire delegation from Ganjam stood behind the young Biswanath and praised his act with great satisfaction. Biswanath's emotional intervention saved the Sammilani from a great debacle, and rest of the session could progress smoothly. It was the first time all assembled there could think of a separate state for Orissa based on language.

The second resolution in the same session was that the Utkal Sammilani was expressing its heartfelt gratitude to the Honorable Viceroy for his welfare proposal to keep the entire Oriya-speaking areas under one political administration. Sri Harihar Panda of Ganjam proposed the resolution, Sri Nilamani Vidyaratna approved it and Ganjam's Pundit Sri Biswanath Misra supported it.

In April 1906 Utkal Sammilani held its Third Session at Balasore. In that convention Sri Biswanath Misra was the supporter of the second and fifth proposals. The second proposal was brought forward to extend hearty thanks to the representatives of the King of India for their measures to include the Utkal Pradesh and Sambalpur under one political administration; and in the resolution it was further expected very earnestly that Ganjam along with all other Oriya-speaking tracts would be brought under one political administration soon.

The fifth resolution was meant to look after the work of executive committees established at different places in Utkal Pradesh to carry out their activities in soil testing, finding out what kind of soil would be good for what kind of plantation, and what kind of manures would be appropriate for the different kinds of plantations; and to oversee the work of Inspectors Government was intending to appoint for the purpose. The Sammilani felt that it was an opportunity and the Inspectors should be offered all cooperation; and under their advice quality and proper seeds be distributed to the farmers. That apart, the Sammilani lauded the Government's efforts to train the sons of the farmers in the Cuttack Model Agriculture Center. The Sammilani also expressed its intent to help them financially; and further appreciated the Government's efforts in that direction too. In that regard, the Sammilani felt that the efforts of the government not only deserved attention; but also they needed to be supported; which the Sammilani took upon itself as its responsibility.

In December 1906 the Sammilani met for its Fourth Convention at Berhampur. Since that session was held at Berhampur, the Ganjam members were basically organizers. The young and energetic Biswanath, as a member representing Ganjam, played his role as a key organizer in that convention and left no stones unturned to make it a success.

The Fifth Convention of the Utkal Sammilani was held at Puri in April of 1908. As per the first resolution of the session, it was decided that a District Committee would be formed in every district and efforts would be made to raise the number of membership. Biswanath Misra was inducted into the Ganjam District Committee along with others. The third resolution of the session was approved by Biswanath Misra; which dealt with recommending the District Committees to send two or more deserving people at their cost to the Model Agriculture Center established by the Government at Cuttack for learning better methods practiced in agriculture. They also needed to make attempts to draw the attention of more farmers to the Model Agriculture Center in the interest of more effective farming.

Biswanath Misra could not be a part of the Sixth, Seventh and Eighth Conventions of Utkal Sammilani, as he was in London pursuing his Bar-at-Law studies.

The Ninth Convention of the Sammilani had taken place at Puri in December 1913. In that convention Barrister Biswanath Misra (the First London-returned Barrister of Orissa) played an important role in the first, seventh and ninth resolutions, and contributed immensely.

On behalf of the Oriyas living in Bihar-Orissa state and Madras state, the first resolution of the Sammilani condemned severely the attempt made on the life of Hon'ble Lord Hardinge and expressed its deepest gratitude to the Almighty for saving his life. Barrister Biswanath supported the resolution.

The seventh resolution dealt with a very important matter of which Barrister Misra was the approver. The proposal was about establishing an engineering school in Orissa, as the Sammilani felt it was direly needed in the state. Further it was decided to pray the Government for the early fulfillment of the demand. Its proposer was Ray Bahadur Sudam Charan Nayak and its supporter was Sri Madhusudan Panigrahi. To make the resolution effective Biswanath had extended powerful arguments in support of the issue. He had said that a long introduction to the issue was unnecessary. Engineering School would be of immense help to the Oriyas. Some might feel that not a lot of students would take admission in the school, as not a single Oriya had gone to Calcutta Engineering College to study engineering. Even not many students went to study in the Cuttack Survey School. However, the trend of the old times had changed a lot. Gradually the consciousness for higher studies was spreading rapidly amongst Oriyas. Oriyas were moving forward to undertake different kinds higher studies. The government had said that if twenty thousand rupees were deposited, engineering school could be opened. It could be clarified here that the Maharaja of Athgarh had promised since long, to donate twenty thousand rupees for the purpose. The proposal only had to be placed before him; which he would certainly fulfill.

The ninth resolution of the session was that in Singhbhum district Oriya was not the official language adopted in courts of law, and hence Oriyas there faced a lot of problems. In view of that, necessary steps be taken. Barrister Biswanath Misra was the approver of the proposal. It is needless to mention here that while Biswanath was practicing as a pleader in Aska, he had successfully implemented Oriya language as the medium of submitting petitions and arguing in the courts of Ganjam.

The Tenth Convention of Utkal Sammilani was held at Parlakhemindi in 1914. Barrister Misra put forward the second proposal of the session; which dealt with the offering of condolences to the departed wife and son of Lord Hardindge. The sixth proposal was also placed before the Sammilani by the fierce Oriya linguaphile Barrister Biswanath. It dealt with the use of Oriya language in the courts, and spreading of Oriya education in a massive scale in Singhbhum under Bihar-Orissa, Jeypore under Madras, and Phuljhar, Padmapur, Chandrapur, etc. under Central Province.

Barrister Biswanath was also the approver of the eighth resolution, which concerned itself with the appointment of Oriya teachers and mentors in the schools of Oriya-speaking tracts; the absence of which would lead to Oriya students suffering severe long-term setbacks.

The observation and analysis of the above resolutions could clearly point to the fact that how keen the London-educated first barrister of Orissa was in the matters of the amelioration and preservation of Oriya language. He was a great Oriya whose every breath was dedicated to proliferation of Oriya language and a separate language-based state for Orissa.

The Eleventh Convention of the Utkal Sammilani was held at Sambalpur in December of 1915. The sixth resolution of the convention again dealt with the implementation of Oriya language in proceedings of the courts in Singhbhum under Bihar-Orissa, Phuljhar, Chandrapur and Padmapur under Central Province. Besides, the Sammilani also expressed concern over the nonproliferation of Oriya language in the education system in those areas. The proposer of the resolution was Gopabandhu Das and the approver was Barrister Biswanath Misra.

The ninth resolution in that session was a milestone resolution, which dealt with the bringing of law education to Orissa. The Sammilani felt that there was a need of opening B.L. class in Ravenshaw College for the benefit of Oriya-speaking students. Barrister Biswanath Misra did not only propose the resolution; he also put all his efforts to see that it saw light of the day. In that context, a letter of great importance by Barrister Biswanath was published in the "Utkal Deepika" on 4.11.1916. The title of the letter was, "B.L. class in Cuttack." In that letter he wrote:

'Esteemed Editor of Utkal Deepika

Honorable Sir,

Readers must be aware that the "New University in Bihar-Orissa" bill has been brought to the Indian Legislative Assembly. The speed with which it is progressing, it is evident that the new university will be operational from

1917. The readers must not also have forgotten that the demand for opening law classes in Ravenshaw College for the benefit of Oriya students has been advocated for long. The newspapers also have been discussing the issue.

Whenever a new project is undertaken, its necessity must be probed into. The intelligentsias have to ponder over it and its efficacy. A big question commonly discussed is whether the investment made for opening law classes would be justified by the students' intake. Such a question can also arise in the minds of the authorities naturally. The readers would not deny that to solve the issue, the citizens of the country must come forward and put their best efforts.

As a matter of fact, Cuttack's Ravenshaw College, in no way, has less student intake than colleges of other states. That apart, not only Oriya students of estranged Ganjam, but also Telugu students from there, are likely to join the course. Two students from Ganjam have recently completed their course in law and have come back from Calcutta. A lot of relatively middle class meritorious students of political Orissa do not dare to go to Calcutta for their higher studies due to paucity of funds. If the law courses start at Cuttack, students not only from political Orissa; but also from Ganjam and Midnapore of natural Orissa would join the course due to incurrence of lesser expenditure. Besides increasing the intake, new graduates joining the course would gradually enhance the image and elegance of the college.

Although it cannot be said that the Honorable Government is totally callous about the demands of the

Oriyas; yet people should know that in any big project just by discussing across the table casually, positive result couldn't be expected. In any good endeavor, determination ultimately produces positive result.

The present new university matter, once solved, the law class in Ravenshaw College issue would be shelved for next eight or ten years, unless the people of Utkal together apply themselves with mind and heart for the purpose.

In the next convention of Utkal Sammilani at Balasore to be held in the current year, the issue should find a prominent place. The Sammilani should take it on itself to send a deputation of eminent people to the Departmental Head for discussion of the issue and its proper implementation. I hope, the President and Secretaries of the executive body of the Sammilani would take it on themselves to ponder over the issue and decide on the course of action to be undertaken.

Faithfully,

Biswanath Misra

President

Utkal Samiti, Calcutta'

The Twelfth Convention of Utkal Sammilani was held at Balasore in December of 1916. The second and third resolutions passed in the session were approved and supported by Barrister Biswanath respectively. Sri Fakir Mohan Senapati proposed the second resolution. The resolution concerned itself with tendering of condolences to the families of the two well-wishers of Utkal Sammilani, the king of Bamanda Sachidanand Tribhubabanpati and Ray Bahadur Samant Radha Charan Das, on their untimely sad demise. In the third resolution of the session it was proposed to declare Jeypore, then under the Madras Presidency, as a separate district; and to promote Oriya as a language there in all its needs. The Sammilani also felt seriously the necessity of making the Madras Government aware of its gravity.

In March of 1918 the Thirteenth Convention of Utkal Sammilani was held at Cuttack. Barrister Biswanath supported the first resolution in the session; which dealt with backing up of the British King in his involvement in the European Great War along with his allies against Germany to keep the prestige of the human race intact. The Sammilani wished luck to the King to win the war and offered its prayers to God for the purpose. Further the Sammilani recorded, on behalf of the people of Utkal, its untarnished respect for the British throne and belief in it.

After the March Convention, the same year (1918) in the month of September, a Special Convention (the Fourteenth) was convened at Cuttack. The fourth resolution in that convention was, "That while thanking the Right Honorable the Secretary of State and His Excellency the Viceroy of India for recognizing the necessity and importance of the principle of constituting homogeneous administrative units on the basis of language and race which the Oriya-speaking people have been urging for many years past, this conference places on record its deep sense of disappointment in finding no definite provision in the Report for the amalgamation of the Oriya-speaking tracts under one administration and is of opinion that unless the desired amalgamation precedes or accompanies the reform, the Oriyas will not only be deprived of the benefits of the scheme itself; but will also be placed under serious disadvantages owing to the fact that they would be in the minority under several existing administrations." Barrister Biswanath Misra was the supporter of the resolution. It was a resolution; which came as the aftermath of Montague-Chelmsford Report.

In the month of December 1919 the Fifteenth Convention of the Utkal Sammilani was held at Puri. Barrister Biswanath Misra proposed the first resolution of the convention. The resolution concerned itself with the extension of gratitude to the Emperor of India for making a welfare announcement in the Royal Declaration for promulgation of the India Reformation Act, with consideration to have good rule for Indians and their contentment.

The observation and analysis of Barrister Misra's work schedules clearly point at his soulful dedication at one direction, and he was extremely emotional about it. It was the protection of Oriya language and formation of separate state for Orissa. His priorities and emotional bonding with Oriya and Orissa later saw him seceding from the Utkal Sammilani.

It was a travesty that the Utkal Sammilani, which was created for protection of Oriya language, and Oriyas ultimately gave way to national interest relegating the interest of Orissa to the back seat. The following news release in the 16th edition of "Asha" published from Berhampur on 10.01.1921 Monday, carried news about Utkal Sammilani. It said that the Sixteenth Convention of

Utkal Sammilani had been effectuated in Chakradharpur in Singhbhum on 30th, 31st and January 1st. A huge pavilion was built in an expansive field in the middle of the town. On the first day of the convention two thousand people attended it. Almost two hundred representatives were in attendance.

As representatives of Ganjam Sri Sribatsa Panda, Sri Harihara Panda, Sri Rajgopal Achary, Sri Ramkrushna MIsra, Sri Jagannath Panigrahy, Sri Nand Kishore Khadanga, Sri Gopinath Nath, Sri Anant Acharya, Sri Ballav Narayan Pattjoshi, Sri Narsingh Panigrahy, Kabiraj Kamakshya Prasad Sharma and Barrister B.N.Misra had joined the convention.

On the first day a meeting was held from evening 9 pm to 11 pm to decide on the matters to be discussed in the sessions to follow. There was big debate and fracas on the issue of making the Utkal Sammilani a part of Indian National Assembly. More than one amendment proposals were also discussed. Babu Brajasundar Das, Barrister B.N.Misra, Babu Bichitranand Das and Babu Biswanath Kar were vehemently in opposition to the basic proposal and showed their severe discontentment and indignation on the issue of making Utkal Sammilani a part of Indian National Assembly.

Making Utkal Sammilani a part of Indian National Assembly, i.e., Congress, meant total noncooperation with the British Government. It was not acceptable to Barrister Biswanath Misra and other like-minded members of the Sammilani. The reason was obvious. From the inception of the Sammilani, its objective priorities were to give protection to Oriya language and forming a separate state for Orissa with all the segregated Oriya-speaking tracts included in it. Such objectives could only be fulfilled with the cooperation of the British Government. The sudden decision of Pandit Gopabandhu Das along with his Satyabadi teammates to join the Congress made it a forced compulsion on the part of Utkal Sammilani to oppose the British Government. It was not at all acceptable to Barrister B.N.Misra and many other stalwart leaders of the Sammilani. The issue, 'whether Orissa first or India's independence first,' became an extremely controversial subject of the time. On the issue, the Oriya population virtually became two clearly divided groups. No wonder, Utkal Sammilani had landed in a big messy controversy leading to serious internal crisis.

Under the circumstances many moderate leaders like Barrister Biswanath seceded themselves from the Utkal Sammilani. Sri Madhusudan Das, the creator of the Sammilani, virtually withdrew himself from all its activities thereafter. Utkal Sammilani became a part of the Indian National Congress. Barrister Biswanath Misra was never a member of Congress; but he had attended a few Congress conventions as an invited guest or observer.

MAHATMA GANDHI AND BISWANATH

In the month of March 1921 Biswanath had met Mahatma Gandhi at the residence of a friend of his, Sri Madhusudan Panigrahy, at Berhampur. The meeting was a turning point in Biswanath's life. Neither Biswanath was in unison with Gandhiji's ideologies nor was he hopeful about the results of noncooperation movement; but as a token of respect to Gandhiji, he did not keep any ties with the British courts from March of 1921 till the withdrawal of the noncooperation movement. It was his dedicated assurance and selfless cooperation for the movement. However, in his heart of hearts, his first priority was protection of Oriya language and the formation of Orissa, a separate Oriya language-based state. He was thoroughly aware that without the cooperation of the British Government, it was not possible. In that light, he was never able to mentally accept the movement of noncooperation with the British. Oriya language and Oriya language-based separate state were deeply ingrained in his flesh and blood. As a consequence, he could never accept any theories or movements that came as obstacles on the way of the Oriya and Orissa movement.

An excerpt from Biswanath's letter published in the daily "Asha" of October 18, 1920, given underneath, justified the above statement more than adequately:

"Everybody is aware of my ceaseless efforts with regard to keeping all the segregated Oriya-speaking tracts under one administration. Not only here, even during my stay in England I had continued my efforts in this regard. As a result, I could gather the sympathy of a lot of responsible politicians towards my movement. My efforts in England could convince Mr. Mac Callum Scott, M.P., and he argued in favor of the Oriyas in the House of Commons. Similarly Mr. E.S.Montague, then Under Secretary of State, also fully agreed with the idea of creation of a separate state for the Oriyas."

BISWANATH AND SEGREGATED ORIYA-SPEAKING TRACTS

Nineteenth century was coming to an end and twentieth century was dawning. Ghumusar under Ganjam district was under the administration of Madras presidency then. The present name of Rasolkonda under Ghumusar is Bhanjanagar. It was the birthplace of Kabi Samrat Upendra Bhanja. It was the citadel of Oriya culture and the throne of the great past of Orissa; but unfortunately the official language practiced there was English and Telugu. After long revolt and unfathomable protests, Oriya was introduced in the schools and colleges. The happiness of Oriyas knew no bounds, as a result. However, a funny situation arose because of that in the birthplace of Upendra Bhanja, the "Kabi Samrat". There was a serious dearth of instructors to teach Oriya. The teachers were mostly Telugus. To eradicate the problem Madras Government adopted a crazy subtle way out. Teachers training institutes were instituted to train the prospective teachers. Those institutes started training the prospective teachers to become "Ubhay Bhasha Prabin (UBP)", that is, experts in both Telugu and Oriya; and they earned the certificate of U.B.P after taking only six months of training in Oriya. The travesty was that Telugu teachers trained that way, also became eligible to teach Oriya language to Oriya students. The ill effect of it has been exemplified below.

The matriculation final history examination papers of Oriya students from one of the schools in Koraput district were sent for evaluation to an Oriya teacher in the Orissa Division. All the students in their answer to a question had written, "Observing the patience of King Pouras, Alexander entered into truce with him." The words "Patience" and "Truce" in Oriya stood for "Dhairya" and "Sandhi" respectively. However, the Ubhay Bhasha Pravin (UBP) Telugu teacher had used the words "Manchi" and "Odambadike" in his notes dictated to the students in the class. No wonder, all the students had used the same terms in their answers; which were not used in Oriya. The Oriya teacher from the Orissa Division while evaluating the papers got flabbergasted when he saw those words of which he could not make out anything, as they were either Telugu words or their corrupt versions. Such was the pitiable condition of Oriya language at the time, in the segregated Oriya-speaking tracts.

After completion of F.A. in 1904, the segregated Oriya-speaking tracts of the south became Biswanath's most liked places of work. He started his active life by dispensing knowledge of Oriya language to the Ubhay Bhasha Prabin teacher-students. After that, he passed his pleadership examination from Madras and started his judiciary career. Subsequent to his completion of pleadership towards the end of 1905, he had gone straight to his village Nua Someswarpur from Madras. If he had wished for it, he could have gone straight to Cuttack for starting his legal practice; but he was always disturbed by the thoughts of the deplorable plights of the Oriyas in the segregated Oriya-speaking tracts and the miserable condition of fragmented Orissa. That was the reason why Biswanath, the sympathetic friend of the sequestered Oriyas, chose Aska as his place of work. He left for Aska straight from his village. Before reaching Aska he had attended a special meeting of Utkal Samiti at Berhampur, where again the problems of segregated Orissa was discussed, reinforcing his determination to serve the people of the area.

BISWANATH THE PLEADER

It was the time when the eminent pleader Harihar Panda of Aska was practicing in Berhampur and Sri Nilamani Vidyaratna was editing a newspaper named "Prajabandhu." The Utkal Samiti meeting at Berhampur bore a lot of importance, which gave the required fillip to the future Oriya language movement. The details of it were published in the weekly, 'Star of Utkal' on 13th January 1906. The news release was as following: "Ganjam Utkal Samiti in a special session, proposed that the Oriya pleaders of Ganjam be urged to write the petitions, applications and proceedings placed in the courts of Ganjam in Oriya. Barrister Biswanath proposed it and Sri Harihar Panda approved it. Both of them are pleaders. We are excited that these two gentlemen have selflessly stuck to their commitments. We believe that the essence of the proposal is to carry out all the court proceedings in Oriya rather than Telugu. On this count, they may lose Telugu clientele. That is the reason why we term this proposal as a self-sacrificing ordinance. The two gentlemen truly deserve our praise because of their selfless effort and endeavour."

It appears as if Biswanath was under oath to do everything, like writing applications, petitions, delivering lectures, making arguments, in Oriya before joining the Aska court for his professional legal career. It was a great challenge for the time, as half the judiciary magistrates in Ganjam courts were Telugus. Even more than half the people involved in litigations were Telugus. Biswanath knew it very well. He was well aware that, to begin with, a new comer to the legal profession must embark on his practice by giving top priority to the wishes of his clients. The more serious matter was that a newcomer from a different state, far away from his birthplace, in a different politically administered state was making such radical decision. The severity of the after-effect was really thought provoking. However, Biswanath was a strongly determined person. For him, Oriya was his mother tongue and Orissa was his motherland. Nothing was more important than those for him. Even he did not consider his profession more important than the protection of Oriya language and formation of a separate Orissa state. He was always disturbed and perturbed by the fragmented look of Orissa; and was prepared to sacrifice anything for its sake. May be, his above oath was only a part of it. He did fulfill his oath with dignity. The apprehension of 'Star of Utkal' that he would be losing his clients came out true. However, the problem lasted only for a few days. Despite being stubbornly determined in his beliefs, he was so well mannered and suave that soon both Oriya and Telugu clients were drawn towards him like iron particles drawn towards a magnet. Clients, whether Telugu or Oriya, once they joined Biswanath's chamber, they never left him and accepted him as the protector of their interests. Thus, Biswanath started his legal profession in Aska, while protecting the interests of Oriya language and Oriyas in the segregated Oriya-speaking tracts. Later he started his unification activities of the sequestered Oriya-speaking tracts through various stints of his.

Although Biswanath had started his next level legal career at Calcutta High Court after obtaining his Bar-at-Law in 1913 followed by his stints at Patna and Madras High Courts, his heart and mind were always devoted to the segregated Oriya-speaking tracts, protection of Oriya language and formation of separate Orissa state. He had evidenced it by being the representative of Ganjam all along, in the Utkal Sammilani. All his activities in Utkal Sammilani were dedicated to the unification and development of the sequestered Oriya-speaking tracts. The examples cited earlier with regard to his propositions and partaking in the Sammilani conventions were ample proof of the above statement. Even the reason of his quitting Utkal Sammilani was founded on the same ground.

BARRISTER BISWANATH AND CALCUTTA

After coming back from London as a Barrister, it was only obvious for BIswanath Misra to start his legal practice in a High Court. Calcutta was the nearest to him with a High Court. At the time, Calcutta did not have even an Oriya lawyer. Madhusudan Das had left Calcutta since long and had started his practice at Cuttack. Calcutta at that time was mostly the habitat of only the lower income group Oriyas. Although Calcutta boasted of three or four times more Oriyas than any city of Orissa, the people predominantly belonged to the classes of laborers, craftsmen, cooks, coolies and masons. For Biswanath to pursue his legal practice, he had to take those people as his clientele. It was a time when in the Calcutta High Court the English and Bengali barristers ruled the roost. Even Bengali lawyers practicing in the High Court shammed as greater than the barristers. In an environment like that, Biswanath, being the lone non-English and non-Bengali barrister knew it well that how difficult it would be for him to pursue his profession in law.

Oriyas in Calcutta did not like to introduce themselves as Oriyas at that time. The reason was their poor lifestyle and rural background. However, Biswanath was cut out of different material. He was a proud Oriya and spruce gentleman. He believed strongly in uniting the Oriyas and inculcating Oriya pride firmly in them. He was convinced that it was the only way he could fruitfully spend his life as a law practitioner.

Repeating his old habit of a simple lifestyle, he rented out House No. 275 in Bow Bazar Street of Calcutta, and started living there. The area was flooded with Oriyas. After gradually improving his practice, towards the end of 1913, he established his position and settled in Bungalow No. 1945 in Dharamtala Street. He came to Calcutta as a helpless person; but in a few days after his arrival there, could render a lot of help to lakhs of Oriyas in Calcutta. He came to Calcutta almost penniless; but quite soon he could establish himself firmly. His place of residence became the central meeting place of the migrant Oriyas and the rendezvous for hundreds of visiting gentlemen, aristocrats, intelligentsia, and people seeking employment, students, laborers and visitors.

His love for the poor was evidenced from the beginning of his career as a barrister at Calcutta. It was a great example of his character. To bring it to light, an article published in "Utkal Deepika" of 09.07.1913 could be cited here. The article laid down that Barrister Biswanath had fought a case of murder and torture (IPC 307 and 324) in Calcutta high Court, and that too without any fees. The name of the accused was Jogen Ghose. His appeal was accepted; but only Biswanath out of all the barristers present in the court agreed to fight the case without charging any fees, as Jogen was a person of hardly any means. He presented himself in the court for two consecutive days and fought for his client honestly, dedicatedly and brilliantly. The jury after long hours of discussion and deliberations declared Jogen Ghose as 'not guilty.' "Utkal Deepika" wrote in its conclusion of the article, "We congratulate Biswanath Misra and applaud his efforts for this. We also wish him all the success and honor in his profession."

Earlier too, on 1913 April 26th "Utkal Deepika" had written in their commentary, "Pleader from Aska, Ganjam, Sri Biswanath Misra had spent two years studying Bar-at-Law in London. After becoming a Barrister, he has started practicing in Calcutta High Court. During his stay at Aska he had made a name for himself as a pleader; and we hope, our youth would not fail to emulate him in pursuing higher education and take steps to eradicate poverty from our country. There was no Oriya Barrister in Calcutta so far. That's why seekers of justice had to suffer a lot. Mr. Misra has helped in overcoming that lacuna; and consequently, earns our thanks, as well as, that of the nation."

Although professionally Calcutta was the headquarters of Barrister Biswanath, his real work place was Orissa, especially, segregated areas like Ganjam Agency and Vizag Agency. He started the Oriya movement at Calcutta; but spread it over to the segregated Oriya-speaking tracts and the whole of Orissa. From 1913 to 1918 nobody had come forward to put the sequestered Oriya-speaking tracts in the main stream of Orissa and the Orissa unification movement. Interestingly, Barrister Biswanath's stay at Calcutta aided the movement. It was all because Calcutta was the central place for all the educated and elites from the sequestered Oriya-speaking tracts to meet each other. That was how Biswanath could keep in touch with the bordering tracts of Orissa and the problems associated with them; which helped him in taking steps for their eradication. In that light, he became a strong viaduct for the Utkal Sammilani.

During his stay at Calcutta, he was deeply involved in the activities of Utkal Sammilani. For the purpose, his efforts were also unprecedented. To instantiate it, his itinerary post Ganjam Convention in 1913 September is worthy of a scrutiny. He attended the Ganjam convention of Utkal Sammilani; and immediately thenceforth he went through such a hectic work schedule that anyone would raise his eyeballs in wonder, as to how a person could be so mobile when the communication network was so awfully poor then. During that period, to arouse the Oriya pride, he traversed from the southern point of Orissa to Northern point, despite the lack of proper mode of transportation. During his whirlwind tour, he travelled extensively through Berhampur, Aska, Rasolkonda (Bhanjanagar) and reached Kharsuan on October 24th 1913. It simply was ample proof of his tenacity in pursuing the Orissa and Oriya causes.

In "Utkal Deepika" of 8.11.1913 Pundit Krushna Chandra Acharya, the Kharsuan Sirastadar, had written that Barrister Biswanath Misra, taking the advantage of Puja Holidays, toured Sambalpur, Bamanda, Patna, and Sonepur to awaken in the people love for the Oriya country; and finally arrived at Kharsuan on October24th. On receiving prior intimation, the King of Kharsuan had made all arrangements to welcome Barrister Misra from Amada station. Mr. Misra was welcomed in a meeting after his arrival. In his reply to the reception, he thanked the organizers and the people gathered there; and offered some valuable suggestions. In the evening he conversed with the talented new king. Then on 25th he and Sirastadar Pandit Acharya made themselves available at the capital of Sareikala. He was received warmly again by the young able prince. Thereafter, Barrister Misra delivered a lecture on the development of Oriya language issues and motivated all members present there. It was very strongly appreciated by all. In Singhbhum district the mother tongue of Sareikala was Oriya. Not only that; it was also the most used language amongst the people. Besides, the king and prince themselves were Oriya poets of good standing. After having a fruitful conversation with the king about the protection and development of Oriya language, a contented Barrister Misra left for Calcutta the same night by train. The article had ended with eulogies for Barrister Misra for his exemplary behavior with regard to serving the Oriyas and Orissa. Finally, Pundit Acharya had brought the article to an end by profusely thanking Barrister Biswanath Misra for his love of Oriya language and Orissa.

The lightning tour of Biswanath gave him a lot of experience about the segregated Oriya people. He also had gathered enough understanding of the students' power and the necessity of students' organizations. Basing on that knowledge, he was determined to set up a powerful students' organization in Orissa. He had felt that through the students' organization, he could arouse Oriya pride and make the unification of Orissa movement active in both Orissa division and the sequestered Oriya-speaking tracts of the time. His second experience and realization was that the kings and maharajas of Orissa were not able to put their best efforts for unification of Orissa or its development because of the political climate of the time, albeit they were sympathetic towards it. As a consequence, Biswanath's next objective was to utilize the rajas and maharajas of the princely states for the proliferation of Orissa's culture and higher education. The essential targets were to open M.A. in Oriya in the Calcutta University and opening up of science classes and library in Ravenshaw College. Apart from those, one of his primary objectives was to introduce Law education at Ravenshaw College.

On 27.12.1913 "Utkal Deepika" had published a news item; which was as following: "In a telegraphic message from Calcutta, it has been communicated that Barrister Biswanath Misra had organized an evening meet on Thursday at his residence for the Oriya students of Calcutta. Most students and other honorable people like Sonepur Maharaja and prince, Bamda Raja Bahadur and prince, kings of Chikiti and Kanika, Ms. Das (Smt. Sailabala Das, adopted daughter of Madhusudan Das), Lochan Prasad Pandey, Editor of Bharat Mitra, Padmalochan Mohanty, Chandra Chatturjya and Harish Chandra Dutta, M.A., etc., were present at the meet. The dignitaries delivered speeches of motivation and advice to the students. The meet finally came to an end with light snacks and tea." The same day another telegraphic message communicated that on December 31st of the ongoing year, a special convention would be held at Puri, specifically for the students. The meet organizers had requested the students to join the convention in large numbers.

The effect of students and the elite guests present at the evening meet at Barrister Misra's residence was far reaching; and it could be clearly observed from the news published in "Utkal Deepika" on 11.04.1914. The news item stated that, "A meet of the Orissa Union (Utkal Samiti) was held on 5th last. Barrister B.N.Misra presided over it and many members of the Union participated in it. Honorable King of Kanika and Honorable M. S. Das, C. I. E, agreed to provide for all the scholarships required for funding the studies of the students of Utkal in M.A. and Law classes in Patna University, till a new university was founded in Orissa. The President, Barrister B.N.Misra, thanked the two generous members profusely for their noble gestures. In the same meet, another proposal was passed; which dealt with the opening of B.Sc. classes in Ravenshaw College at the soonest.

As a result of the above movement, the Maharaja Science Laboratory was opened in Ravenshaw College through a hefty donation of Maharaja of Mayurbhanj. In the same way, Kanika Library was established in Ravenshaw College by the unflinching donation of King of Kanika. Barrister Biswanath had put all his efforts for the spread of higher education in Orissa since 1913. It had become an uninterrupted dream project of Biswanath all his life. Observing and analyzing his activities of later days, it could be clearly perceived that he put all his efforts for the unification of Orissa and making it a separate state first, and then it was all for the advancement of higher education for the Oriyas, their training and employment. During his entire tenure at the Central Legislative Assembly too, he had devoted all energy and labor towards the same objectives.

In that context, if his activities at the Utkal Sammilani are contemplated on, his efforts in the direction of development of higher education in Orissa can be clearly marked. It is known to all, how his relentless work towards introduction of engineering and law education in Orissa has been glaringly exemplary. In the light of the above, the seventh resolution of the ninth convention of Utkal Sammilani and his letter published in "Utkal Deepika" of 04.11.1916 are worth citing for critical readers and historians.

It is interesting to note that from the day he stayed at Calcutta, every convention of Utkal Sammilani contained resolutions about amalgamation of the segregated Oriya-speaking tracts, formation of a separate Orissa state, the introduction of higher education and training. Not only they became the primary issues of the time; but all efforts were directed towards their accomplishment too. The main spokesman of all those resolutions about higher education and training, the use of Oriya language in the courts of the Oriya speaking tracts was Calcutta Utkal Samiti's president, Barrister Biswanath Misra.

His frequent visits to the various segregated Oriya-speaking tracts convinced him that to form a separate state of Orissa, strong and powerful students and youth organizations had to be formed. It was the reason why, he often tried to convince the kings and maharajas of the princely states to cooperate in the Oriya movement and participate in the development of higher education and spread of Oriya culture. Because of his efforts only, the Maharaja Science Laboratory could be established in Ravenshaw College with the contributions from

Mayurbhanj Maharaja. In the same way, in the same college, Kanika Library could be founded by the generous grant from Raja of Kanika. With the aid of Sonepur Maharaja, postgraduate class in Oriya could be opened in Calcutta University and a chair could be created in Rabindranath Tagore's Rabindrabharati University (Shantiniketan) for research in Oriya language and literature.

Later Orissa division was removed from Bengal province and merged with Bihar, Patna being declared as its capital. Consequently, Biswanath left Calcutta and started his legal practice in Patna High Court, as Oriyas and Orissa were his main concern. In the meantime another opportunity came in his way. Because of his intimacy with Ganjam, he always represented it in the movements for amalgamation of the sequestered Oriya-speaking tracts. In an occasion like that he had the opportunity to meet the Governor of Madras in March of 1920 along with Sri Shashibhusan Rath to present the demands of the Oriyas. In that assignment he had to go over to Madras frequently. His repeated visits prompted him to pursue his legal career in Madras and he was accepted in Madras High Court as an Advocate. At that time only barristers could become advocates. Others were termed as pleaders.

He never missed any Utkal Sammilani Conventions and joined them irrespective of wherever they were held. In the meets, he motivated and encouraged the Oriyas of segregated Oriya-speaking tracts to jump into the movement for amalgamation of Orissa and formation of separate Orissa state. Later, after he completed his stint as a Member of the first Legislative Council, he came back to Patna and continued his practice there.

BISWANATH AND CUTTACK

Before 1921 there was no indication of the non-cooperation movement. By then Biswanath had set his mind to shift his practice to Cuttack. That apart, there was not enough opportunity for practicing in Calcutta High Court after joining the Patna High Court. There was another worry that was bothering him. Pursuance of his legal career at Patna kept him away from Ganjam and Orissa; which was unbearable for him. It simply implied that continuing his practice at Patna for a long time was not possible. Apart from that, Mahatma Gandhi's call for non-cooperation movement started taking shape from March of 1921. Biswanath was under oath and had pledged to Gandhiji that he would not participate in any kind of legal practice in the British courts till the non-cooperation movement was withdrawn. Under the circumstances, he thought it was the right decision to shift to Cuttack.

At Cuttack he set his household in a big expanse of land at Purighat across River Kathjodi. The house was pretty large and it was named as "Bharati Kotha." It was the place where his new work center gradually grew and "Bharati Kotha" became the destination for many legends of Orissa. Biswanath strongly believed that for the amalgamation of the cut-off Oriya-speaking areas and formation of a separate Orissa province, it was mandatory for the youth and the students to join the movement. Even during his stay at Calcutta, it was evidenced from his activities. He had continued with his belief of involving the students and youth power in the movement at Cuttack too. By his efforts many student and youth summits were held in Orissa. He was elected as President of Students' Society at Cuttack. During his time as the President of Students' Committee (Society), many students leaders like Jadumani Mangaraj, Harekrishna Mahtab, and Nabakrishna Chowdhury were members of it, who went on to become eminent leaders of Orissa at subsequent times. Sri Chintamani Acharya, who became the Vice Chancellor of Utkal University at a later time, also cooperated with Barrister Biswanath in the endeavors of the Students Society. Biswanath always motivated the students and their leaders to fight for the union of the Oriya-speaking tracts and protection of Oriya language. For the purpose, he incessantly inspired and motivated them.

Dr. Harekrushna Mahtab and some of his friends who were active in the Oriya movement, actually stayed in some vacant rooms in Biswanath's "Bharati Kotha" by making a students' mess there. As a consequence of it, they always got the knowledge and direction for the separate Orissa state movement and got trained under the tutelage of the great man. More importantly, they continuously stayed in proximity with Barrister Biswanath; which itself was a great motivating factor.

BARRISTER BISWANATH AND SIMON COMMISSION

The Indian Statutory Commission was formed with seven British Parliamentarians as members in November 1927. The Chairman of the Commission was Sir John Simon and his chief deputy was Clement Attlee. Attlee went on to become the British Premier later. The Commission arrived in British India on February 3rd 1928. Its objective was to study the constitutional changes and reforms in the largest and most significant possession of Britain. Even earlier, the British Government had appointed a committee with Edwin Samuel Montague, then Secretary of State for India, and Lord Chelmsford, then Viceroy of India. The Committee had given its report in 1918, on the basis of which the Indian Act 1919 was formed. At that time the British Government had committed that it would be revisited with regard to its efficacy measures after ten years. As a result of that commitment, the Simon Commission had come to India. Its objective was to place a detailed report on the efficacy of Indian constitution prepared on the basis of the Indian Act of 1919 and its benefits, after making a proper evaluation.

However, after the arrival of the Commission in Bombay, it had to face dreadful resistance. It was black flagged at all places. The "Simon Go Back" revolts spread all over India. It was probably the beginning of India's freedom movement. A very sad repercussion of the revolt was the death of Punjab Keshari Lala Lajpat Rai by severe caning on 17th November 1928. As a result of that, anti-Simon uprising had intensified and spread all over India.

PHILIP-DUFF COMMITTEE

In this respect, to know in depth, one has to go back a few years to 1924. Due to Barrister Misra's repeated appeals and arguments in the Central Legislative Assembly for the formation of a separate state of Orissa, Government of India had appointed the Philip-Duff committee. At the time Mr. C. L. Philip was the Political Agent of the princely states of Orissa and A. C. Duff was the Collector of Vishakhapatna. Barrister Biswanath Misra was espoused with the responsibility of visiting the Oriya-speaking border tracts along with the Committee to find out the views of the people of the areas with regard to their amalgamation into one unit. The Committee had laid down a well thought-out report about the amalgamation of the Oriya-speaking tracts. The report was highly influenced by the tremendous efforts and dedication of Barrister Misra. The excerpt from the report given below had great impact historically: " it has been found out from our investigations that the educated Oriya mass in the Oriya-speaking areas of Madras have a long cherished honest wish. It is about amalgamating the Oriya-speaking tracts of Madras and keeping them under one administration in Orissa."

When such a conducive environment had started prevailing, Birkenhead, the Secretary of India, made a controversial statement; which indicated the rift between Hindus and Muslims in India. When Simon commission was appointed, no Indian member was nominated into it. In that context, Birkenhead had again said that Indians were not designated in the commission because if he were a Hindu, the report would have a Hindu bias and if he were a Muslim; it would have a Muslim bias. Therefore, the Commission could not have made a report befitting to all Indians.

Birkenhead comment was insulting to Indians. Hence the front-ranking leaders of India decided to promulgate a constitution acceptable to all Indians. In order to materialize it, a committee lead by Motilal Nehru was formed in February of 1928. In the committee Tej Bahadur Sapru was a member who was a liberal constitutional expert. In 1928 August the draft constitution was in circulation; and formal discussions and debates had already started.

In the report of the committee, Motilal Nehru after making necessary investigations into the financial situation of Sindh, had recommended it to be a separate state. Unfortunately, however, after years of demands and movements, the committee ignored demands of the Oriyas. It had altogether disregarded the demand for uniting the unjustifiably segregated Oriya-speaking tracts under different provinces, and putting them under one separate state of Orissa. Such an action of the Committee hurt all the Oriya language lovers and the leaders fighting for a separate state of Orissa got extremely annoyed. Needless to mention here, Barrister Biswanath also got hurt and became exceedingly exasperated. As a result of it, going against the general mood of India, Barrister Biswanath and Brajasundar Das, etc., met and welcomed Simon in 1929 at Patna with the demand of separate statehood for Orissa. It was totally against the pan Indian situation and environment of the time; but it was the only option left for the revolting Oriya language-based society.

The efforts of Barrister Misra and the like-minded people yielded some result, as Lord Simon ordered for the formation of a subcommittee of which Major Clement Attlee was declared as the Chairman. Clement Attlee later became the Prime Minister of United Kingdom. It was Attlee under whose supervision India's independence was realized.

To collect opinions and witnesses in favor of formation of a separate Orissa state, Major Attlee Subcommittee had visited all the bordering areas and had met the local pro-Oriya and anti-Oriya amalgamation movement people. Besides, the Attlee Subcommittee had met the representatives of the Oriyas of Madras Presidency at Vishakhapatna. Although officially the future King of Jeypore, Vikram Dev Verma, was head of the representatives, the real main spokesperson of the group was Barrister Biswanath Misra. He had prepared all the memoranda and presented the Oriya viewpoints in a logical order before the Attlee Subcommittee.

Interestingly though, it was noticed later that Simon Commission and the Attlee Subcommittee had not recommended the amalgamation of all the Oriya-speaking border areas for putting them under the separate Orissa state. Biswanath was awfully disturbed by that. Without losing hope, to arouse the aspiration of Oriyas and reorganize the Oriya movement in Madras, Barrister Biswanath wrote a lot of thoughtful articles in English; which were published in the newspapers like "The Hindu" and "Madras Mail," etc. Underneath are given the essence of the articles.

ORIYAS OF MADRAS AND SIMON COMMISSION

In this article, it was mentioned, "In the Simon Commission Report, a recommendation has been made to form a Boundary Commission for Orissa. In the report some sympathetic sweet words have been said for Oriyas. Some of our friends have become out and out elated by it. The readers must realize that the problems of Oriyas are totally different from that of India. The mentioned target may be desirable; but it is not realizable at the time. Firstly, the problems of the Malayalam language people be considered. They may not be too keen to have a separate state for them till princely states like Cochin and Travancore are merged with it. Next the case of Assamese people be brought to the fore. Assam may not stand as a state on its own after the Bengali speaking people have been added to the Surma valley. And, Sindhu is a state that somehow can live on forever with the aid of the League of Nations. Orissa with its one and half crore population cannot wait till a commission is setup and decides about its statehood after solving the various questions raised. Besides, Political Supervisors in India will not welcome such a commission until basic political relationship between India and England is resolved. Therefore, a proposal to recommend a

Boundary Commission is meaningless at the time and should be avoided too."

This article had a subhead, which was:

Still Recommendation

Under that title it was written, "We have crossed the stage of recommendation since long. From 1902 to 1905, people reading the government documents can easily find that the government of Lord Curzon made its recommendation. In 1911 at the time of the coronation ceremony of the Emperor, a lot of letters were interchanged; which clearly indicated that a whole lot of injustices have been done to Orissa. However, the result was, 'confusion, worse confounded'. For example, the political Orissa Division of today got merged with a new state called Bihar-Orissa.

Thereafter came the Mont-Ford report. In it too, a special recommendation was made. The government, formed after the administrative reformation, was recommended to take an urgent step on the issue of Orissa and Bihar; and effectuate the decision treating it as an exigency. People had continued their protest movements all along. All over the Oriya-speaking areas continuous movements and unyielding protests continued. The public opinion was so strong that to make a detailed inquiry, the government was forced to set up the Philip-Duff Commission. That apart, Orissa government also appointed a special officer for it to collect more proof. Simon Commission had appointed the subcommittee from within. The subcommittee was made responsible to give detailed proposals. After all that, what is the point in appointing another committee to make fresh inquiries? Why is it being considered as a national issue when it is the demand for a language-based separate state of the Oriyas. It clearly indicates that under the pretext of a fresh inquiry, effort is being made only to subvert public opinion."

Under this article, the last subheading was:

Regarding the Inquiry

In this part of the article, it was written, "The subcommittee constituted by the Simon Commission have neither been able to deal with the issue in a justifiable manner nor have conducted it properly. Especially, the recommendations made by them for the Oriya people are faulty to a great extent. No reason has been cited as to why Vizag Agency and Sompeta, Parlakhemundi and Tekali taluk under Ganjam district would not be amalgamated with Orissa. Esteemed Sri Biswanath Dash had raised a few questions in the Madras Legislative Council, in answer to which the Madras Government had accepted that the Commission had not asked for any information about the number of Oriyas staying in VIzag Agency. Madras Government had given only those numbers and information; which the Commission had inquired from them. All these clearly point to the fact that the Subcommittee has not felt the necessity of considering the amalgamation of Vizag Agency with Orissa at all. In my articles published in the magazine 'Eastcoast' and other English newspapers of Madras, I had clearly shown that as per all government reports, Vizag Agency was overly populated with Oriyas. The government has also accepted it in all their reports and publications. The majority of the populations in the Agency are Oriyas. Oriya is the official language there. Even Oriya has been the medium of instruction for the Kandha tribe in the Agency since its possession by the British Government. Besides, the Kandhas have their relations in the neighboring Oriya-speaking areas and they maintain their marriage alliances there too. It also spreads all over the princely states of Orissa and the British occupied India. I have only quoted these from the reports of Mr. McPherson and other officers appointed especially for the purpose who said in their reports that from their investigations they have found out that in the latter fifty years of the last century, the Kandhas have established their closeness with the Oriyas and they maintain it even today. I had also quoted the views of military specialists in that regard in my article."

O'DONNEL COMMITTEE AND THE QUESTIONS OF PARLIAMENTARIAN BISWANATH

The First Round Table Conference was held over a period from the November 1930 to January 1931. In the Conference a white paper was published to make Orissa a separate state. For the purpose, O'Donnell committee was constituted. Sir Samuel O'Donnell was designated to head the committee. The other member of the committee was Sri Phookun Mehta. Both the members had recommended the inclusion of Parlakhemindi and Jeypore in the proposed Orissa state; but later O'Donnell changed his mind. At that time Barrister Biswanath Misra was already a Member of the First Central Legislative Assembly. He had mentioned on the floor of the House during his speech that the infamous British practice of "Divide et Impera" was being adopted by O'Donnel thoroughly well. O'Donnell could do it because of the nefarious activities of some of the anti-Orissa state formation elements. In that context Barrister Misra's question in the Central Legislative Assembly was not only extremely important; but also it showed his courage and character. The question asked was very exciting too. For sure, at the time, i.e.; 24th September 1931, no Indian was aware of the private letter of Lord Birkenhead, Secretary of

State, British Empire in India; but Biswanath Misra could sense it by the actions of the British rulers with regard to India; and had asked the mind-boggling question. The question went in the following way:

"(a) Is the government aware that on 14th May 1859, the Governor of Bombay in a transcript of his had mentioned 'Divide et Impera' (rule by dividing), the ancient Roman precept, would remain as our guiding pledge?

(b) Is the government prepared to say that they are not practicing the precept in their administration?

(c) Is the government aware that the general public as well as the newspapers and debating platforms have been discussing and declaring that India's administration is running on the policy of "Divide et Impera?"

In his answer to the question, India's Home Minister, Sir James Crerar, had emphatically said that "Divide et Impera" had not been the policy of the British Government. Even he went on to the extent of saying that he had not been able locate any so-called transcript of Lord Elphinstone, which was mentioned by Barrister Misra.

Birkenhead's private letters were made available later much after India got its independence and powers were transferred to the Indian authorities. Had they been made available earlier, the contradiction between Barrister Biswanath's questions and the answers given to it in the Central Legislative Assembly could have been noticed. Anyways, the questions of Barrister Misra were undoubtedly brilliant for the time and highly investigative.

It was the time when some anti-Orissa elements were trying to sabotage the Unification of Orissa and the separate Orissa state formation movement. Some Oriya language lovers and separate Orissa movement fighters raised their voices in scathing attacks against the traitors who tried to spearhead the sabotage. Barrister Biswanath, the Mr. Orissa, was the leader of the group. His role was that of the kingpin and most vital. The reason was obvious. Barrister Misra was the pioneer of the unification of Orissa movement, as the spokesperson of Ganjam. His work and words with regard to the unification of Ganjam and Koraput with Orissa were absolutely invaluable.

Barrister Misra's emotional attachment with separate Orissa province formation was always at the extreme. The perspective was very clear when he asked the following question on the floor of the Central Legislative Assembly on August 22nd of 1933. The question is recorded on page 7 of the fifth volume of the annals of arguments of the legislative assembly. In his question he had kind of warned the government with regard to formation of the separate state of Orissa by unifying the Oriya-speaking tracts of the border areas. His question was:

(a) Is the Government aware of the displeasure and anger of the Oriyas because of non-inclusion of the following areas in the proposed Orissa state?

1. Singhbhum district (Bihar-Orissa)

2. South Midnapore (Hijli district of Bengal)

3. Parlakhimindi, Urala, Manjusha, Tekali etc. of Ganjam district

4. Phuljhar from Central Province

A little investigation into the situation could clearly reveal that from the beginning of 1933 to the month of September of 1933, when he passed away, the only worry for him was the boundary determination and formation of separate state for Orissa. They were the sole reasons for his mental turmoil and depression. That apart, he was in an awfully melancholic state and woe, as the places dearer to his heart belonging to Ganjam were not considered for inclusion in the proposed Orissa state. More than that, he was extremely perturbed because of the treacherous acts of some of the well-known elites who had backstabbed the long cherished movement. He lost his health fast because of the sorrowful circumstances of the time.

BARRISTER BISWANATH AND THE DAILY "ASHA"

The daily "Asha" was the only Oriya newspaper that was published from Berhampur, Ganjam, at the time. Well-known Oriya-movement leader Sri Shashi Bhushan Rath was its editor. "Asha" had published a number of news items on Barrister Misra's activities. Some such published news clips have been laid down below because of their historical importance. However, the clips are from 1919 to the subsequent period, as the same from the era before was not available.

22nd December 1919

Barrister Biswanath Misra and eight others have been elected to represent Ganjam at the 15th convention of Utkal Sammilani scheduled to be held at Puri.

29th December 1919

Barrister Misra proposed the first resolution of the convention. The President approved the resolution.

2nd February 1920

Twelve members are elected from the Ganjam District Oriya Committee for the Utkal Sammilani Council this year. Barrister B. N. Misra is one of them. The Ganjam District Oriya Committee meeting was held on January 28th last at the Khallikote Diamond Jubilee Town hall at Berhampur to elect the members. B. N. Misra in his acceptance speech acknowledged his election by saying that he felt proud to be a part of the Oriya race. That apart, he gave a highly motivational speech to the gathering present there. After his speech, the President delivered his vote of thanks.

8th March 1920

Sri Shashi Bhushan Rath and Barrister B. N. Misra have left for Madras on last 4th to raise the demands of the Oriyas before the Governor of Madras.

18th October 1920

Barrister Biswanath Misra had sent a letter to "Asha;" which was published on the above date. A verbatim copy of it is given below.

Dear Sir,

Many of my friends and quite a number of voters have been inquiring me whether I am going to stand as a candidate for the reformed councils. I take this opportunity to inform such of them as are interested in the matter that I have decided to stand for the Bihar - Orissa Council from the urban Constituency of Orissa from the Municipalities of Cuttack, Puri, Balasore, Jajpur, Kendrapara and Sambalpur.

I am the first and only Barrister in the Oriya Country. Owing to practice in Patna, Calcutta and Madras High

Courts and Moffusil Courts, I have gained plenty of experience of the Oriyas living under different administrations. There is almost no part of the country unknown to me. My past record as a public man will enable you to judge that I can successfully represent the interests of Oriyas in the Bihar - Orissa Legislative Council. As you are doubtless aware, I belong to the District of Puri and to the class of Brahmans and that I hold advanced views on matters social and political. I believe that the Reforms inaugurated are a stepping-stone to the attainment of Responsible Govt. in India and co-operation with Govt. in interests of the country is essential. I hold also that the Govt. should be opposed when necessary. I do not have any faith in Non-Co-operation, the new political shibboleth that is being preached by a certain section of the people.

My experience as a public man has been of a varied kind and has been acquired during a period of service done for the good of the public for over 20 years in Ganjam and Orissa.

My work in connection with the movement for amalgamation of the Oriya-speaking tracts under one administration needs no special mention. Not only here, but while in England also, I carried on the agitation and secured sympathetic consideration at the hands of responsible statesmen. As a result of my labours, Mr. Mac Callum Scot, M.P., advocated the cause of the Oriyas in the House of Commons and Mr. E. S. Montague, then Under Secretary of State was convinced of the desirability of the formation of one province for the Oriyas.

This problem of amalgamation of the Oriya tracts will surely come for discussion before the new Councils and need I here assert that my experience in the cause will serve the country in good stead?

I have been connected with almost all the social, literary and political movements and associations of Orissa and Ganjam for over a decade. Should the voters support my candidature I shall spare no pains to represent their interests faithfully and espouse their cause to the satisfaction of all concerned.

Yours truly

B.N. Misra

27th December 1920

B. N. Misra joins the First Ganjam Pundit Sabha. This is a great proof of his knowledge in Oriya language and his dedication to Oriya language and literature.

10th January 1921

B. N. Misra and others representing Ganjam attended the sixteenth convention of Utkal Sammilani at Chakradharpur. Barrister B. N. Misra, B. N. Kar, Brajasundar Das and Bichitranand Das, and some others gave their opinions against the idea of subsuming Utkal Sammilani under Indian National Congress.

14th February 1921

Barrister Biswanath Misra has been elected as a Member of the Kallikote College Committee.

28th February 1921

Major news published was "Desha Mishrana Issue" (Amalgamation of Oriya-speaking tracts). In the special meeting of Ganjam Oriya Samaj held on 18.02.1921, the main issue discussed was, which Oriya-speaking regions of Madras need to be amalgamated with Orissa. The assembly formed a non-government commission to probe and decide about it. They appointed Barrister Biswanath Misra as the President and Sri Lal Mohan Pattnaik as the Secretary of the commission. As soon as the Commission was formed, Barrister Misra jumped into action discharging his responsibility.

28th February 1921 (same day)

An advertisement was published in "Asha." It said that Oriya Border Commission would meet at the following places on the following dates to determine the Oriya-speaking regions. Hence the sympathetic presence of all the members and local gentlemen was solicited.

Place
  Date

Manjusha
  5th, 6th, 7th March
Sompeta

12th, 13th March
Barua
  12th, 13th March
Jalantar
  19th, 20th March
Tekali   and
Parlakhimindi   25th,
26th, 27th, 28th March

      Signed: Biswanath Misra

        President

18th April 1921

The Bihar-Orissa Governor Honorable Lord Singh and Honorable Madhusudan Das are stationed at Puri at present. Taking advantage of it, Barrister Biswanath Misra and others have expressed their willingness to be part of the deputation to meet them at Puri with the problems of the amalgamation of Oriya-speaking tracts.

6th February 1922

On account of the resignation of Ray Bahadur Nimai Charan Mitra from the Central Legislative Assembly, a vacancy has been created in the Assembly. To fill up the vacancy some candidates have shown their willingness on last 31st. To fill up the vacant position, Barrister Biswanath Misra, Bipin Bihari Mitra and Jyotish Chandra Chakravarty have come forward as competing candidates.

13th March 1922

A reception meet was held to felicitate Barrister Biswanath Misra, as he was elected to the Central Legislative Assembly.

The same day it was also published that to join the Central Legislative Assembly, Barrister Misra has left Berhampur for Delhi the previous day.

Again on the same day, Sri Shashi Bhushan Rath also wrote in his editorial eulogizing Barrister Misra for his successful election as Member of the Central Legislative assembly. He wrote:

Barrister Misra

Barrister Biswanath Misra has been elected to the Central Legislative Assembly in place of Ray Bahadur Nimai Charan Mitra. Barrister Misra is a capable person. He is the first Barrister of Orissa. He had gone to England despite the social sanctions and castigation forced on him. This is the main evidence of his moral strength and character. He is a sweet-talking and affable person. In his election every Oriya should be happy. We also hope that he would display his patriotic attitude in the works of the Central Legislative Assembly.

Barrister Misra's Gratitude

Dear Electors

You will all be happy to know that I have been elected as Member of the Central legislative Assembly. My special gratitude is for those who have put their efforts for my election and sympathized with me. I would feel obliged if I could do something in the Central Legislative Assembly with your cooperation. I hope, you will always be with me in my activities and progress in the Assembly and keep me updated with anything special happening.

Yours Sincerely

Biswanath Misra

(Barrister)

20th March 1922

Barrister Biswanath Misra took oath in the Central Legislative Assembly on 14th of this month and officially became a part of it.

3rd July 1922

Barrister Biswanath Misra, the Member of Central Legislative Assembly, has sent a proposal in the following manner to be discussed in the forthcoming session of the Central Legislative Assembly.

"The Central Legislative Assembly recommends the Chairman of the Assembly, the Governor General, that approval from the Secretary of India and the all-powerful Emperor be sought to unite the adjacent Oriya-speaking tracts, now under the administration of the four governments of Bihar-Orissa, Madras, Central Province and Bengal, under one administration of a Governor or Deputy Governor, as deemed suitable."

12th March 1922

Information has been made available that the issue of amalgamation of Oriya-speaking tracts is likely to be discussed in this session of the Assembly. Barrister Biswanath Misra will raise the issue.

13th August 1923

In this issue of "Asha" the item that drew the most attention was a letter from Barrister Misra. The letter is quoted underneath.

Dear Sir,

Although over last two decades the Oriyas of Ganjam and Jeypore are moving for the amalgamation of Oriya parts of Madras with Orissa, it seems that no criticism was offered to the publication of certain matters which the Govt. of Madras did in reply to the resolution of Mr. S. B. Rath M.L.C. in the Council. The Oriya public are utterly ignorant of any such publication.

In spite of the official reports of the Collector, the Agency Commissioner, the Board of Revenue, Madras, has not published any white paper affirming the strong desire of the Oriyas for the amalgamation, the Madras Govt. now says that the Oriyas are not very keen over the matter as no criticism was offered to their publication so called.

I therefore request you to wake up Oriya feeling in Ganjam and Jeypore and ask the Oriyas of Madras to express their feeling in as many memorials, resolutions and telegrams to the Govt. of Madras and the Govt. of India as they can and as early as they can.

Yours sincerely

B. N. Misra

10th September 1923

Barrister B. N. Misra has been chosen as the Editor of the weekly, "Utkal Herald." Barrister Misra has replaced Khan Bahadur Abdul Mazid as the Editor.

8th October 1923

Barrister Biswanath Misra and Sri Bichitrananda Das have shouldered the responsibility to form the District Committees in Balasore and Singhbhum; and undertake the general propagation of the Oriya amalgamation movement. They are scheduled to complete their mission before 25th of October.

22nd June 1925

On the sad demise of Deshbandhu Chittaranjan, a condolence meeting was held in the Town Hall of Cuttack on 18th. Barrister B. N. Misra presided over the meeting. Mr. M. S. Das, Biswanath Kar, Nilakanth Dash, Ramkrushna Bose, etc., eulogized the acts of Deshbandhu and praised him in their speeches.

17th January 1927

In his editorial Sri Shashi Bhushan Rath wrote that in the meantime Barrister Biswanath Misra had written a long, well thought-out reasonable letter of prayer to the Viceroy about amalgamation of Oriya-speaking tracts.

In view of the Ganjam and Sambalpur agitation for amalgamation; and proposed resolution in that context in the legislative Assembly, Barrister Misra, in his prayer, had requested not to dare delay the decision any further on the issue.

26th January 1931

The news came out under the heading, "Separate Province Questions in the Assembly." Barrister Biswanath Misra has sent a copy of the questions raised by him in the Central Legislative assembly, which is given below.

Separate Province Questions in the Assembly

1. (a) Is the Government aware that Bihar and Madras governments have stopped the work in the departments of Barbers and Masons in Orissa and Ganjam.

   (b) If a separate state for the Oriya-speaking areas is not formed, one has to undergo through these difficulties. Does the government not realize it?

2. To pacify the excitement of the Oriyas, would the Government inform when the border determination

committee would meet for the purpose?

3. In view of the answer to my question in the Simla session and in view of the recommendation of the Simon Commission, would the Government inform how the commission would operate and what would be Government's modus operandi?

4. Is the Government aware of the proposals approved in the Utkal Samaj meeting held in Vishakhapatna on 07.12.30?

(a)   This committee has condemned Simon Sub Committee's recommendation of taking out the Jeypore tribal areas from Orissa.

(b)   Is the Government aware that a proposal has been made to leave the Vishakhapatna tribal areas in the hands of the Boundary Commission?

5. If the Government is aware, would they leave the decision in the hands of the Boundary Commission?

6. Is the Government aware that there are Oriya-speaking areas out side the map of Oriya-speaking tracts provided to the Simon Commission?

7. The tribals like Kandha, Saura and others do not have any written language. Hence they are influenced by Oriya language and Oriya civilization. Would the Boundary Commission not take that into account?

26th January 1931

The proposal to form a Nationalist Committee before the start of the Viceroy's session has been materialized. This committee will oppose the government budget, as it comes. In this committee both the members, Barrister Biswanath Misra and Sri Bhubananada Das, are there.

2nd February 1931

The salt rate has come down drastically in

India. Government came up with the proposal in the Central Legislative Assembly to form a committee to find out the ideal rate of salt and suggest mechanism to utilize the unused salt lying in abundance. Sri Biswanath Misra in his answer said that from the Orissa coast in 1822, Salt Taxation of Rupees 18 lakhs were collected. Now it has been stopped altogether. Government by stopping salt harvesting in the Orissa coast has lost the revenue.

5th December 1932

It was special news because it concerned formation of a separate province for Orissa.

Question- Answer in Legislative Assembly regarding separate province for Orissa

This week Government will send its report.

New Delhi 29.11.32

Last week Oriya Member Barrister Biswanath Misra had asked some questions in the legislative assembly relating to separate state of Orissa. Arising out of those questions, a few others were raised. Underneath the questions with answers are given:

Barrister Misra: What is the opinion of the Government with regard to the formation of a separate state for Orissa?

Member, Home Affairs: I am not in a position to express the view of Government of India.

Barrister Misra: What report concerning it, has the Government sent to the Secretary of India?

Member, Home Affairs: I have just said that I was not in a position to express the view of Government of India.

26th December 1932

Sensational news of "Asha"was:

"Orissa Became a Province"

London 24.12.32
26th December 1932

"Oriya Deputation in Delhi"

An Oriya Deputation has gone to meet India's Viceroy.

24th April 1933

Barrister B. N. Misra, Member of Legislative Assembly, has written:

A word about the Oriya Witnesses

'It is in the air that those who would go to London to represent the Oriyas, as witnesses for amalgamation of Oriya-speaking tracts would take care of the interest of their own parties in Orissa apart from the border issues of the separate Orissa state. How much truth is there in it, is unknown; but if it were true, it would not be in the interest of the country. If representatives selected for border movement taking advantage of their selection, look after their own interest, it would not be decent. Separate Orissa formation and the border determination movement are right now on. Hence the representatives should work towards them. It would be an act of shame and lowliness if they act for their own interest. Hope, representatives would pay special attention to it.'

BARRISTER BISWANATH AND CENTRAL LEGISLATIVE ASSEMBLY

Edwin Samuel Montague, the then Secretary of State, and Lord Chelmsford, the then Viceroy, jointly had prepared a report in 1918. The report was named as Mont-Ford Report. Basing on that, Government of India had prepared Indian Act 1919; which was mainly concerned with the constitutional reforms. Basing on it Central Legislative Assembly was formed. It was the one that gave birth to the Lok Sabha (Lower House) of the present times. The Upper House (Rajya Sabha) was named as Council of States.

Legislative Assembly (the Lower House) had tenure of three years and Council of states (the Upper House) had a life of five years. The Lower House (Lok Sabha of today) had 145 members. 104 out of them were elected and rest 41 was nominated members. The Upper House (present Rajya Sabha) had 60 members. 33 of the members were elected and the rest were nominated to represent the Upper House.

******

On 4th February 1922 the Chauri Chaura incident took place at Gorakhpur District in the United Province (present Uttar Pradesh). Disturbed by it, Gandhiji stopped the non-cooperation movement at the national level on the 12th February. Thus came a dramatic end to the Non-cooperation movement.

Barrister Misra because of his commitment to Gandhiji and his non-cooperation movement, had given up his legal practice in the British courts. It had serious repercussion on the financial situation of his family. However, the changed situation created opportunity for him to go back to the courts and practice again. But because of his focus being shifted to the national scenario in the meantime, his thirst for practice had waned. His main objectives had become the eradication of problems related to the segregated Oriya-speaking tracts and their unification. Those being the main concerns, continuing his legal practice was a great difficulty.

******

Two Oriya candidates, Sri Brajasundar Das and Raybahadur Nimai Charan Mitra, were elected to the first Central Legislative Assembly in November of 1920. Nimai Charan Mitra later resigned his membership. It was an opportunity for Barrister Biswanath Misra. To fill up the vacancy, he took part in the by-election. Two other candidates also filed their nominations against him. In the context, "Utkal Deepika" in its 18.02.1922 edition had written, "we are aware that Mr. B. N. Misra has worked a lot in the general public life. The other two are almost unknown and have no known contribution towards public life. We are convinced that out of all the candidates, Barrister B. N. Misra is the most suitable person for such a responsible post. Should the voters not choose the right and befitting candidate?"

Again after a month on 18.03.1922, "Utkal Deepika" had published a congratulatory statement on the occasion of Biswanath Misra's victory. In the same light on 13.03.1922 the daily "Asha" had published the news, "In order to felicitate Barrister Mr. Biswanath Misra on his win to the Central Legislative Assembly, two evening reception meets were organized at Berhampur. Last Friday, Silk merchant and Municipal Councilor, Mr. Nilasibaya and on Sunday, Pleader Sri Madhusudan Panigrahi had organized reception meets to congratulate Mr. Misra."

In the same manner, Sri Shashibhusan Rath had written in his editorial in "Asha", "Barrister Biswanath Misra has been elected to the Central Legislative Assembly in place of Raybahadur Nimai Charan Mitra. Barrister Misra is a capable person. He is the first Barrister of Orissa. He had gone to London without caring for the social sanctions. This is the greatest proof of his moral character. He is an extremely affable and gregarious person. Oriyas in general must feel very contented in his win. We hope, he will prove his mettle and through his deeds evince his patriotism in the Central Legislative Assembly."

On 15.03.1922, Barrister Biswanath Misra took oath in the Central Legislative Assembly, as a Member representing the non-Muslim constituency of Orissa Division.

Underneath all his speeches from 1st, 3rd and 4th Legislative Assembly have been given chronologically and verbatim, as recorded in the annals of the Central Legislative Assembly.

First Legislative Assembly and Barrister Biswanath

Legislative Assembly and Biswanath's Schedule of Questions and Answers

The first speech of Barrister Biswanath in the first Legislative Assembly was scheduled for 20.03.1922, exactly five days after his swearing-in. It was his speech on the Indian Budget or Finance bill.

The Indian Finance Bill (20.03.1922)

(Salt Taxation)

Babu B. N. Misra: Sir, I beg to support this amendment. I rise partly with diffidence, because I am new to this Assembly, and partly with great confidence. I hope I may be excused if I have any shortcomings as a beginner.

Sir, the Honourable the Finance Member said that the present proposal to raise the tax from Rs. 1-4-0 to Rs. 2-8-

0 per maund would not tell very heavily on the poor Indian consumer. He also said that it would cost each member 3 annas more and that if each family consists of 4 members, it would cost the family Re. 0-12-0. He has not, of course, taken into account the fact that each individual has to consume about 6 seers of salt, over and above the salt consumed by his animals. Besides a large quantity of salt is spent in curing fish and so on. Now, Sir, assuming that it would cost 12 annas per each family for salt, perhaps the Honourable the Finance Member who always deals with crores and lakhs, hundreds and thousands, cannot imagine what three annas mean to the poor Indians. (Hear, Hear) Sir, the poor people toil the whole day long and each family can spare to spend about two annas for the whole month for salt. Now if you increase the rate, he will be able to buy only half the quantity of salt, he is now consuming. If he buys one seer now, after the tax is increased, he will have to buy only half a seer or one pound. Now, Sir, how can he buy the salt which is necessary for his consumption with his limited income? You have not given him any more wealth. Suppose he has only one anna in his pocket and he has to buy salt for his use which may be just sufficient for him. Now after tax is increased, how can he buy the necessary quantity?

Now, Sir, let us imagine what he eats. The poor people of this country have not got large tables richly furnished with crockery forks and spoons, as so many fortunate Members of this House have, nor can they afford to eat chops, cutlets, pulses with other side dishes. Sir, the poor have got to live only on rice and a pinch of salt; they have to live on wheat or raggy and a pinch of salt. They have not got side dishes; perhaps there are many who have never seen the face of a curry or a side dish. If you take away half of the salt which is required by him, how is he to live? I submit, Sir, he will simply be driven either to leave half of his food or he must take food without any salt. How difficult it will be for him to live like this I leave the Assembly to imagine. Sir, medical men say that salt is absolutely necessary for our digestion besides being alimentary. A poor man who eats nothing else, but simple rice and salt, if he cannot purchase half of it owing to the proposed increase in taxation, I submit, that not only he will not be able to take his food properly, but perhaps we shall be accelerating his death by making him subject to so many diseases. (Hear, Hear.)

Sir, many Honourable Members have said: 'The income of an Indian family is very limited.' The Indian peasant is always in want. Sir, he always borrows money and takes advances long before his crop is ready for harvesting. We cannot conceive that such a man, who is always in need, will have any reserve to give to Government in the shape of increased tax. I submit, Sir, if you increase the salt tax, it will produce great hardship on the poor peasants, who form about 90 per cent of the population. This tax we should never increase. Of course, the British Government always deals with crores and lakhs. They perhaps think that 2 or 3 annas mean nothing. But, Sir, in these days when we are living on almost famine prices, for almost every necessary article of life, I submit it will be impossible for the middle class or the poor people to save more money to buy their salt. If a man has got one hundred rupees, you can take away fifty rupees from him, or if he has ten rupees, you can take away five rupees from him, or if a man has got only one rupee, you can take away .9 from him; but if a man is always in want and if he has .000 with him, how can you take anything from him? (Laughter.) I would ask the House to consider the condition of the poor people according to their standard of life and not judge them by the same standard of life as we are living.

Now, Sir, much has been said about retrenchment, want of revenue and so on, it will perhaps be preposterous for me to make any remarks about these things. But I believe the whole thing is carried on, on a wrong basis. Sir, I must say that the English people who have come to India, instead of Indianising themselves have Anglicised the Indians. (Hear, hear and loud Laughter.) The English people always live in luxury and their standard of life is very much higher than that of the Indians. The people of India are very poor. Whence are they to get so much money to live like the English? If English methods and English standards are applied, certainly it is impossible for India to be able to cope with them. Of course, all Honourable Members have known their own standard of living. One dinner for them costs Rs. 2 or Rs. 5. On the other hand, do the Government realize that with Rs. 3 an Indian can live a whole month? What is the proportion? English standards and Indian standards are quite different. The whole mistake lies with the English Government. There is also another thing. English people, even retired Governors, Lieutenant Governors and other high officials, when they are in England, can go by penny bus, penny train. But in India, Sir, three first class (fares) are necessary for them. In India, for a Lieutenant Governor, a special train is necessary. I admit that the Englishman is most practical, very business-like and very polite. He is the best friend, companion, helper and sympathizer. But unfortunately the Englishman in India is neither an Englishman of England or in England, but is something quite different. I do not mean that he is transformed into something different from mankind. But, Sir, he is an official. We have to understand the English vocabulary in a different way. We must think that the English people have a different Dictionary for themselves and a different Dictionary for Indians. I may quote to you, Sir, an instance. You all know, even His Excellency the Viceroy when he writes to you, will write 'Your most obedient servant'. Any big official, when he writes to you, subscribes himself 'Your most obedient servant'. What is the meaning of those words? 'Your most obedient servant'? When you implore them that a certain thing should not be done, they will carry it out against your wishes. What sort of obedient servants these Honourable official members are? His Excellency has the power to veto all the resolutions of this House. (No. no') Whenever he wishes, His Excellency has the power to veto although he is the most disobedient (Laughter) 'obedient servant.' He must describe himself either as His Majesty's obedient servant or the Indian Government's most obedient servant.

Mr. President: Order, Order. It was a little difficult to know when exactly the Honourable Member began to go out of order, but he is certainly out of order now.

Mr. B. N. Misra:I am just speaking about the Englishman in India, Sir. Of course my idea is that they should not write 'Your most obedient servant' but either write the most disobedient servant or the most oppressive master or act like obedient servants.

Coming to the subject under discussion, the difference is between the standards, - the point of view of Government and the point of view of the poor Indians. That is why, Sir, we have always a tug of war for retrenchment. I admit that Honourable Members have a very good intention, but they cannot but think in the way in which they have been brought up. That is why the establishment becomes so costly. Sir, India is very poor. India is overwhelmingly poor. The other day an Hounourable Member said, 'We stand by Statute.' But all these statutes are human-made statutes. They can be passed today, amended tomorrow and repealed the day after tomorrow. But there is a Higher Statute, Higher Right, Justice, Equity and good conscience. I appeal to this Assembly that justice should be done. When His Excellency came out to India, he held out all hopes that British justice will be given, the poor millions should be protected. They cannot support a costly Government. Some sacrifice should be made. (Cries of 'Salt, salt'. Dr. Gour : 'Now you stick to salt'.) I submit, Sir, that the interests of the poor Indians should be looked into and any increase in the duty will make the scale go down much below and will hang very heavily on the neck of the poor peasants. There is this difficulty, that money should be scraped by any means — by hook or crook. But I appeal to this Assembly that there are many other ways. Perhaps our official friends will never agree to a proposal for retrenchment. But I appeal to them to make us as the British people are. Let them make us as rich as they are and live in as high a style as they live. We have no objection to grant money. Let them look to our interests and those interests will be served perhaps by opening up many new channels, opening up new mines or starting new industries. In this connection, Sir, I wish to point out to this Assembly that the Orissa coast has a great possibility, and salt can be manufactured there. So long ago as 1822, the then Commissioner of Orissa, Mr. Sterling, wrote that 'First salt of all India' was produced there and the salt Industry could fetch 18 lakhs of rupees as revenue to the Government. This was a hundred years ago. I think if the industry had been taken care of by the Government all these years, it would be fetching a crore now, and this crore would have gone towards meeting the deficit. There was also a resolution about this in the Bihar and Orissa Legislative Council, and the Governor of Bihar and Orissa promised to move the India Government to have salt manufactured there. I do not know what has become of that first proposal. Besides there are many other ways in which the income of the country can be increased and the standard can be maintained. To increase the taxation without increasing the wealth of the poor is, I submit, really a great hardship, and surely the tug of war will never come to an end.

With these words, Sir, I support the amendment.

His appeal to the House was not to increase tax on the essential needs of the poor. He further appealed that the national income could be increased and deficit could be eradicated by cutting Government expenditure. With his views on the floor, he opposed the proposed increase in the tax of salt.

Unification of Oriya-Speaking Tracts

On 01.04.1922 "Utkal Deepika" published a news; which said that Mr. B. N. Misra had asked some questions on the floor of the Central Legislative Assembly to the Government. On 20.02.20 Honourable Member Sachidanand Sinha in the deliberation meet of the Viceroy had tried to bring in a proposal to unite all the Oriya-speaking tracts. The Honourable Home Member had assured that he would seek definite views of all the Governments In that regard. Barrister Misra's questions were aimed at eliciting answers from the Government in that connection.

Mr. B. N. Misrahad asked the following questions:

a. If the opinions of the Governments of other states had been obtained yet?

b. If yes, could the Government be kind enough to place the opinions on the floor of the House?

c. If that had not happened, could the Government ask for the reports of only those Governments who had not done so till the present time?

The Home Secretary, Sir William Vincent, furnished the replies to the above queries in the Central Legislative Assembly. According to his replies, the final answers to questions (a) and (b) had been obtained within the ensuing month. However, they still did not provide all the information. The reason being a local Government was still conducting its inquiry on the issue. Despite that, Government of India would soon initiate action on the proposals. However, there existed no necessity or proposal to put the issues on the floor of the House again. Question (c) did not have any relevance at the time.

"Asha" and "Utkal Deepika" had published the news under the head 'Issue of Utkal Unification' on 03.07.1922 and 08.07.1922 respectively.

Barrister Biswanath Misra had sent a proposal in the following manner to be discussed in the forthcoming session of the Central Legislative Assembly. The Unification of Orissa and amalgamation of Oriya-speaking tracts proposal was as following:

"The Central Legislative Assembly recommends the presiding Viceroy to get the approval of the Secretary, India, and the all powerful British Emperor to unite and put under one administration the political Orissa now under four states like Bihar-Orissa, Madras, Central Province and Bengal, along with the Oriya speaking tracts, both geographically and historically, by uniting them and bringing them under one administration, either under the Governor or a Deputy Governor, as may deem fit."

Indian Finance Bill (Postal Department) (22.03.1922)
Mr. B. N. Misra: Sir, I beg to oppose all these amendments. My sole ground is, of course, quite different from the grounds advanced by the Honourable Members

of this House. My sole ground is this. Does the sender of a letter or post card not get the benefit of the half anna or one anna postage on the letter or postcard sent? That is the sole reason, apart from other considerations. If a man lives a thousand miles away, by spending half anna or one anna he can get every information from a district, a thousand miles away. I don't think there is any reason for him to grudge to pay half anna or one anna. (Hear, hear.) Those who don't go out, don't require to send any letters; it is only those people who go abroad, either for commercial purposes, or for service, or for any other purpose, that require to send letters. I submit it will be quite reasonable for any such man to pay for the benefit he gets out of the letters he sends. If Government wants all these monies for stringency, there, I think, will be strong objection, as really the Department which works so hard is not properly paid or remunerated, so that much of it should go to improve the Department, and there will be no objection to a small portion going to the Government as it is at the head of administration.

On these grounds I oppose all the amendments, and I think Honourable Members of this House will not bring opposition for the sake of opposition but must judge each matter by its own merit, that is, the benefit, which it brings to the sender. I hope that Honourable Members will consider that and give their support to Government.

The Civil Marriage Amendment Bill (12.09.1922)

Mr. Biswa Nath Misra: Sir, I wish to be enlightened on some points, but I believe there is a great misapprehension amongst the Muhammadan as well as the Hindu Members present in this House. I believe many Muhammadan members think that if this Bill were passed there will be marriages between Hindus and Muhammadans which the Muhammadan religion does not allow; and others perhaps think that there will be marriages between Christian and Muhammadan, and Hindu and Christian and so on. I do not think that is what is aimed at, because the statement of Objects and Reasons itself uses the expression 'A civil marriage law, without reference to race, religion or social distinction', so that I do not think that any religious principles are involved at all in this kind of marriage. I think a Hindu can marry a Hindu under the Civil Marriage Act. Ordinarily of course Hindus are required to perform their marriages according to Hindu rites; they have to call the priest, they have to spend so much of money on the marriage occasion and they have to feed many people; they have to pay so much dowry and do this and that. We have heard of all these evils; at any rate these marriages are so very costly that sometimes many do not marry. I have heard of many instances of families of Rajas where, owing to the prohibitive expenses, many girls and daughters have remained unmarried; we have heard of instances in Bengal of several girls committing suicide by burning themselves with kerosene oil because their parents were not able to pay the dowry demanded by the husband or bridegroom. I think if this bill is passed into law it will enable the contracting parties to contract marriage under this Act without making any declaration. The Act of 1872 made it compulsory that the contracting parties should make a declaration that they are not Hindus, Muhammadans, Jains, Buddhists and so on; under that Act these declarations were necessary. Even a Brahmin who wanted to marry a Brahmin girl must go to a priest to get the marriage performed. Now if this Bill is passed into Law a Brahmin can marry a Brahmin girl without undergoing all those ceremonies and formalities that are required now according to the Hindu rites, and the marriage will be a valid one. This is not of course compulsory; it will not make every Hindu go and make a declaration when he wishes to marry a Hindu Girl, or a Muhammadan when he wishes to marry a Muhammadan; it will simply enable those who are willing to contract a marriage in this form to do so without undergoing a prohibitive cost; for instance a Muhammadan must have a Kazi and must perform the marriage in the presence of their vakils and so on, and they have to pay so much dowry to the girl; there may be persons who might wish to get the marriage performed without paying the dowry to the girl and the girl might be willing; but according to the Muhammadan form of marriage dowry must be paid, either prompt dowry or a deferred dowry. I think, therefore, if some Hindus are really sincere in wishing to perform marriages, they may, by allowing this Bill to be passed, avoid those pernicious customs which really tell very heavily against those who perform marriages in the present state of Hindu and Muhammadan society; so that I do not think there is room for any misapprehension on the part of Hindu or Muhammadan members, that, if this law were passed, Muhammadans might not like it and there might be riots and so on. A Muhammadan can marry a Muhammadan girl under this Act without in any way affecting the religious feelings or the religion of Muhammadans. I see no reason at all for any such apprehension. I do not see any reason either why it should affect the Hindus. A Brahmin can marry a Brahmin girl under this Act and I do not think that it affects the Hindu religion in the feast. On the other hand I think that if this bill were passed it would be pleasing and welcome to many. The Bill is not compulsory; it is simply permissive. Those who wish to contract marriages under this Act will have some relief.

I need not make a long speech at this stage, but I wish to do away with misapprehensions that may exist in the minds of members; because I think Dr. Gour really intends that a Hindu should marry a Hindu girl and a Muhammadan should marry a Muhammadan girl in this form and I do not think therefore there should be any objection to it and I hope the House will approve it.

After long discussions, the Motion was adopted.

Double Journeys by Registrars and Cashiers (15.01.1923)

Mr. B. N. Misra: (a) Is it a fact that the Registrars and Cashiers of the Secretariat accompanied by a clerk or menial go from Simla to Delhi or vice versa a few days before the move of their Department and come back after a couple of days' stay to go again with the Department?

(b) Are the Government aware that it costs a large amount twice every year on account of the travelling, daily and other allowances of these officers in addition to the loss suffered by the Departments owing to their absence from duty?

(c) Do the Government propose to consider this question with a view to economy and see whether only one junior man going in advance of the Department would be quite sufficient for the purpose?

The Honourable Sir Malcolm Hailey:(a) The practice referred to by the Honourable Member is followed in only a few of the Departments of Government of India.

(b) The cost in travelling and other allowances is not very appreciable.

(c) This is already the practice in most departments, and those Departments which follow the practice referred to in part (a) of the question will now consider whether it is possible to adopt this suggestion in lieu of the existing practice.

Staff Selection board – Extension of Scope (15.01.1923)

Mr. B. N. Misra:(a) Do the Government propose to consider the advisability of extending the scope of the Staff Selection Board to the Accounts and other offices under the Government of India?

(b) Will the Government be pleased to lay on the table a list of offices subordinate to the various Departments of the Government of India

The Honourable Sir Malcolm Hailey:(a) No

(b) A statement is being sent to the Honourable Member.

Staff Selection Board – Statistics of Examinations (15.01.1923)

Mr. B. N. Misra: (a) Will the Government please lay on the table information on the following points regarding the last examination of the Staff Selection Board for outside candidates?

1. Total number of candidates who applied with necessary fees.

2. Total number of candidates who were allowed to appear.

3. Number of candidates for the upper division of the attached offices.

4. How many out of (3) are to be called for interview.

5. How many out of (3) are to be declared successful.

(b) Will the Government please state if Army Headquarters is regarded by the Staff Selection Board, as an attached or Secretariat office?

(c) Is it a fact that Army Headquarters is not in receipt of Secretariat pay and allowances?

The Honourable Sir Malcolm Hailey: (a) 1. The total number of candidates who submitted applications accompanied by the necessary fees was 1,012.

2. The total number of candidates who were allowed to appear for the examination was 883.

3. The number of candidates for the Upper Division of Attached Offices was 440.

A very large number of these candidates applied also to be registered for other posts, e.g., in the Lower Division of the Secretariat and as clerks in Attached Offices, etc.

4. Of the 440 who applied for posts as Assistants in Attached Offices 55 qualified at the written examination and were called up for interview in order to qualify in that capacity. Many others were called up for interview in connection with other appointments for which they had qualified at the written examination.

5. Of the 55 interviewed for Assistantships 48 were declared successful.

(b) The Army Headquarters are treated as a Secretariat Office for this purpose.

(c) Yes.

Staff Selection Board – Method of Marking (15.01.1923)

Mr. B. N. Misra:(a) Will the Government please state how the marks were allotted under each head by the Staff Selection Board for each of the following at their last examination held in July, 1922, for outside candidates?

Written examination, (2) War services, (3) Special qualification and experience, (4) Interview.

(b) Will the Government please state if any limit has been fixed by the Board for the number to be passed? If so, is the examination intended to be more competitive than a qualifying test?

The Honourable Sir Malcolm Hailey:(a) A maximum of

300 marks were allotted for the written examination and 50 marks at the interview. The marks allotted at the interview were divided under three heads, viz., up to 10 for "Appearance", up to 10 for "Service" and up to 30 for "Intelligence." For active war service the maximum number of marks under "Service" was granted, viz., 10 marks. For other classes of war service marks were granted according to the length of such service. No marks were allotted for special qualifications as such, since no special, qualifications were called for, but those who had special qualifications or experience secured marks either under Intelligence or Service.

(b) The examination is a qualifying one, and no limit as to the number of candidates to be passed was fixed.

Staff Selection Board – Employment of Passed and Unpassed Men (15.01.1923)

Mr. B. N. Misra:(a) Will the Government please refer to the reply given to unstarred question No. 350 on the 28th March, 1922, regarding the unpassed men in the Secretariat and attached offices being replaced by passed candidates of the Staff Selection Board and state how far the promise made therein has been carried out?

(b) Will the Government please lay on the table a statement showing the number of unpassed candidates (including those who have appeared at the recent examination) employed in the Upper and Lower divisions of all the Departments of the Secretariat and the attached offices?

(c) What was the total number of outside candidates

passed by the Staff Selection Board in 1921, and how many of them were employed on 1st September 1922?

(d) How many of the passed candidates were not in service on 1st September 1922, and how many unpassed candidates were in service on the same date?

(e) What steps do the Government propose to take with a view to replace unpassed men by passed men?

(f) Will the Government please call for a list of all unpassed men in service in the various Departments of the Secretariat and the attached offices and state the definite dates by which they will be replaced by passed candidates?

The Honourable Sir Malcolm Hailey: The information is being collected and will be laid on the table when ready.

The Indian Mines Bill (29.01.1923)

Mr. B.N.Misra: Sir, my amendment relates to sub-clause (c) of Clause 3. In this sub-clause 'child' is defined to be a person understood under the age of thirteen years. It appears to me, Sir, as if this Honourable House is going to prepare a dictionary or to give meanings to words, which are ordinarily understood in another way. Generally a child inIndia means a person below the age of 16; that is, up to the age of 15 we generally take them to be children; in law we have minor and major; and a child or minor would mean any person up to the age of 18; above that age he will be a major. In England a child or infant would mean any person up to the age of 22 and after that age. . . .
.

Mr. President: Order, order. The Honourable Member has apparently neglected to provide any description for a person up to the age of 12 years. I cannot allow an amendment to be moved which makes nonsense.

Mr. B. N. Misra: I am sorry, Sir, but this has reference to section 26, and so I have put in this amendment to this section. The law provides that no child shall be employed in a mine or be allowed to be present in any part of mine which is below ground. . . . .

Mr. B. N. Misra: Sir, I move:

"That in clause 3, sub-clause (k), for the words 'the enforced absence of the injured person from', the words 'inability to attend to' be substituted."

Because "serious bodily injury" is defined as injury which involves or in all probability will involve the permanent loss of the use of, or permanent injury to, any limb or the permanent loss of or injury to the sight or hearing, or the fracture of any limb or the enforced absence of the injured person from work for a period exceeding 20 days. I submit, Sir, in this the term "enforced absence" is not quite clear, because who will enforce? Will really the mine owners enforce the labour to absent from work? Certainly they are not going to do that. Their interest is to bring the injured person to work and to show that he has not received any serious bodily injury. I think, it is rather meaningless, because in the Indian Penal Code we have got the term "grievous hurt" defined as "inability to attend to work for 20 days, etc." The words "the enforced absence of the injured person from" is rather meaningless, and if we substitute the words "inability to attend to" it would be quite all right. It would mean the inability of the person to attend to his work. So I move this amendment. The motion was negatived.

Mr. B. N. Misra: Sir, my amendment runs as follows:

" (i) That in clause 23, sub-clause (b) for the word 'sixty' the words 'forty eight' be substituted.
(ii) That in clause 23 (c) for the words 'fifty four' the words 'forty two' be substituted."
Clause 23 runs as follows:
"No person shall be employed in a mine:

a. on more than six days in any one week;
b. if he works above ground, for more than sixty hours in any one week;
c. if he works below ground, for more than fifty four hours in any one week."

My amendment relates to clauses (b) and (c). The first sub-clause says that no person shall be employed for more than six days in one week. Practically a labourer has to work sixty hours in six days, and if he has to work sixty hours in a week, it comes to this, that he has to work ten hours a day. I consider that this ten hours' continuous work is really very unwholesome and it will greatly tell upon the health of the labourers. The object of the bill is to protect the safety and health of the labourers. Generally labourers go to work at about 7 in the morning, come at about 12, prepare their meals, have their bath and so on. They go to work at 3 p.m., come back at 6 p.m. An ordinary labourer works 8 hours a day. That is outside, in the open fields. In this case, if the present conditions are allowed, they will have to work 10 hours. For instance, if they go early morning at 7, they will complete their ten hours' work by 5 o' clock without any recess. If some recess is allowed for their bath and their food, - you must allow at least two or three hours, - even if you allow only two hours, they will have to work till night 7 o' clock. I think two hours' recess is absolutely necessary for their bath and other things. Practically, they will have to work from morning 7 till night 7, if any recess is allowed. If no recess is allowed, as is not contemplated, they will have to work continuously from 7 a.m. till 5 p.m. I wish to point out to Honourable Members that we began just at about 11 o' clock and we went for owe had one hour's ur lunch at 2 p.m. That is, after three hours' work we had one hour's rest. I think Honourable Members will have some sympathy and some consideration for these hard working poor labourers. If two or three hours' work is sufficient for an hour's rest for us, don't you think that these labourers who have to work in the pits deserve your sympathy! I am told sometimes these pits are 5000 feet deep and some are 2000 feet deep, and they have to work at such depths underneath the ground that they do not get any free air, and the pits are very warm and very unhealthy. Do they not, as human beings, require some sort of concession and do you think it proper that they should be so much tormented and work for ten hours a day at such depths? Sub-clause (c) provides that they will have to work only fifty-four hours underground. That means that underground labour is required to be 9 hours a day and aboveground work 10 hours a day. There is no definition of what is aboveground work and what is underground. We do not know which they will call underground work – 200 feet or 300 feet or 1,000 feet under the ground. In these circumstances, to labour for 9 hours or 10 hours a day is very unwholesome for these labourers. Probably my Honourable friend, Mr. Innes, will tell us that we have to conform to the decision of the Geneva International Conference, which has accepted 10 hours' labour to be the minimum. I submit that for this particular kind of work, which is really very difficult, and in a country like India where the weather is really so uncharitable or so specially hot in summer, it is very difficult for labourers to work 9 or 10 hours a day. I think 5 or 6 hours will be really very tiresome for any labourer who really wants to work. If you simply want them to be there even till 10 o' clock, they might be idling away their time. In the interests of hard work you have to give them some rest. If you give less hours, they can work more energetically and more vigorously, and they can turn out more work than if you allow them to be there for 20 hours or 15 hours or any longer hours. The result that the mine owners will get by allowing these people to work more hours, will not be profitable to them, because we must imagine that the workmen are after all human beings and no man can do hard work continuously for more than 7 or 8 hours. If you keep him there for 10 or 15 hours I do not think it will be profitable to the mine owners. Probably, it may be said that these labourers will get more money. As a matter of fact, they do not get more money. The work is carried on on a contract system. Say, the cooly sirdar takes 10 or 12 coolies. He takes a contract and whatever extra money is got is taken by the cooly sirdar from the mine owner or his agent. The actual coolies do not get any profit, because the coolies continue to get the same daily wages. The gain goes to the sirdar, or headman or contractor. I submit therefore that if they work hard it will not benefit them. I do not think that such provision will really bring any benefit to these labourers. Then, probably,

it may be said that in the Factory Act we have also 10 hours labour. I submit to this house that labour in a factory and labour in a mine is quite different. Labour in a factory is more comfortable where they have to work under buildings or in open air, whereas this mine work is really very tiresome and unwholesome work. Ten hours labour is very difficult even above ground and 9 hours a day or 54 hours in the week is really very difficult to do. Of course, we are not making any provision that those who have worked 4 or 5 hours underground should be brought above ground and another set should go underground. If there were some such provision, there might be reason in that, but there is no such provision. So, a man working underground will always be there continuously 9 hours, which is very difficult. In these circumstances I move:
"that the clause (b) instead of '60 hours' '48 hours' be substituted and in clause (c) instead of '54 hours' '42 hours' be substituted.".

Mr. Chairman: Amendment moved:
"That in clause 23, sub-clause (b), for the word 'sixty' the words 'forty-eight' be substituted,"

....

....

....

Mr. Chairman: The amendment before the House is:
"That in sub-clause (b) of clause 23 substitute '54' for '60'."

The motion was negatived.

Mr. B. N. Misra: Sir, …..

Mr. Chairman: Is the Honourable Member formally moving it? He has already made a speech.

Mr. B. N. Misra:I have already made a speech, Sir; that is what I was going to express. I think I have dealt with both the clauses, and I submit that at least this amendment (42 hours a week) for underground work should be accepted. I therefore move:

" That in clause 23, sub-clause (c), for the words 'fifty-four' the words 'forty-two' be substituted."

The motion was negatived.

The Indian Mines bill (30.01.1923)

Mr. B. N. Misra: Sir, clause 26 runs as follows:

"No child shall be employed in a mine, or be allowed to be present in any part of a mine which is below ground."

My amendment is;

"To omit the words 'be employed in a mine, or'."

This will mean that a child can be employed above ground in the mining work. "No child shall be employed in a mine." Here "mine" must mean above ground as well as underground. The other part of the clause is "or be allowed to be present in any part of a mine which is below ground." The phrase "which is below ground" qualifies only "or be allowed to be present in any part of a mine." If the construction of the clause is that no child shall be employed or shall be allowed to be present in any part of a mine, which is below ground, I have no objection. But my point is that a child should be allowed to work above ground. The construction of this clause as it is, is that no child should be employed in a mine. I submit it is rather injurious to the laboring class. My proposal is that the words "be employed in a mine" should be omitted from the clause. This will give an advantage. We have defined a "child" to be one under the age of 13. We are aware that these labourers always have children and the children always assist their parents in their work. The Honourable Mr. Innes has already said and we all very well know, that it is the poor agriculturist class that comes for this labour, and we know that in poor agriculturist families, the children always help their parents in their work. If they have children of 6, 7, 8 or 12 or 13 years of age, they help their parents in the fields. They accompany them to the fields and help them there. They may not go underground, but they can work above ground and help their parents similarly. They can carry the baskets of coal. They can do some minor work, which is not very hard, they can earn some money in that way. Children of poor labourers very often never see schools. We, rich people, who send our children to schools cannot expect these labourers to send their children to any boarding schools or even to any primary schools. They always work jointly with their parents. If we keep them from laboring even above ground or doing some work near about the mine, it will mean not only loss of their earning to the family, but it will also mean that the parents will have to provide for their children and maintain them. Not only that. The children will ruin their own career, because they are not accustomed to go to school, they naturally waste their time in playing, they will not be of any use in future to themselves or to the family. They won't get used to work. In England even a cobbler's son or a shoe-maker's son can become a Prime Minister, and any poor man or a man of the laboring class can occupy very high positions. That is not so with Indian labourers. You cannot expect from this poor laboring class to get men who will get so much educated or who will rise so much above their class they can occupy any high position in life. Generally these people continue to be labourers. We know very well how our caste system is working and we know that in India a peasant is always a peasant, a Brahman is always a Brahman, a blacksmith is always a blacksmith.

Mr. President: Order, order. Caste has nothing to do with employment of children in mines.

Mr. B. N. Misra:I am simply showing the analogy. The labourers who work in a mine cannot suddenly turn so rich and earn so much money that they can afford to send their children to schools. If the words, I propose, are omitted, the children will be given an opportunity of working near about the mine and they will earn a livelihood, and help their parents and also learn how to work so that when they grow up, they can work in the mines or even elsewhere. In these circumstances, I submit that this Honourable House will accept the amendment. If my amendment is accepted, the objection on the part of the mine owners that they will lose labour and the industry will be ruined for want of labour will not hold good and the people will be allowed to work as much as they can above ground. With these words, Sir, I move my amendment, which runs as follows:

" In clause 26, the words 'be employed in a mine, or' be omitted."

The motion was negatived.

The Workmen's Compensation Bill (03. 02. 1923)

Mr. B. N. Misra: May I rise to a point of order. My amendment runs 'or such others as being closely related absolutely depend on, or are entitled to maintenance by law and custom'. This will cover the persons that have been proposed by Mr. Joshi. So, practically, if this amendment is voted against, my amendment will be rather weakened. I think, my amendment being of a more general character, it ought to precede his amendment.

The President: As regards that, Honourable Members may in this case simply vote against Mr. Joshi and then move their own.

Mr. B. N. Misra: Sir, my amendment is rather different from the amendments put forward by other Members. I move my amendment, which runs as follows:

" In sub-clause (d) of clause 2 (1) after the word 'sister' the following be inserted:

'or such others as being closely related, absolutely depend on, or are entitled to maintenance by law and custom'."

Sir, some dependents of the workmen have been included in the clause, but as far as I understood the Honourable Member of Commerce, Mr. Innes and Mr. Joshi, they said that they do not want a large number of dependents as it will complicate matters, there will be difficulty and litigation, the amount they will get will be very small and so on. But I do not contemplate such a case. What I contemplate is where there is a person absolutely dependent on the workmen, say, for instance, grandmother

– mother's mother. The mother's mother owing to natural affection brought up the grandson. In fact, the mother's mother spent all her earnings and income for the grandson and brought him up. When the grandson grew he earned money and helped the grandmother. Btut when the grandson passes away, the grandmother is really at a disadvantage, having spent all her income and property over the grandson, on whom she was absolutely dependent. I do not contemplate a case in which if the grandson dies there are others living to help her. Take the case where there is a grandmother and grandson. The grandson grew up and was employed in some factory or somewhere else and died on account of some injury or accident. Then, the grandmother is, I think, in justice entitled to have a share from the compensation given to such a deceased workman. I consider it is only just to classify her as dependent or relation absolutely dependent upon the deceased workman. I think there will be no objection to giving some compensation or classifying her as a dependent. Here are two brothers. The elder brother died and the elder brother's wife brought up her husband's younger brother. When this boy grew up, he got employed and supported his brother's wife, because she spent all her money over him and took so much trouble over her husband's brother. If this man dies, the woman should be entitled under those circumstances to get compensation, because she was absolutely dependent on the deceased workman. The present definition covers minor son. But sometimes there may be a grown up son, who is blind, or a grown up son either deaf or dumb. Such incapable persons who are unable to earn are naturally dependent upon the income or earning of their father. In such cases even the Hindu law states that such blind, deaf or dumb sons or a son who suffers from leprosy or other incurable diseases should be maintained by the father even if they are grown up. There is no such provision. The provision only enables the minor son to be a dependent on the workman. But, in such cases, as I have pointed out, according to Hindu Law, the father is bound to maintain them. When such a workman dies, I think these blind, deaf or dumb sons should be classified as dependents and they should get compensation. I think, Honourable Members of the House will not view my amendment as adding to the list. My amendment meets such other urgent and exceptional cases. I hope Honourable Members of the House will accept the amendment. And then the second part includes those who by law and custom are entitled to maintenance. I think all the lawyer Members of this House will agree with me that the grandfather or grandmother or grandson are real dependents. Such persons ought to be allowed to be classified as dependents of the deceased workman, because they are entitled to maintenance by law. With these words, Sir, I move my amendment.

The Workmen's Compensation Bill (05.02.1923)

Mr. B. N. Misra: Sir, I beg to move:
"In sub-clause A (i) of clause 4 (i), for the word 'thirty' the word 'sixty' be substituted."
This clause provides that in the case of death of a workman only thirty months wages will be paid as compensation; that is quite sufficient. Sir, probably some

of the Honourable Members will call me very greedy as I am asking for a little more. But I think Honourable Members will find that this proposal to raise thirty to sixty months' wages will not entail such hardship on the mill-owners, factory owners and rich people, nor will they find it difficult to make that payment for it will be a payment in the interests of labour itself. Sir, the workmen that are in view come mostly from the laboring class who get say say about Rs. 15 to 20 or say 25 a month. The amount contemplated under this section will probably be from Rs. 600 to Rs. 800. Rs. 20 to 25 has been ascertained to be the average monthly wages of the workman. Now, Sir, will this payment really entail hardship upon the millowners? It has been said that it is a new Act and that industry will perhaps be ruined if workmen are allowed such compensation. Sir, this is not a general order of things. Accidents are, of course, rare. For instance in the case of agriculture or in the case of landowners, we get famine or we get floods occasionally. We do not get them often. What is done in such cases? Whenever there is a flood or a famine, even the benign Government not only gives up the rent from the poor tenants but also comes to the relief of the famine-stricken or the flood-stricken people. I think that is a very wholesome rule observed by the Government.

Mr. President: Order, order. The Honourable Member has wandered very far from his own amendment.

Mr. B. N. Misra: Sir, I was giving an illustration.

Mr. President: The illustration is out of order.

Mr. B. N. Misra: The mill-owners, factory-owners, are not such poor people as will find it difficult to meet these occasional accidents which will be due to the negligence or it may be really due to some actions on the part of the owners themselves or it may be due to some natural causes. But these rich people amass their wealth with the labour of these poor labourers. The prosperity of these industries is due to the workmen's labour. If the workmen are not properly looked after or if there is not sufficient inducement to workmen, I think these industries cannot prosper. These small payments, instead of being a hardship to the mill-owners or factory-owners or mine-owners, will really do good to them inasmuch as it will induce the workmen to readily come forward and join the factories, etc. Now, Sir, the amount that has been fixed is thirty months' wages in case of death. Is that the value set upon a man's life – whether he be a workman or any other man? I f you put it at thirty months' wages, I think it is too little. If it is intended to help his dependents, then also it is very little. Of course the maximum is fixed at Rs. 2,500. Probably that may help the higher paid men such as engineers and others who get perhaps Rs. 200 or Rs. 300 a month. In their case Rs. 2,500 may be sufficient. But in the case of poor workmen, thirty months' wages is very small. The Honourable Mr. Innes said that even when a man is murdered, nobody compels the murderer to pay compensation to the relations of the deceased. When a man has murdered, the amount it is found out, he is hanged by the neck and nobody lives to pay compensation. Our civil law lays down that no man's heirs or successors are responsible for the guilt or criminal action of his predecessors. That is why the heirs or successors are not asked to pay compensation. The man is either transported to the Andamans or is kept in jail for several years.

Mr. President: Order, order. The Honourable Member is getting even further from his amendment.

Mr. B. N. Misra: Sir, my submission is, it is really a moral duty on the part of these owners who are rich men to meet this occasional expenditure, which will really be a relief to the workmen and will not really tell so much upon the industry. I therefore submit that thirty months' wages is too small and that it ought to be increased to sixty months' wages.

Mr. President: Amendment moved:

"In sub-clause A (i) of clause 4 (1), for the word 'thirty' the word 'sixty' be substituted."

The question is that that amendment be made.

The motion was negatived.

In that connection, many Honourable Members raised the issue in different forms but with the same intention. However, the Government, as usual, negatived the motion with their veto power. Barrister B. N. Misra made a serious comment in that regard.

Mr. B. N. Misra: Sir, if I am not mistaken, probably many of the Honourable Members want it to rain copious showers over the middle of the ocean but they do not want even a drizzle over the scorched and dry land. Their attitude has been always to support the man of wealth. I have already submitted my arguments in my last speech and I do not wish to say anything more here. I respectfully submit to the House my amendment:

"That in sub-clause B (i) of clause 4 (1) for the words 'forty two' the words 'eighty four' be substituted."

The motion was ultimately negative.

The Indian Penal Code (Amendment) Bill (26.02.1923)

(Amendment of Sections 362 and 366)

Mr. B. N. Misra: Sir, I move that in clause 2 the words "or of abuse of authority" be omitted.

The words are rather vague. There may be authority of many kinds, such as natural authority, official authority and other kinds of authority; natural authority would mean the authority of the parents, of the father or mother or natural guardian; and if that kind of authority is meant I think it will be very difficult to ascertain where the abuse lies. Take the case of a girl who is reading in a particular school and the school mistress sends the girl to attend some meeting or a tennis party or to some church to attend prayers, and there she meets some young men and somehow or other gets into bad company and is seduced for the purpose mentioned in the Bill. There is the difficulty. It may be said that the girl went to such a place, and having gone to such a place, was seduced. It may be wrongly construed against the schoolmistress for abuse of authority. Probably it may be said that nobody accompanied the girl, and the girl having gone alone, such an occasion arose. It will be very difficult to put a proper interpretation on the words "or abuse of authority." It is liable to be abused in other ways as well. If you put a strict interpretation on these words, you may say that the natural authority did not exercise proper care or caution and so there is an abuse of authority. We know that in some societies girls are allowed to go out, there may be abuse, there may not be abuse of such a system. But it will be very difficult to fix the guilt of a person in authority. I suggest the omission of the words 'or abuse of authority' in clause 2.

The Honourable Sir Malcolm Hailey: I would explain very briefly why the words 'or abuse of authority' were placed in the Bill. They are necessary in order to meet our obligations under the Convention. Its Article II runs as follows:

"Whoever in order to gratify the passions of another person attempts by fraud, by means of violence, threat, abuse of authority or any other method of compulsion, to procure, entice, etc."

I cannot agree with my Honourable friend that these words constitute any sort of danger. I do not indeed think that the cases put by him are in any way relevant to the section as drafted. Abuse of authority could not be argued against any person who had merely been guilty of carelessness or omission to provide proper precautions, for this possibility was evidently at the back of Mr. Misra's apprehension. He will see that it is necessary not only that a person should be guilty of abuse of authority, but that by so doing he should induce any woman to go from any place with intent that she may be, or knowing that it is likely that she will be, forced or seduced, etc.

Finally the amendment was, by leave of the Assembly, withdrawn.

Mr. B. N. Misra: Sir, I have got a very difficult task now before me. The amendment I have proposed is:

"In clause 3 in proposed section 366 A for the words 'to do' substitute the word 'does' and in the same clause omit the words 'or seduced' wherever they occur in proposed sections 366A and 367B."

I do not move the first part to substitute "does" for "to do." I shall deal with the other part of my amendment, namely, to omit the words "or seduced." I wish to make it clear to the Honourable House that I do not yield to anybody in this House in my desire to see that the procurer is punished. I do not wish to support such a heinous crime if it really is committed. Well, Sir, we are a body here sitting as legislators, and we should do what is practicable and what is workable, and this must be reasonable and workable thing. Sir, it is laid down that whoever induces any minor girl to be seduced to illicit intercourse with another person shall be punished, it is also said that the procurer alone is to be punished and not others. Sir, the original object of this Bill was for the suppression of the white slave traffic, which meant that it wanted to stop trafficking in white slaves, i.e.; Europeans or white girls from a foreign country. The section as it appears in Penal Code has really lost that object and it applies now to India and becomes a part of the Indian Penal Code. I submit, Sir, if this is allowed, it will be really a hardship in India for reasons that I am going to place before the Honourable House. Sir, if it is taken that seduction is to be punished, or the procurer is to be punished, he is punishable under section 366 of Indian Penal Code and I think there will be absolutely no necessity for having this amendment. Section 366 says:
"Whoever kidnaps or abducts any woman with intent that she may be compelled, or knowing it to be likely that she will be compelled, to marry any person against her will, or in order that she may be forced or seduced to illicit intercourse ......"
If that be the object, such person is convicted under

section 366. We have got other sections, regarding enticing away married women and so on. Sir, the object is to punish a procurer so that he may not carry on his nefarious trade and it is for this purpose that this amendment is proposed. I submit really this does not affect India. I do not think in a country like India such actual trafficking in girls exists because Indian society, whether Hindu or Muhammadan, is such that it always takes care to get its girls married. Under the Hindu law it is religious injunction that the girls must be given in marriage, and you will find in the higher societies such as Kshatrias, Brhmins and others that they get their girls married at a very early age, at an age, which would be surprising to Europeans. The ninth year is described by Manu to be the best year when a girl should be given in marriage. Practically before 12, before a girl attains puberty, she must be given in marriage. That is the Hindu idea of marriage. Also we find among our Muhammadan friends, although some of them marry after the girls attain puberty, most of them marry their girls at an earlier age. I am speaking of the picked society of Muhammadans, where the marriage law is so much in vogue that there would be no such fear of any girl being seduced, and there would be no such traffic in girls as to be supplied for immoral purposes. But even assuming that there are societies and people of lower orders living in India, where seduction of girls is possible. I submit, Sir, that really if you do not punish the seduction or illicit intercourse with a girl. I see no reason why the procurer should be so vehemently condemned in this House. Sir, I would point out that you, Sir, want meat, Honourable Members want meat and the country wants meat. That is why the butcher keeps a stall and sells meat. Sir, we all want mat to buy, w relish it and we never condemn ourselves for eating it. Because the butcher supplies it for our convenience and for our rquirements, we want him to be punished, why? Is it not the same in this country with these women, whether you call them dancing girls, or devadssis or ordinary dassis or prostitutes. It is not an unknown thing. I think all Honourable Members have seen everywhere this kind of women. (Cries of "No, no."). You pass through any street and you will find them, you find them existing in very large numbers. They have existed fom time immemorial; they have not come into existence under British rule or under Mughal rule; they have existed perhaps from the times spoken of in the puranas. They are regarded as a necessity even for marriage and other parties and for singing songs in invocation of God. Perhaps every Member of this House might have heard of ceremonies in temples of ......

Mr. President: The Honourable Member will discuss his amendment now.

Mr. B. N. Misra:I am only pointing out, Sir, that girls have been necessary for the purpose of certain religious ceremonies. (Cries of "withdraw, withdraw.") I come, now, Sir, to (Cries of "withdraw, withdraw.") to Mr. Kinney, the eminent English lawyer, who in his Book on Criminal Law at page 143, says:

"Hence a voluntary illicit intercourse of the sexes, even though it may take the form of mercenary prostitution or an adulterous violation of marital legal rights, furnishes no ground for criminal indictment."

That is the state of things in England. Even in cases of divorce, we find that the seducer is not punished; he appears as the co-respondent and is liable civilly and not criminally. Much has been said about girls being disposed of to Zemindars and Rajas. I submit, Sir, it is not a fact. Neither Dr. Gour nor anybody else has really represented the true state of things.

Dr. H. S. Gour:I rise to a point of order. I never made any statement that girls were disposed of either Zemindars or to Rajas.

Mr. B. N. Misra: Zemindars never get any girls from procurers, as has been said. What happens is this. When Zemindars or Rajas marry, their wives or Ranis bring with them some girls as maid servants; that is how they come to live in Raja's palaces. Such a thing as procuring of girls does not exist and no gentleman, whether he be a Zemindar or a Raja or any ordinary man, would ever adopt such a nefarious means to procure girls. (Cries of "Withdraw, withdraw.") I am sorry, Sir, my friends who have been staying in towns do not know what happens in the mufassil and in the country. I will just tell you, Sir. This penal code will apply all over India, and, as the Honourable Sir Malcolm Hailey pointed out to you, to many advanced tracts occupied by Bhils and Gonds, etc. I was Public Prosecutor in Agency Tracts and I know among the Khonds they have a system whereby the grown-up men and women live in their houses and all grown-up boys and girls from the same village or from three or four villages go to a particular house called Dhangar House. The unmarried boys are called dhangars and the unmarried girls are called dhangris. Supposing a dhangari says to a girl friend of hers "Let us go to a certain place and sing songs." Suppose she spends a night there and does what she likes, are you going to punish her because she called her friend to have a dance and sing a song? (Cries of "Shame, shame.") Surely you will not say that such a girl who has asked her girl friend to go to the dhangar house should be punished for illicit intercourse. Why should we think so much about these people who are able to take care of themselves? Surely this House is not going to maintain all the people in the street or is not going to make provision for them. (A voice: "You wait and see" and cries of "Withdraw, withdraw.")

Then, Sir, we find another point. Under section 366B the age is fixed at 21. I do not think really that girls from foreign countries are so dull or so low in intellect that they do not know what they are about. Why should the seducer be punished in such cases, and where is the element of seduction? The girl is quite intelligent and understands where she is going. Perhaps she goes for her best interests. So why should you protect and why should you punish the seducer of a girl who is, say, 20 years of age? Do you really think that the man has committed any offence when a girl of 20, with full deliberation, comes with him to any place? (Loud cries of "Withdraw, withdraw.") (Sir Jamsetjee Jejeebhoy: "Now you have made your speech, withdraw.") Sir, this House has not really realized where the shoe pinches. With these words I move my amendment.

The motion was negatived.

Mr. B. N. Misra: Sir, my next amendment is:

"In clause 3 at the end of the proposed section 366B add the following:

'In the case of compulsion or use of force for illicit intercourse and with fine only in the case of simple seduction for the same'."

My object in moving this amendment is the same as that of

the Mover of the previous amendment – that in the case of simple seduction, where no force or violence is used, the punishment should not be so severe as 10 years but that it should be fine only. This is the object of my amendment. I think that in the case of consent there should not be such severe punishment and as we say in common parlance "do not place the same value on a diamond as on an ordinary stone." The punishment for stealing a rose from your table and Rs. 10,000 from your pocket, though they are both thefts, is not the same. You would not inflict the same punishment for both; and in this case I submit that for simple seduction without any force or violence the punishment should be fine only.

The motion was negatived.

Clause 3, as amended, was added to the Bill.

Statement Laid on the Table (28.02.1923)
The Honourable Sir Malcolm Hailey: Sir, I lay on the table the information promised in reply to a question by Mr. B. N. Misra, asked on the 15th January, 1923, regarding the passed and unpassed candidates of the Staff Selection Board.

Information promised by **Sir Malcolm Hailey**on the 15th January 1923, in reply to **Mr. B.N. Misra's**starred question No. 14 regarding passed and unpassed candidates of the Staff Selection Board.

(a) No promise was made in the answer to question No. 350 on the 28th March 1922.

(b) A statement giving the required information is being placed in the library.

(c) and (d). The information will be found in the answers given to questions Nos. 86 and 148 on the 7th September 1922.

(e) and (f). Indication of the action taken will be found in the statement mentioned above.

Departments are taking action to replace unpassed men by passed men, but the process of elimination will inevitably be gradual so as not to disturb the work and organisation of the Departments.

Index to Legislative Assembly Debates (28.02.1923)
Misra, Mr. B. N. –
Budget. General discussion of the - for 1923-24. First stage 3072-74.
Budget demands for grants. Civil works. 3661-62.
Budget demand for Indian Postal and Telegraph Department. 3574-75.
Budget demand for the staff household of the Governor General. 3444-45
Code of Criminal Procedure (Amendment) Bill:
Consideration of –
Clause 11. 1128-29.
Clause 14. 1202.
Clause 15. 1209-10.

Clause 16 as passed by the Council of State. 1245-46.
Clause 21 as passed by the Council of State. 1391.
Clause 24. 1478.
Clause 27. 1545-47, 1553-54.
Clause 28. 1561-62.
Clause 45. 1822-1823.

General Discussion on the Budget (06.03.1923)

Mr. B. N. Misra: Sir, I do not think really the congratulations or the curses of Honourable Members on this side affect the Honourable Members on Treasury Benches. They are doing their duty that appertains to their office; we have to do also a certain duty as representing the people. If we go through the whole budget we find, Sir, that it is practically a budget for the maintenance of the administration. As pointed out by Dr. Gour, the whole money that you find is to be spent upon administration and administration alone. Sir, when the tax-payer pays his hard-earned money, he expects also some benefit. What benefit does this budget provide for the tax-payer? Sir, the only benefit that the tax-payer can ever get is from the improvement of industries and agriculture or from irrigation and such other works and projects by which the people really get the benefit that they desire. I am sorry if I do not swim with the current and with other Honourable Members in talking about retrenchment, in certain directions especially. Sir, I find really that a very very poor provision has been made in the budget for what are called nation-building Departments. India is an agricultural country, and it is known that most of the Government revenue about 31 crores, is realized from the land. But what actually are we spending for the improvement of

Agriculture? I see from the Budget Demand, No. 32 I think, that a very small sum has been asked for for improvement of this Department. For Agriculture they have asked for 7 lakhs, and for industry only Rs. 44,000. Sir, everyone knows the abject condition of Indian industry. I will ask you just to turn for a moment and look at the articles on your desk, the ink bottle, the pen, the writing paper, the blotting pad; look at all those things and you will find that they are of foreign manufacture. Can you point out anything of Indian make? Is not such a vast country entitled to provide those things the trade in which is dominated by foreign countries? I will ask the Honourable Members also just to look around at the clothes they wear. Of what make is the cloth? All is foreign, Sir. Everything is of foreign manufacture, the thread with which their clothes are stitched and the needle, which has been used for the purpose, all are of foreign make; nothing is made in India. (A voice: "What about yourself?"). I am also one of you, not from outside. I wish to point out really the wretched condition of Indian industry. I think that any amount spent on improving Indian industry will not be objected to by any Member of this House and will not be spent uselessly.

As regards agriculture also we find a very small sum of money budgetted for. I speak subject to correction, but from a Year Book I have ascertained that in a country like Ireland, of which, Sir, you are well aware of the size and which also from your travels in India you know to be a fraction of the size of India, I found that in the year 1916-17 the Board of Agriculture in Ireland demanded 76,177 pounds for the improvement of agriculture. They provide there for all kinds of agricultural education; they conduct scientific research in agriculture, and they also provide for lectures on agriculture, horticulture, book-keeping, butter-making, and so forth. But what is being done in India on those lines to improve agricultural conditions or industry? Ireland is perhaps less than one-twentieth the size of British India, yet we only are asked for Rs. 44,000 for industry. I submit, Sir, this expenditure on Indian industry is really farcical. Perhaps some Members may say that it is a provincial subject. Sir, we all know what the condition of provincial finance is. The ministers are everywhere crying themselves hoarse for money. We take provincial contributions; we take the income tax; the Central Government takes in many other ways the income of the provinces. They have nothing and those Departments are starving. I submit, Sir, that more money ought to be spent on Indian industry and agriculture.

Sir, I do not wish to travel over the same grounds, which other Members have covered in regard to the expenditure, especially on railways and on the military. Strictly speaking, the working expenses of railways have increased abnormally. In the budget of 1913-14 you will find that the expenses amounted to 49.26 crores; the estimate for 1922-23 amounts to 94.72 crores. I do not think that the increase is at all justifiable. Honourable Members will see that the same figures have been used, 4 and 9, but the 4 and 9 have been reversed and 94 makes a vast difference. I find from the replies given to some questions which I put that the railway staffs have been greatly increased. I do not see what the justification is for increasing staffs by 30 or 40 per cent on some lines, as far as I have been able to gather. I cannot understand why the staff should be increased when they are working the same length of line and the same number of stations. Probably the reason was to provide employment for war-returned men. That seems to be the only object. An increase might reasonably have been expected on account of the increased price of coal and other commodities but not on account of staff.

As regards the military, there is no doubt that we do not know whether we are living in peace or war. Certainly during the war, in a time of emergency, demands on account of military expenditure have to be met anyhow. But the war ceased in 1918; five years have since nearly passed, but still we are living in war conditions. I fail to see why. Sir, as regards Waziristan and the Mashud country it is admitted on all hands that it is not at all a productive country; also the Honourable Mr. Bray has said that Government have no intention of occupying it. If so, why should we waste so much of our money upon it? It is described as a rugged, hilly country, but I think so far as our money is concerned, it is a bottom-less pit. You can pour in any amount and there will be no result. Before so many of our soldiers were not located there, and the people of the province managed very well for a long time, the people for whom my friend, Mr. Abdur Rahim, has pleaded so vehemently. But now for three or four years the province has been kept filled with troops, because the frontier tribes are coming and making raids and committing dacoities and so forth. Are our brave soldiers to be kept there to arrest those dacoits? That is the duty of the chaukidars or of the police. The duty of our soldiers is to fight. Are those people waging war against us? They are not doing anything of that kind, and why should our brave soldiers be wasted there simply to catch dacoits and raiders. I have read in the papers that even in the broad streets of Calcutta dacoities are committed, and also in the streets of London; but no soldiers are kept there to catch the dacoits. I believe that the people could very well deal with the situation themselves. It is only the Arms Act, Sir, which brings all this trouble upon those people. If they are exempted from the operation of the Arms Act they can very well defend themselves against the dacoits. What is the good of keeping soldiers if a dacoit comes after midnight and if he will shoot me and carry away my property? What will the soldiers do? Sir, really, if we are exempted from the Arms Act, if we, Indians, are provided with our own arms, I think we can defend ourselves, and, Sir, there will be no need for our soldiers to defend us and there will be no need for so much money being spent. I won't detain the House much longer. I will only say something, Sir, about taxation. It was my unpleasant duty last year to oppose taxation vehemently, and also I think nothing has been changed, or no case has been made out, why these poor men should be taxed. Sir, of course, some people say, these poor men are smoking cigarettes, also that the rich men are spending money on motors and on petrol. But granting all that, so far as human nature goes, there must be some waste, but that is no reason why there should be this taxation of poor. There is one thing. If such a Government as this deals in crores and crores of rupees, it will not be respectable for a Government like this to go to these poor people. Sir, if you are in need, perhaps if you are failing in business, you can approach your respectable banker or you can approach some respectable friend to accommodate you in your difficulties, but, Sir, I ask you, if you go to your own chaukidar or to your own mehtar and say, 'give me something,' what would be the result? I think it would be against your own sentiment, and what will those people be thinking? They would think that this Government has gone bankrupt, this Government has no prestige, they are asking us for even a pie, what is their worth? Sir, it will create a very bad impression amongst the poorer classes of the people; they will say, "Government is doing nothing; the Honourable Members are only sitting there to get us taxed." That will be the feeling no doubt. With these words, Sir, I oppose the salt tax.

Staff and Household of Governor General – Tour Expenses (15.03.1923)
Mr. B. N. Misra: Sir, I beg to move:
"That the provision for Tour expenses under sub-head 'Staff and Household of the Governor General' be reduced by Rs. 20,000."
We find in last year's budget the sum asked for was Rs. 3,65,000. We find that in the revised estimate the sum actually demanded was 4,32.700. Now we have been asked Rs. 4,26,000. We do not know whether when a supplementary budget comes like last year we shall be asked to vote for another Rs. 70,000. However, assuming this figure to be correct I submit that the tour expenses form a very large amount. I do not mean to repeat my remarks of last year. I do not mean to say that His Excellency should not take special trains whenever His Excellency thinks this desirable. What I submit to the house is this. What object is gained by these tours of His Excellency. We know in olden times our rulers, the Rajas and Maharajas, used to go in disguise and find out what

really the complaint and grievances of the people were.

The Honourable Sir Malcolm Hailey: How do you know that the Viceroy does not?

Mr. B. N. Misra: If that be the object even 40 lakhs may be spent to remedy the grievances of the people. We find that His Excellency's tours are either public or private. If it is a private tour, we find it in the papers that His Excellency will arrive on such and such a date at such and such a place and so on. Whether it is public or private, so far as the general public is concerned, they know very well where His Excellency is. Then, Sir, wherever His Excellency goes, we find that interviews are allowed. They are all practically arranged through application to the Private Secretary or whenever he happens to be in mofussil through the District Magistrate and so on. And who are the persons that are allowed to interview His Excellency? If you will see the list of interviewers, you will find that they are Rai Bahadurs, Rai Sahibs, Khan Sahibs, Khan Bahadurs and so on.

The Honourable Sir Malcolm Hailey: You might include Mr. Gandhi.

Mr. B. N. Misra: So far as I read the papers, Mahatma Gandhi came to see His Excellency. These men are generally either semi-Government men or demi-officials. I mean Rai Bahadurs and Khan Bahadurs or the officials. Further I do not know if my Honourable friends have read of or come to know of any instances in which His Excellency paid any visit in disguise and learnt from the common people their complaints against his administration or the oppressions of his subordinate officers at any place. I speak subject to correction. But as far as I know the papers say that His Excellency attended a ball, or a dance or gave a party or held a Durbar. This is all that we find from paper and programmes published in Gazettes, etc. We see after the transfer of capital to Delhi His Excellency has been invariably going to Calcutta and some other places every Christmas. Of course no other place can provide amusements and other things which Calcutta provides. If really the object is to find out how the people are living and how the administration is going on, His Excellency ought to divert his attention to other directions and I see no reason why he should always go to Calcutta and Burma and not to other parts of the country. We find also that when complaints are made to His Excellency personally, these complaints are sent to be dealt with by the departments and as a matter practice that is systematically followed. These are forwarded to the local Governments who forward it to the Commissioners who forward it to the Collectors and District Magistrates who forward it to the sub-inspector of police and who again makes inquiries from the village chukidar or dafadar and complaints are again submitted to the District Magistrate, the Commissioner, the local Government and so on.

The President: The Honourable Member cannot embark on a discussion on the entire administration on a vote for tour expenses.

Mr. B. N. MIsra: My object is to show that the grievances of the people are not taken into consideration by His Excellency in his tour programmes. Many of these tours are made to the states, from which the British tax payers do not really derive any benefit. Most of these tours and tour expenses consist in visiting big States ....
(Cries of "Withdraw.")

Well. I do not mind withdrawing, if you think it is much smaller a matter. You propose to impose an additional tax on salt on the poor people and spend lakhs here. If that be the object, then I withdraw.

The Budget – List of Demands (16.03.1923)
Mr. B. N. Misra:I think the Honourable Sir Sivaswamy Aiyar is going to move a general reduction. I shall speak on that reduction.

Mr. B. N. Misra: Sir, I beg to move:

"That the provision for Working Expenses under the head "Indian Postal and Telegraph Department' (page 31) be reduced by Rs, 25,000."

When I sent this amendment asking for reduction of working expenses, I made up my mind to point out the top-heavy administration of this Postal and Telegraph Department. Sir, if we compare the increase of work since 1913-14 to about 1921-22 and if we compare the increase of the officers and staff, we find that really the increase of officers in the Postal and Telegraph Department has been nearly 32 per cent, whereas in regard to the staff the increase is by about 17 per cent. In the two departments really the officers have been increased in such large numbers that it costs much more than is really desirable in the interests of the working of the departments. The staff has been increased only by 17 per cent. Moreover I find the increase in expenditure is more in the Telegraph Department, although the Department, as was pointed out by the Honourable Mover, is a commercial concern. The Postal Department pays more revenue to the Government and it transacts much pecuniary business, Savings Bank, Registration, and many other branches which fetch more revenue. But I see less money has been spent on it; whereas on the Telegraph Department much more money has been spent and the increase of revenue has not been really so much. Of course there is no separate account and we do not find the income separately shown; but really that will be found to be the case if the matter is scrutinized. Then, Sir, we find the pay in both the departments is very disproportionate. In the Telegraph Department you find the pay of these officers is much more, whereas people who transact very responsible business such as receiving money orders or savings bank deposits and have heavy and responsible transactions in money are paid much less. I beg to point out to the House that even in England these services are not paid on a separate scale. They give the same pay to both the branches. I fail to see why in India a separate pay and a very much higher scale of pay should be paid to the Telegraph Department, and why the Postal Department should not be paid on the same scale. I had in my mind several other details to point out but I do not do so now. The Retrenchment Committee desire retrenchment of some items which are very undesirable. They propose to take away some postal peons and take away some small officers whose pay is very small but who render much service to the public and whose retention will be very beneficial to the public, but they want to keep many highly paid officers at the top who really do nothing except perhaps supervise, and do not really do useful work for the public. I find there are several amendments in this matter and especially one by Dr. Gour who asks for a reduction of 10 lakhs, and as I ask for a small sum, I must leave my arguments to be advanced by Dr. Gour. I wish him success and I hope he will get this 10 lakhs. In his favour, I withdraw.

Election of Members for the Public Accounts Committee (28.03.1923)

The President: Before adjourning, I would invite the attention of the Assembly to the fact that at the end of the business today an election of Members to serve on the Committee on Public Accounts has been set down. Eight Members have to be elected by a procedure, which ought by now to be familiar to Members. The following candidates have been proposed for election to the Committee:

Mr. Braja Sundar Dass

Mr. B. N. Misra

Mr. N. M. Joshi

Mr. Syed Nabi Hadi

Mr. Ambica Prasad Sinha

Mr. K. Ahmed

Mr. K. G. Bagde

Mr. K. C. Neogi

Rao Bahadur P. V. Srinivasa Rao

Sardar Gulab Singh

Rai Sahib Lakshmi Narayan Lal.

Questions and Answers (02.07.1923)

Clerks Employed on Bengal-Nagpur Railway

Mr. B. N. Misra: (i) Will the Government be pleased to state the total number of clerks employed in the District Traffic Superintendent's Office at:

(a) Khurda Road
(b) Kharagpur
(c) Salimar
(d) Adra
(e) Chakradharpur Stations on the Bengal-Nagpur Railway Line?

(ii) Will the Government be pleased to state the number of Oriyas in the same offices?

The Honourable Mr. C. A. Innes:I propose to reply to this and the following two questions together.

Mr. B. N. Misra: Will Government please state – (i) the total number of clerks employed in the several booking offices, parcel offices and goods offices on the Bengal-Nagpur Railway:

(a) Between Kharagpur and Navpara.
(b) Between Kharagpur and Bilaspur.

(ii) The number of Oriyas in the offices referred above?

Employment of Oriyas on Bengal-Nagpur Railway

Mr. B. N. Misra: In view of the paucity of Oriyas in Railway service on the Bengal-Nagpur Railway line do the Government propose to advise the Bengal-nagpur Railway authorities to employ more Oriyas to mitigate the inconvenience of Oriya passengers and dealers?

The Honourable Mr. C. A. Innes: Government do not possess the information asked for. Nor do they propose to address the Agent in the sense suggested. The question was brought to the Agent's notice on Mr. Braja Sundar Dass' representation last September, and the Government have no doubt that, subject to consideration of efficiency, the Agent fully recognizes the desirability of affording Oriyas equal opportunities with other classes in the Railway Service.

Questions and Answers (23.07.1923)

Military Force for Quelling Disorders
Mr. B. N. Misra: Will the Government be pleased to state the strength of the Military force maintained for quelling internal disorders in India?

Mr. E. Burden: The attention of the Honourable Member is invited to the reply given on 15th January 1923 to the question asked on the same subject by Mr. Ginwala, No. 4.

Internal Disorders Quelled by Military

Mr. B. N. Misra: Will the Government be pleased to state on how many occasions Military was employed to quell internal disorder during (a) 1912 to 1917, (b) 1917 to

1922 and the number employed and expenditure incurred in each year during the above mentioned period?

Mr. E. Burden: The only information available in regard to the first part of the Honourable Member's question is for the period 1st January 1921 to the 31st December 1922. During this period, the aid of the military was resorted to an approximately 170 occasions and the total number of troops that were employed was 9 cavalry regiments, 36 infantry battalions and 7 sections of armoured cars. These figures, I may mention, are exclusive of the troops used in connexion with the Malabar rebellion.

The information desired in respect of the earlier periods mentioned by the Honourable Member is, I regret to say, not available.

As regards the second part of the question, for the reason given in reply to similar questions asked by Mr. Bagde and Sir Montague Webb on the 11th February and the 23rd March 1922, respectively, I regret I am unable to furnish the information required.

Mr. B. N. Misra: Is the Government aware of the discontent amongst Europeans in the Civil Service of India owing to their pay and prospects not being prosperous?

The Honourable Sir Malcolm Hailey: The answer is in the affirmative.

Railway to Bhubaneswar

Mr. B. N. Misra: (1) Is the Government aware that Bhubaneswar is a place of pilgrimage; not only Hindus from different parts of India but non-Hindus also visit the Temples from Archaeological and Architectural point of view?

Is the Government aware that the Railway station, although it goes by the name Bhubaneswar, is located at Budheswar, about 3 miles from the temples, and the road being infested with wild animals becomes dangerous and inconvenient for passengers to travel from the present station to the town?

Is the Government aware of the repeated demand by the public to remove the present Railway Station from Budheswar and to locate it within Bhubaneswar at a place on the same line, which is half a mile from the main Temple?

If the answer is in the affirmative, are the Government prepared to advise the Railway Board to locate even a Flag Station in the vicinity of the Temples within the ambit of the Bhubaneswar Town?

The Honourable Mr. C. A. Innes: (1) Yes.

(2) Some inconvenience is admitted but the Government has no information regarding   the depredations of wild animals.

(3) Yes.

(4) Government do not propose to issue orders for the removal of the station to a new site as it is not considered that the expenditure would be justified. The present station contains adequate facilities for pilgrim traffic and the provision of a new station at the proposed site would involve costly regarding of the line.

Booking Office at Badadanda, Puri

Mr. B. N. Misra: (1) Is the Government aware of the

demand of public to start a Third Class Booking Office at Badadanda in the Town of Puri (Jagannath)?

(2) Is the Government prepared to advise the Railway Board or the Traffic Manager, Bengal-Nagpur Railway, to open a Third Class Booking Office immediately in Badadanda, Puri?

The Honourable Mr. C. A. Innnes: (1) Yes.

(2) The Railway Authorities have given the suggestion careful consideration and are of opinion that in view of the adequate arrangements which exist at Puri station there is no need for a branch booking office at Badadanda.

In the circumstances Government do not propose taking any action in the matter.

Irregular Running of Trains on Bengal-Nagpur Railway (27.07.1923)

Mr. B. N. Misra: (a) Is the Government aware of the inconvenience and hardship caused to passengers by the irregularity and frequent delay of Bengal-Nagpur Railway Trains running between Howrah and Khurdha Road Stations?

(b) In view of the difficulty of the passengers who are frequently disappointed to catch the corresponding trains from Khurdha Road station to Waltair and vice versa are the Government prepared to direct the Bengal-Nagpur Railway Administration to make necessary arrangements to obviate the hardship and passengers and run

8 Up (Puri Express),

24 Up (Khurdha-Waltair Passenger),

and

10 Up (Puri Passenger)

22 Up (Khurdha-Waltair Passenger),

as corresponding trains?

The Honourable Mr. D. T. Chadwick: (a) Government has received no representation on the subject.

(b) The matter will be brought to the notice of the Agent, Bengal-Nagpur Railway.

Mr. B. N. Misra: Has the attention of Government been drawn to the articles, which have appeared in the local papers, namely, "Utkal Dipika" of Cuttack, the "Shakti" of Puri and the "Asha" of Ganjam?

The Honourable Mr. D. T. Chadwick: I have seen none of the publications referred to.

Bengal Nagpur Railway Platforms (27.07.1923)

Mr. B. N. Misra: (1) Is it a fact that there are only 15 stations out of 61 between Howrah and Puri, that are without raised platforms? If so, are the Government prepared to ask the Bengal-Nagpur Railway Administration to provide for raised platforms at these stations for the safety and convenience of passengers, e.g., Byree, Laskshan Nath Road, Malatipatpore and Jagatpore?

(2) Will the Government be pleased to ask the Bengal-Nagpur Railway Administration not to open any new station without raised platform?

(3) What is the total annual income of the Bengal-Nagpur Railway from passenger traffic between Howrah and Puri? What percentage of it will be expended in constructing raised platforms at the above-mentioned 15 stations?

(4) Is it the duty of Railway Administration to provide for the safety and convenience of passengers at all stations, irrespective of the income derived from any particular station?

The Honourable Mr. D. T. Chadwick: (1) and (2). Yes, the policy of Government is to leave it to the discretion of Railway Administrations to provide high-level platforms at stations where the passenger traffic justifies their provision. Government do not, therefore, propose to address the Bengal-Nagpur Railway Administration in the matter.

(3) The figure asked for are not available.

(4) The provision of reasonable conveniences as high-level platforms depends upon the volume of traffic offering at each station.

Jellasore-Contai Railway Extension (27.07.1923)

Mr. B. N. Misra: Is it a fact that the Bengal-Nagpur Railway intends to open a branch line to Contai in Midnapore District from Jellasore Station?

The Honourable Mr. D. T. Chadwick: A scheme for a branch line to Contai from Jellasore is under consideration by the Bengal-Nagpur Railway Administration.

Oriyas in Government Service (04.02.1924)

Mr. B. Venkatapatiraju: Will the Government be pleased to give the information that is being collected and promised to be given in reply to the question No. 553 put by Mr. B. N. Misra on the 12th March 1923 regarding Oriyas in Government Service?

The Honourable Sir Malcolm Hailey: A statement containing the information, which was supplied to **Mr. Misra**on the 21st May 1923, is laid on the table.

Statement showing the number of Oriyas employed in the Government of India

Secretariat and certain other Departments.

Departments	Number of Oriyas employed
Post and Telegraph Department	1,419
Income Tax Department	7
All Departments of the Government of India Secretariat	(i) On a salary of Rs. 500 or upwards Nil.
	(ii) On a salary of Rs. 100 or upwards Nil.

Opening of a Town Booking Office at Puri (16.09.1924)

Mr. Nilakantha Das: (a) Are the Government prepared to consider the question of opening a town booking office in the town of Puri, specially during festival times if not all around the year?

(b) Is it a fact that the local people approached the authorities in the matter in various ways?

Mr. A. A. L. Parsons: (a) and (b). The Honourable Member is referred to the answer given, on 23rd July,

1923, in this Assembly to question No. 292, asked by **Mr. B. N. Misra.**

Resolutions in the Assembly (15.01.1928)
Mr. B. N. Misra: Will the Government be pleased to state the number of:

(a). Resolutions sent by (i) Official, (ii) Non-official Members of the Assembly during 1921 and 1922, respectively?
(b). The number of Resolutions admitted by the Hon'ble the President?
(c). The number of (i) Official, (ii) Non-official Resolutions that came up for discussion before the Assembly during each year?

Sir Henry Mancroff Smith: A statement is laid on the table, which gives the information asked for by the Honourable Member.

Statement showing the number of resolutions (official and non-official) received, admitted

and actually moved in the Legislative Assembly since its inauguration in 1921.

Session	Total number of Resolutions of which Notice Received	Total number of Resolutions Submitted (Official and on-official)	Total Number of Resolutions Actually moved Official	Total Number of resolutions actually moved Non-Official
Delhi Session, 1921	9 (Official) 138 (Non-Official)	129	8	25
Simla session, 1921	9 (Official) 220 (Non-Official)	204	8	20
Delhi session, 1922	3 (Official) 264 (Non-Official)	224	3	35
Simla session, 1922	7 (Official) 255 (Non-Official)	236	6	9

Resolutions not Discussed in the Assembly (15.01.1928)

Mr. B. N. Misra: (a) Will the Government be pleased to

state how many of the admitted Resolutions could not come up for discussion before the House and the reason why they could not be reached.

(b) If for want of time the Resolutions could not come up before the House for discussion, will the Government be pleased to allow sufficient time this session so that all the Resolutions may come up and be discussed before the House?

Sir Henry Moncrieff Smith: (a) The number of admitted Resolutions, which did not come up for discussion can be ascertained from the statement, which I have just laid on the table in answer to the preceding question. The figures are as follows:-

1921	Delhi Term	94
Resolutions		
	Simla Term	176
Resolutions		
1922	Delhi Term	186
Resolutions		
	Simla Term	221
Resolutions		

It is obvious that the reason why these Resolutions did not come up for discussion is that there was not possible to allot sufficient time for the discussion of so many Resolutions.

(b) Under rule 6 of the Indian Legislative Rules the power to allot time for the discussion of non-official Resolutions is vested in His Excellency the Governor General and not in the Government of India, and I would invite the Honourable Member's attention to the instructions contained in rule 6 for the exercise of power. I may also state for the Honourable Member's information that there are now more than 250 admitted Resolutions undisposed of.

The Code of Criminal Procedure (Amendment) Bill (17.01.1928)

Mr. B. N. MIsra: Although my motion comes under amendments, what I have really proposed is not an amendment or alteration of a sentence or word in clause 14, but what I have proposed, is an explanation of certain words. So it will be necessary for me to read the clause itself, and then point out why this explanation is necessary in this case. Sub-section (1) of section 88 runs as follows: "The court issuing a proclamation under section 87 may at any time order the attachment of any property, movable or immovable, or both, belonging to the proclaimed person." In sub-clause (3) of the same section we find: "If the property ordered to be attached is a debt or other movable property, the attachment under this section shall be made:

(a) by seizure; or
(b) by the appointment of a receiver ; or"

 and so on . Then we find also in sub-section (4):

"If the property ordered to be attached is immovable, the attachment under this section shall, in the case of land paying revenue to Government be made through the Collector of the district in which the land is situated, and in all other cases:

(a) by taking possession; or
(b) by the appointment of receiver;"

and so on.

Now the explanation that I want to be added, is this: The words 'belonging to the proclaimed person' are capable of interpretation in such a way that they will entail hardship unless they are explained and probably the whole object will be spoiled. That is why I wish to add an explanation that when the offender is a member of a joint family, 'property belonging to the proclaimed person' means the specific interest of such a person. Sir, perhaps, in a country like England or France, or other countries where people generally live separately, the explanation will be absolutely unnecessary. In a country like England or France probably, as soon as an infant grows up, and becomes a man or a major and wants to marry, he will seek a home of his own, and unless he has a home of his own, probably he will not marry, so that practically all grown up men live separate. But in the case of India, whether they be Hindus, Muhammadans, Indian Christians or Parsees, or hold other religious beliefs, generally live in joint families. You find in a family a grand father, grand mother, father, son, uncle, nephew, niece, perhaps a great grand father and a great grand son all living together, and if a son wants to live in a separate home, he is looked down upon as having broken the home and having separated from his parents. It is looked upon with disapproval if a son or brother should live separate, but in other countries it will probably not be looked at in the same sense. The result is, in India, people almost invariably live in joint families. As regards the rights of different persons, it may be different. In the case of a Hindu who is governed by the Mitakshara law the right of survivorship and co-partnership come in. Hindus living under the Dayabhaga law, the Indian Christians and the Muhammadans, Sikhs and others also live in joint families. They may not have ancestral property, but still they hold property jointly. If a person, who has committed an offence does not appear, somehow or other, the court is justified in issuing a warrant and then a Proclamation and attachment side by side. Under section 87:

"If any court has reason to believe (whether after taking evidence or not) that any person against whom a warrant has been issued by it has absconded or is concealing himself so that such warrant cannot be executed, such Court may publish a written proclamation requiring him to appear at a specified place and a specified time not less than thirty days from the date of publishing such proclamation."

And section 88 provides:

"The Court issuing a proclamation under section 87 may at any time order the attachment of any property, movable or immovable, or both, belonging to the proclaimed person."

The Court is not to wait even 30 days after issuing the proclamation, but may at any time order the attachment of any property, moveable or immoveable, or both, belonging to the proclaimed person. Now if such a proclamation is issued, what will be the result? Really a person may have gone to any interior part of the country on business or trade. Then what happens? We know that every place is not accessible to the railway; nor have got postal or telegraphic communication. A man may go into the interior somewhere where you cannot get a letter even in a fortnight, and if he seeks to come home from there to a railway station or a distant place, it may take a fortnight to travel from such interior place to the headquarters station. And in the mean time a proclamation will have been issued against him without his knowledge. Of course it will be to the interest of the complainant to represent that he is concealed, or if the police do not find him in the house, and do not take further steps and say, the man is concealing himself, what has the Magistrate to do? A warrant has to be issued, a proclamation has to be issued and the man's property is to be attached. I must say here, before any guilt is established, not only is the man punished but all the members of his family are punished by the attachment order because the attachment order provides that the property can be taken possession of and so on. To be more clear I shall say, for example, several persons are living jointly; they have no ancestral property, but have acquired a house. No sooner the attachment order is issued, what will be the result? The Receiver will come and take possession of the house. Suppose I am living with my brothers and their wives and children in a house. Suppose the house belongs to A, B, C, and D jointly and attachment orders are issued against the property as belonging to D, there is no wrong in taking possession of it, because it belongs to D as well and you cannot find fault with a Magistrate because he has issued an order of attachment against the same property for it belongs to him. Suppose I have a cow and my brothers and other members of the family have a share in the cow and my children and their children are living upon the milk of the cow. Now, if I have committed some offence, or if for some offence alleged against me, the police comes and takes possession of the cow, under an attachment order by a Magistrate, you cannot blame the Magistrate for his action saying it belongs to me. There is no safety in such procedure. If the cow is taken possession of, my brothers' children or my own babies would be deprived of her milk. Say I have a house and am living under the Hindu Mitakhshara family law. There is my wife who has got a right of residence in the house. Now are you going to punish my wife and turn her out although he has committed no offence, simply because a case has been filed against me rightly or wrongly and I have not appeared before a court not having any knowledge of such a fact? Will that law be sound and for the benefit of the society and even in the interests of criminal law? I submit, Sir, this will be really a very hard and very unwise law, if it will be a law where an innocent person can be turned out of a house because it jointly belongs to another. If for instance there is a joint partnership, business or firm and a case is filed against one of the members of the firm for some supposed crime. Suppose he has gone away somewhere on business and other members are carrying on the business. If this is really the law, you cannot blame the Magistrate for attaching the partnership property or joint property belonging to the firm. It also belongs to the offender undoubtedly. He may have a hundredth share or tenth share, but it belongs to him, and the property may be attached and taken possession of.

I need not multiply instances to show how this law will entail hardship on innocent members of a family because by the custom of the country they are living together. No provision has been made in this case. I submit, Sir, the House will consider the reasonableness of the explanation I have given, not only in the interests of members of joint Mitakshara families but of all members of the Hindu or Muhammadan community, or Parsees or Indian Christians, or any community that is living jointly. Other members should not be punished for the alleged offence committed by an accused person.

Now, Sir, I have explained the other difficulties. Probably the prosecution may say , if a man is concealing himself , 'Attach the property and the other members of the family will be compelled to produce him.' The object of our criminal law is never to punish innocent people. It is a very laudable object to punish the guilty and I have never said a thing whereby a guilty person should escape or not be brought to trial. What I say is that the other members should not suffer. Supposing a man in a village has committed an offence. There is the complainant to produce him, there is the police also to find him out, there are so many agencies really to find out the man. It may be the case that a complaint has been lodged against a person who has perhaps gone away on business or without his knowledge some false complaint has been filed against him and it has been made to appear to the Magistrate that the man is absconding or concealing himself. The section says:

"If any Court has reason to believe (whether after taking

evidence or not) that any person against whom a warrant has been issued by it has absconded or is concealing himself, etc."

So that as soon as a representation is made, the Court can issue an attachment. It generally happens that the police comes and says 'so and so is concealing himself' we cannot find him, issue a warrant against him and also this proclamation and attachment order.' Then, the result is that we have to punish the other members of the family who are quite innocent, who would themselves be interested to point out the accused if he could be found.

Now, Sir, probably it may be said 'Well, there are already provisions for a claim; if any person's property is attached, the other members having any right or claim to the property can lay a claim.' My submission to this House is, that is really the most undesirable part of it. Now, Sir, the average family is not rich nor can they file a claim. You cannot simply go to the court and file it; you must come with money to file a claim. You must substantiate your claim, and by that time what has happened? Your wife, who never came out, is in the street and your children are somewhere not knowing where to get their food. If you had any granary; or paddy or gram or wheat in your house, all that is attached. You have no food, no house to live in and no cloth to wear. Can you imagine anyone in such circumstances coming and laying a claim very easily? He must pay his pleader, his mukhtear or his petition writer, whoever, whoever he may be, and must pay, and must pay his court fees and adduce evidence. After all these paraphernalia has been gone through, he does not know what the decision of the Magistrate will be in such a case. If the whole provision was not on the Statute Book, it would be really wholesome, but, since there is a provision, and since some offenders may evade a trial, I think, when the Crown is prosecuting or when the Crown is the complainant, as the burden of proof always lies on the prosecution, this burden must also lie on the prosecution to specify the interest of the accused person. The prosecution can very easily find it out; I do not think there will be any difficulty. If a particular person lives in a family, his relations and interests are known complainant or to the police, whoever lodges the complaint. Under the Hindu law the complainant knows this man has got a certain share in the property. Even under any other system of law you must know that he has so much share or that other persons like his wife and mother have got a right of residence or his old grand-mother or old grand-father has got a right of residence. These things can be known very easily and it ought to lie on the possession to show the interest that an accused has in a property. Of course, so long as you do not proceed against property, there is no trouble, but once you attach property you do not touch the accused alone, you touch all the relations, all the surroundings, all the members. For instance, a poor tenant has some fields and you come and take away the paddy heaps you have harvested. The poor tenant has toiled the whole year to get some paddy from the field and you come and take away his paddy, simply because it belongs to the landlord. This morning we had so much discussion about the attachment. I submit this House will remember these difficulties of attachment and the trouble and expenses one has to undergo over these attachments. Why put a man to all this trouble, why drag him to Court and then so charitably release his property after putting him to so much trouble.

This House will also remember that, even in the Civil Procedure Code, when you attach property, at least some things are exempted from attachment, for instance, the implements of workman or some paddy grains or paddy seeds for the poor peasant or some other things, which are absolutely necessary. I think that is not at all illiberal. Will our Criminal Procedure Code be so illiberal as not to leave anything? You will attach everything without exception. No exemption of property is made under this, you lose everything. Supposing there are two brothers who have got a pair of bullocks for ploughing the land. One brother has committed or supposed to have committed some crime. You come and take away the pair of bullocks and do not spare for the other brother even one bullock with which he could otherwise have cultivated his land. It is very hard to attach the property of a proclaimed person who is responsible for all this business, because it may belong to ten persons as well as to the proclaimed person.

Then, Sir, for wrongful attachment under the Civil Procedure Code there is some remedy. But supposing a man wrongfully applied to the Court and said 'So and so is concealing himself' and the Court issues an order of attachment for all the property, there is no provision for protection against the wrongful attachment of his property under this Code. If it is done under the orders of the Magistrate, the civil court will say 'You can not proceed, you have no remedy practically, it is an act of the Court.' It would mean an action and then you would have to make the Secretary of State for India a party. But in practice this is never done. The interest is never specified. So in the case of joint families it is absolutely a hard and difficult procedure that has been laid down here. Under the circumstances I propose that this explanation should be added, so that the Magistrates, whether they be third class or second class, whether they be new men or experienced men, may not commit an error and innocent people may not be harassed. With these words I propose that this amendment should be carried.

After some further arguments on the motion by some other Members, Mr. Deputy President negatived the motion.

Mr. B. N. Misra: Sir, I beg to move the following amendment:

"In clause 15 insert the following at the beginning:

'In sub-section (1) of section 103 for the word 'two' the word 'five' shall be substituted'."

Sir, as regards searches it is provided that there should be two or more respectable inhabitants of the locality to attend a search; the officers generally take only a small number, say two persons and they are really the village headman or some others who are really interested in the prosecution. Now under clause (5) of this section we have "Any person who without reasonable cause refuses or neglects to attend and witness a search under this section when called upon to do so by an order in writing delivered or tendered to him, shall be deemed to have committed an offence under section 187 of the Indian Penal Code." So strictly speaking there will be no difficulty in getting more witnesses.

In excise and other cases where smuggling of opium and

other drugs are in question, generally the department comes forward with one or two informers who attest the search list when it is made. In these cases other villagers or respectable men are not called to attach the list. Strictly speaking, in any village two or more people can be found, and there will be no difficulty to get more persons to avoid suspicion. There is another difficulty, Sir. Sometimes you have got only two witnesses in the search list; sometimes they fall ill or they don't come, and when the case comes up it has to be adjourned from time to time till those witnesses turn up. (A voice: "There is a word 'more'.") Well, if you take the word "more", accept them as five, there is no objection to that; but the difficulty is, if there is only a small number of witnesses, it is not good, because some of them may happen to be interested only in the prosecution, or sometimes they may not be present when they are called, on account of illness or other cause, and the case will have to be adjourned many times. It is of course a simple matter, my amendment does not really deal with the substance, but it is simply a safeguard. If there are more persons, it is better. That is why I have put the word 'five' in place of the word 'two'. Instead of giving the option to two, you can have more than five and there will not be any hardship. With these observations, Sir, I commend my amendment to the House.

Mr. Deputy President negatived the motion.

Third Legislative Assembly and Barrister Biswanath

Demands for Supplementary Grants (10. 07. 1930)

Mr. B. N. Misra: As this is a demand for Round Table Conference, I believe, this House is entitled to know whether it would consist the representatives of British India alone. We have already in the newspapers that there will be twelve members from the Indian States and the States' people. Sir, up till now, in the annals of British History, there has been no occasion when the Indian states, or their people joined the British Indian Administration or the British Indian People. Sir, when the Princes' Protection Bill came before this House, it was thrown out because it was said that we had nothing to do with Indian States' Administration, nor had the Indian States anything to do with the British Indian Administration. We were told all along that we were separate and that British Indian people have nothing to do with states, which have nothing to do with us. The states have not advanced in education to the same extent as we have advanced in the British territories. With the greatest respect to the states and their Rulers, they have never been accustomed to the same system of administration and education as we enjoy in the British portion. With due respect to the Rulers and Princes, although they enjoy vast territories and possessions, I must say these are the very cause of the misery of the Rulers. Probably they do not enjoy the same freedom as we ordinarily enjoy …….

Mr. President: Order, order. The Honourable Member cannot go into the internal administration of the Indian States.

Mr. B. N. Misra: I was only pointing out that they not advanced to the same extent as we have. Probably it will be difficult for them to appreciate the position in British

India. They have never taken any interest in the progress of the British Indian People. So it will be very difficult for the Rulers of the States or their people to join with the British Indian People in their aspirations and in their demand for self-government. Therefore, I submit, that they will not be proper associates with the British Indian people in their demand. I have some doubts and misgivings about their coming for the first time to join with us in the Round Table Conference. It is probably to frustrate the demands of the British Indians that the scheme has been devised.

Then, Sir, so much has been said about the Simon Commission's Report. In spite of all that has been said about the much-maligned Commissioners, I must say that we have talked only of what they have not given. The Honourable Members on the Treasury Benches have not thought of giving effect to their recommendations. I refer to their recommendations in respect of the Oriya-speaking people. In their Report, on page 312 of the second volume, they have stated that, as regards provincial areas, the question whether some redistribution is desirable should at once be taken up and they mention that the case of Sind and the Oriya-speaking people will be the first to be considered. My submission is this. Whatever may come out – we all assume that some golden egg will come out as a result of the Round Table Conference deliberations – be it Dominion Status or be it Autonomy – it will be of no use to the Oriya-speaking people. We are in a minority in four provinces. This House is very keen and the Indian Government is also very keen and very anxious about the interests of the minority communities. We are a minority. What has been done for us in spite of so many declarations? Sir, Lord Curzon's Government in 1903 made a declaration that the Oriya-speaking tracts should be joined in one province; also from the Montague-Chelmsford Report we got something in 1917. They said that a new province should be formed at an early date. The Simon Commission recommended that it should be done at once. We, Indians, are not very familiar with the meanings of English words and expressions. According to the Britisher, does early date mean 20 years or 30 years or 100 years? We have learnt to believe that at once means at once, not 100 years or 10 years or a month. Honourable Members on the Treasury Benches have not taken any action in the matter. They have not brought forward any proposal for the formation of an Oriya province at once. Whatever may be the reforms or new constitution of the Local Governments or the Central Government, in any case they will be of no use to the Oriyas, unless the formation of a new province is taken up at once. Sir, the Treasury Benches ought to realize that the Simon Commission should not form the basis or the only basis in considering the interests of every class and community in the country. As regards other matters His Excellency has very kindly announced that the Conference will be free to consider any matter. The only objection is that we should be asked to mix with the Rulers of the States. It is left to them to follow our system or not. My point is that the question should first be decided for British India alone. Let other people come in or not, as they like.

Discontent and Hardship caused by Duties imposed under the Salt Act (14.07.1930)

Mr. B. N. Misra: Are Government aware of the great discontent and hardship caused by the duties imposed under the Salt Act of 1882 and the subsequent Acts amending the same?

The Honourable Sir George Schuster: Government do not consider that the existing salt tax is the cause either hardship or legitimate discontent.

Convictions under the Salt Act (14.07.1930)

Mr. B. N. Misra: (a) Are Government aware that there have been several convictions under the Salt Act in different provinces of India?

(b) If so, will Government be pleased to state:

(i) the total number of convictions under the said Act during the last six months in British India;

(ii) the number of convictions in which sentences of fine only have been imposed;

(iii) the number of convictions in which sentences of imprisonment up to six months have been passed; and

(iv) the number of convictions in which sentences of imprisonment of over six months have been passed?

The Honourable Mr. H.G. Haig: The information required is being collected and will be furnished to the Honourable Member in due course.

Assaults on Satyagrahis by the Police (14.07.1930)

Mr. B. N. Misra: Are the Government aware of the discontent on account of the dealings with and assaults on Satyagrahis by the police and other officials of Government?

The Honourable Mr. H. G. Haig: I would recall to the Honourable Member the observations made in this matter by His Excellency the Viceroy in his speech to the Indian Legislature on 9th July, 1930.

Resignations of Members of Legislatures as a Protest against Repressive Measures (14.07.1930)

Mr. B. N. Misra: Will Government be pleased to state the number of Members who have resigned as a protest against the repressive measures of Government:

(a) in the Assembly; and
(b) in the several Provincial Legislative Councils during the last six months?

The Honourable Mr. H. G. Haig:
(a) Eight, I should judge so far as reasons for resignation have been given.
(b) With regard to the Provincial Legislative Councils a statement is laid on the table giving the information so far as it is known to the Government of India.

Statement giving the number of Members of the Provincial Legislative Councils who resigned as a protest against the repressive measures of Government during the last six months

Madras

....*8*

Bombay

....*20*

Bengal

....*1*

United Provinces...... 8

Punjab

....*1*

Burma

....*1*

Bihar and Orissa 7

Central Provinces 8

Assam

....*3*

Coorg

....*Nil*

Total.......................... 57

Redistribution of Areas of the Oriya-Speaking Peoples (15.07.1930)

Mr. B. N. Misra: (a) Are Government aware of:

(i) the recommendation of Mont-Ford Report in 1919

"that a sub-province for Orissa should be formed at no distant date";

(ii) the recommendations of Simon Commission "that the question of redistribution of the areas of the Oriya speaking people will be first considered" besides the long standing agitation of the Oriyas and promises by Government in the same matter?

(b) If the answer to part (a) is in the affirmative, will Government be pleased to state:
(i) whether they intend to make a redistribution of the Oriya speaking areas on the existing materials before them, collected during the last 30 years; or
(ii) whether they propose to appoint a fresh committee of officials and non-officials to inquire into the same; or
(iii) whether, in the latter case, Government are prepared to name the personnel and appoint such a committee immediately to begin their work ?

The Honourable Mr. H. G. Haig: (a) (i) and (ii). Government are aware of the references to Orissa in paragraph 246 of the Joint Report, and of the recommendation of the Indian Statutory Commission that the Boundaries Commission should be set up to investigate the main cases, including Orissa, in which provincial readjustment seems called for.
(b) The recommendations of the Commission are now being considered by Government. In the mean time I regret that I am unable to make any statement in reply to

the points raised in this part of the Honourable Member's question.

Mr. B. N. Misra: May I ask the Honourable Member whether at any rate it will be done before the proposed Government of India Act is introduced in the House of Commons?

The Honourable Mr. H. G. Haig: I am afraid I cannot give any definite assurance on that point until we explore the matter further.

Fourth Legislative Assembly and Barrister Biswanath

The Suppression of Counterfeiting Currency (International Convention) Bill (22.01.1931)

Appointment of Select Committee

Dr. Ziauddin Ahmad: Sir, I beg to move that the Select Committee to which the Bill to give effect to the International Convention for the suppression of counterfeiting currency was referred, do consist of the following persons, namely: The Honourable Sir George Schuster, Sir Lancelot Graham, Sir Hari Singh Gour, Mr. Muhammad Azhar Ali, Mr. B. R. Puri, Sardar Sant Singh, Mian Muhammad Shah Nawaz, **Mr. B. N. Misra**, Mr. G. Morgan, the Deputy President and Mover, with instructions to report by the 4th February, 1931, and that the number of Members whose presence shall be necessary to constitute a meeting of the Committee shall be five.

The motion was adopted.

Election of Committee to consider Proposals on Salt Industry (26.01.1931)

Mr. B. N. Misra: Sir, now a days, the trend of thought has advanced in such a way that we always think of scientific methods, machines and engines. But we forget that hand-made-engines are nothing in comparison with the natural engines that we have got. On the Orissa coast, particularly, I am aware that throughout the coast, salt was manufactured to such an extent that a great historian, Mr. Sterling, stated that, in the year 1822, the revenue from salt was 18 lakhs of rupees, and the time has come now when we do not get even one pice worth of salt from our own sea or from the Lake Chilka. These were the natural sources from which we were getting salt and the rich people then were only those who had industries in salt, or what they called nimak. They were the only people who were doing it. Then science had not advanced so much as it has today. This must be said to the discredit of East India Company. Though the coast of Orissa was only conquered in 1803 and there was then perhaps no proper control, salt was manufactured to such large extent, that Orissa not only supplied its own needs, but supplied the needs of the Central Provinces, Bihar and other provinces too. Then, what happened? With the advent of scientific arrangements, probably certain officials were put in there where salt was manufactured, or in places like the Chilka Lake. The officer who was sent there, instead of helping the poor manufacturer of salt, instead of assisting the process, as one could have naturally expected him to do, instead of devising ways and means for increasing the production, instead of that, he managed to send a report to the effect that there was no good production of salt there; that it was not a proper place for the manufacture of salt, and so on, with the result that salt manufacture was stopped there. In those days there were no machines. Nothing but the sun - the great natural engine – was used in the manufacture of salt. Salt water used to enter the fields or the salt pans and the sun used to dry up the water and salt would settle on those very fields, and in this way salt was easily manufactured. By this process, they supplied salt to all the provinces, and the revenue from salt was something like 22 lakhs of rupees. From this you can very well imagine, how much money could be earned by the people, and how much employment it gave to the coolies engaged in the process of manufacture of salt. With the stopping of the manufacture of salt, the people lost their employment. There was also a resolution in the Bihar and Orissa Council about this. The Government said that science was a great boon, but the people think that it is such a boon that it kills all our enterprise, all our industries and manual labour. The Government think that salt must be scientifically produced and so they will not consent to revive our old method of manufacturing salt. The Government think that they must have big machines and large sums of money to manufacture salt and without this equipment they could not manufacture salt. Perhaps they then requested the Tata Company, who were managing their steel concern. They did not agree, and perhaps as no rich man or millionaire came forward, it was not done. But it can be very easily done by an individual or any villager if salt is permitted to be manufactured on the Orissa coast. But the scientific method of manufacturing salt, as in the case of Liverpool or Madras Salt, requires great capital and also great many machines. You want to encourage these scientific methods but not these natural methods. You want only artificial methods. That is why the salt industry has been killed in Orissa, and also I believe in many places. The natural method has been killed perhaps on account of the commercial spirit and commercial jealousy and not by allowing the natives of the soil to manufacture salt. But salt can be manufactured very easily, as was proved by the salt satyagrahis last year, who showed how it could be manufactured without any detriment to the Government revenue and without any cost to the people.

Sir, as a Committee is going to be appointed, I hope they will thoroughly examine not only the scientific method of manufacturing salt with the aid of machinery, but the natural method as well, whether on the sea coast or in the salt mines in Sambhar, where salt can be naturally manufactured. They should also consider whether the stringent rules against salt manufacture should not be abolished. It will also be of benefit to the Government because they will realize some duties and it will also be beneficial to the people.

Sir, I thank the Honourable the, Finance Member for bringing this up for consideration and I hope the Committee will have both the methods of view.

The President: The question is:

"That this Assembly do proceed to the election in such manner, as may be approved by the Honourable the

President, of a Committee consisting of 10 Members of the Assembly to which shall be added two Members of the Assembly to be nominated by the Governor General for the purpose of considering the proposals contained in the Report of Indian Tariff Board on the Salt Industry in India and making such recommendations in regard to them as they may think fit. One of the Members so nominated shall be the Chairman of the Committee."

The motion was adopted.

Policy of Repression (05.02.1931)

Mr. B. N. Misra: Sir, the Honourable the Leader of the House just now said that the object of the Congress was the subversion of the Government established law. I think he has entirely misunderstood the whole object of the Congress. Certainly, the Congress has nowhere done anything to subvert the Government established by law. All that it has preached and is preaching is about the swadeshi movement and the Khaddar movement. Is that tantamount to subversion of Government, I ask? Does it show that the Congress wants a different Government by a different nation? Sir, the Congress also carries on a vigorous propaganda against drinks. Sir, whatever may be the feeling about liquor amongst European community, Indians are unanimous on the point that drinking of liquor should be stopped. It is only moral dictate that would compel any people to prohibit liquor, and if the Congress has endeavoured to carry on a propaganda against the evil of drink and to prohibit the sale of drink, does it amount to subversion of Government established by law? If the ladies picketed, have they done anything to subvert Government? It was merely moral preaching. The same thing with regard to salt. We cannot enter into the details at the present time, but these are the things that the Congress has done. How can the Honourable the Leader of the House and the Honourable the Home Member then say that it is an action calculated to subvert the Government? Now, take the ordinances. They are never passed by any Legislature. They are made by particular person for a particular purpose. Therefore, I submit that the whole spirit of the Congress has never been to subvert the Government. On the other hand, the Government have done many things which compels Indians to resort to measures which are made punishable under the ordinances. In other word, let me say that the Congress is like Ram India fighting against the stealing away of Liberty Sita from India. If Indians want to prepare their own cloth and ask their compatriots not to use foreign cloth, is that a sin? You have right to ask your brethren, your villagers, your countrymen not to drink. Ii is a just right, it is a piece of social service; but the Government interpret it as subverting the Government. I do not know what their universities teach them, what their Bible teaches them, or what their law teaches them; but we have been taught in our schools to be temperate, not to smoke cigarettes, not to drink. These are the things; which we were taught in our schools and the Government regard them as subversion of Government established by law. I do not know what is meant by subversion of Government. What is the aim of Congress? Have they done anything to turn out Sir George Rainy, or Sir George Schuster, or any other Member of Government? They have done nothing of the sort. Simply they preach what is natural, what any man with a conscience, with any education, with any knowledge, with any sincerity, would preach. They are described as encouraging violence and things of that sort. Who has done it? It is the Government by these lathi charges. You drive innocent people away with lathis as if you were lathials of petty Zamindars or goondas. That has been the attitude of Government in dealing with Congress or the temperance movement. The Honourable Member told us that there is a no-tax campaign. No no-tax movement has ever been begun in any part of the country. But Government imagine all sorts of things. You must remember that in this country ladies burned themselves to death to save themselves from violation of their chastity, and no lady will be afraid to do the same on behalf of her country if there be oppression. Let me tell the Government that if you want to suppress ladies, we Indians believe in Punarjanma, regeneration, in re-birth. We always believe in the immortality of soul, and we have been taught by the Bhagavat Gita and other sastras not to care for these mortal bodies. I ask, have the Government succeeded in suppressing the people anywhere in India? Have they done it in Bombay, in Madras, in Punjab or anywhere else? Have they killed their spirit? No, On the other hand, the suppressive, repressive or oppressive policy of the Government will only encourage their spirit and they will rise more and more. I am reminded at this stage of our Chandi judh where out of a drop of blood that fell, up sprang thousand of Chandis. I submit, Sir, that the present struggle is one of Ram-India against the stealing of Liberty-Sita by the British policy, by the kind of policy, like Churchillism, or Dyerism or O'Dwyerism. (An Honourable Member: "or 'Arthur Mooreism'.") Now, let me say that Mr. Ramsay MacDonald has made a declaration. He has come like Vibhishana to help in the fight of India, and it is for the officials, who have eaten the salt of India, to come and lend their aid, When Queen Victoria assumed the Government of India, she did so under an Act entitled, "For the better Government of India". Do you think that you will have better and better government by imprisoning thousands and thousands of people, or by taking away the liberty of the Indian people? What has the Congress done to destroy the commerce of India, or the industries of India? They have simply said, that foreign goods should not come to this country. That exactly is the thing that India wants. But what the Commerce Member or the other Members of the Government want is the betterment of their own country, England. Let them place their hands on their breasts, let them feel in their heart of hearts, and say whether the Congress has done anything to harm Indian interests? Sir, I do not think that I need take up the time of the House any more, but I would implore the House to support the Resolution and I would request my Honourable friends Mr. Amar Nath Dutt and Seth Haji Abdoola Haroon to withdraw their amendments.

After long debates the House was adjourned till Eleven of the Clock on Monday, the 9th February, 1931.

Employment of Mr. Hughes in the Horticultural Division

New Delhi (19.02.1931)

Mr. B. N. Misra: (a) Is it a fact that Mr. Hughes has been called on deputation by the Public Works Department, Delhi, to be attached to the Horticulture Division, as Superintendent of Gardens?

(b) If so, will government please state what technical qualifications does he possess, what pay he was drawing while in the employ of the Punjab Government and what pay he has been offered by the Public Works Department, Delhi?

Mr. Tin Tut: It has been decided to revert Mr. Hughes to his post under the Punjab Government.

The Railway Budget - List of Demands (24.02.31)

Mr. B.N. Misra: Sir, I rise to support the motion. Unfortunately we lost yesterday the bigger cut. Sir, the Budget shows a very gloomy feature, and that is that we have to appropriate Rs. 10 crores from the Reserve Fund and so on. We are thus in a difficulty, and no one will deny that. The real point, however, is how to meet it instead of drawing from the Reserve Fund this Rs. 10 crores which we have to draw. The position is otherwise. The Honourable Member said that if we propose any cut of even 5 or 4 ½ per cent or any per cent, in the salaries of the highly-paid men, they will find it very difficult; and so also if we cut from the salaries of the lower-paid men, that is of those on Rs. 30 and upwards, they will also feel it much. No doubt everybody would feel it. It would touch his pocket, but we have to see, Sir, who can bear it – from which source we have to retrench. It is not by retrenching so many officers or so many men, but the retrenchment must be confined to those who can bear the loss. It is surely not reasonable to ask that those who cannot bear the brunt, namely, the poorly paid men, should have a reduction in their salaries. The Railway Member said yesterday that the salaries of the highly paid men should not be touched because they have to provide for so many luxuries and comforts and there are so many demands on their purse to meet the amenities of life. But one thing is clear. Whatever it may have been in the past, and whatever hopes and expectations may have been formed, let us all understand now that these high salaries should not be paid in future and hereafter. Sir, it may not be this year that shall succeed in effecting retrenchment of 5 to 10 per cent, but let it be clearly understood that reduction must henceforward begin and that it must continue. It may not be done in one or two years, but it must be done sooner or later. It must be treated as commercial concern. In business and commerce everybody makes a profit. Even an oil seller who invests one rupee in a tin of oil sells that tin for Rs. 1-4-0 or Rs. 1-6-0. Making a profit of 4 or 6 annas. But why cannot these railways, which have a capital of hundreds of crores, make any profit at all? It is a shame. From the layman's point of view one cannot believe that such a commercial concern cannot earn anything and cannot show any profit. Whether it is to their credit or their discredit it is for them to consider. Not to speak of respectable people, they cannot even go to an ordinary man in the street and convince him. We are not experts; we are poor people who do not even deal in hundreds. But here they are dealing in crores and I find it a little difficult to understand myself how these crores are made up. For Repairs they have 37 crores, for Inspection they have so many crores,

For Railway Board they have so many crores. They are always dealing in crores, which I find it somewhat difficult to understand. But to come back to the main point, there must be retrenchment. I have got a motion for cut of Rs. 100 to discuss the policy. I think I shall speak a few words on that too. But retrenchment must begin. The Honourable the Railway Member said that he will not think of reducing the salaries of those who draw salaries up to Rs. 30. I thank him for his kindness and mercy, but I think it very grudging mercy, a stinting mercy and a very miserly mercy that he has shown. I say and I maintain that those who draw salaries upto Rs. 100, i.e., junior servants, clerks, etc., should not be touched. They must not have an eye upon these poorly paid men. They must think of the men above that, and as regards that, many of my friends have said that there must be sliding scale. I think for people drawing from Rs. 100 to Rs. 500 there should be a reduction of 5 per cent; for people who draw a salary of Rs. 500 to Rs. 1000 there should be a reduction of 10 per cent; and those who draw a salary of Rs. 1000 and upwards should have their pay reduced by 20 per cent. It will not be a great loss to them. Supposing there is a man who gets Rs. 2000 and his salary is reduced by 20 per cent., he will get Rs. 1600, and it will not be a great loss to him. They should think of the fate of their money unfortunate brethren who are serving in the same line who are equally educated, equally competent, equally fit and are drawing a much smaller pay either in the railway service or in other services. If they kill the goose that lays the golden eggs how can they live themselves? If the railways become bankrupt in few years what will be their position and how can they maintain themselves? If a man begins on a low salary, and then after some years is fortunate to get Rs. 2000 or more, he should think of his less fortunate brethren and try to live on a lower salary so that he may not feel it. It is only greed that makes man love these fat salaries. Who does not wish to get more money? If I get Rs. 2,000 I shall wish get Rs. 4000, and if I get Rs. 4000, I shall try for Rs. 10,000. But we must now make up our mind to cut our coat according to the cloth we have, and must practise simple living, as Mahatma Gandhi said the other day. No man is a Ravana with 10 mouths and twenty bellies. If one man can live on Rs. 100, there is no reason why another should want Rs. 5000. Therefore I say to the Railway Member that this will not all be a hard thing. You have only to make up your minds. If a man makes up his mind that he will be satisfied with Rs. 1000, certainly he will be satisfied and that will suffice for his requirements. You can also get good service and contented men. There are thousands of people who get much lower salaries, but they are contented, honest and competent men and they are as hard-working as men in any other service. Therefore I appeal to the Honourable the Railway Member and the Railway Board that they must make up their minds to have retrenchment. If they do not want to have it all at once it may be done gradually so that the men may get used to it. What cannot be cured must be endured, and therefore the men must consent to retrenchment and get used to it. The retrenchment must be not only on this item but on every item.

This is about retrenchment. I have one other question to deal with. It is neither a communal question nor a racial one. I do not plead for any community on the ground of race or caste or religion. I am simply urging my case on the ground of convenience and facilities to the passengers and travellers. Sir, Bengal Nagpur Railway runs over the whole Oriya-speaking country over 800 miles.

Maulavi Muhammad Yakub: Sir, is the Honourable Member relevant in talking about the Oriyas on this motion?

The President: The Honourable Member must restrict his observations only to retrenchment.

Mr. B. N. Misra: Very well, Sir. Then I have nothing more to say.

Recruitment of Ministerial Establishment in the Foreign and Political Department (05.03.1931)

Mr. B. N. Misra: (a) Is it a fact that all questions relating to the ministerial establishment of the Foreign and Political Department are dealt with by the Under Secretary of that Department?

(b) Is it a fact that similar questions in the other Departments of the Government of India are dealt with by Deputy Secretaries of those Departments?

(c) Is it a fact that the foreign and Political Department of the Government of India has the largest ministerial establishment of the Government of India Departments?

(d) Is there any reason why this distinction has been made and the Foreign and Political Department observes a principle different from that observed in the other Departments in regard to matters relating to ministerial establishment?

(e) Is it a fact that, owing to the Under Secretary in the

Foreign and Political Department being normally a junior and inexperienced official, his work mostly is done according to direction from the Assistant Secretary?

(f) Are Government aware that this practice is the cause of discontent in Foreign and Political Department?

Mr. J. G. Achison: (a) yes. But the Under Secretary has not the final authority in more important cases such as confirmation of probationers, and the most important questions, such as promotions to the Superintendent's grade, dismissals, reduction or stoppage of increment are decided by the two Secretaries jointly.

(b) Yes, this is the usual practice. But, for the reasons given in answer to (d), this arrangement would not be feasible in the Foreign and Political Department.

(c) Yes.

(d) Yes, to relieve the Deputy Secretaries, who are already over-burdened with important work, of routine work and petty matters relating to establishment; and also to provide a link between the Foreign and Political sides of the Department. It should be pointed out that the Under Secretary is himself usually an officer of many years' responsible administrative experience.

(e) and (f). No, Sir.

Appointment of Stenographers in the Foreign and Political Department (05.03.1931)

Mr. B. N. Misra: Will Government be pleased to state whether it is a fact that Foreign and Political Department of the Government of India has employed some stenographers who have not passed the Public Service Commission examination? If the answer be in the affirmative, are Government aware that there are over half-a-dozen candidates on the list of Public Service Commission who have passed the shorthand test of the Commission? Are they entitled to be employed in preference to those who have not passed the test of the Commission?

Mr. J. G. Acheson: Yes, Sir. Two temporary vacancies of stenographers have been filled by men who have not passed the examination. In one case it was desired to adjust the proportion of Muslim to Hindu stenographers, and since there were no Muslims available who had passed the examination, the present incumbent was selected on the recommendation of the Public Service Commission. The second vacancy was originally for two months only, and it was not possible to find a fully qualified candidate for such a short period. This appointment will shortly expire.

Election of Members to the Standing Committee for the Department of Education, Health and Lands
Mr. President: I have to inform the House that Khan Bahadur Maulavi Raffiuddin Ahmad, Kumar Gupteshwar Prasad Singh and **Mr. B. N. Misra**have been elected to the Standing Committee for the Department of Education, Health and Lands.

Resolution Re Appointment of A Committee to Advise on the Purchase of the Bengal and North Western and Rohilkund and Kumaon Railways (01.04.1931)

The Honourable Sir George Rainy (Member for Commerce and Railways): Sir, I move a committee consisting of Dr. Ziauddin Ahmad, **Mr. B. N. Misra**, Mr. Muhammad Azhar Ali, Mr. Maswood Ahmad, Mr. Gaya Prasad Singh, Pandit Ram Krishna Jha, Rai Bahadur Sukhraj Rai, Lala Rameswar Prasad Bagla , Lala Hariraj Swaru, Mr. Muhammad Anwar-ul-Amin, Mr. E. Studd, Mr. L. V. Heathcote, Honourable the Finance Member , and the Honourable the Railway Member be appointed to consider what action should be taken when the opportunity to purchase the Bengal and North Western and Rohilkund and Kumaon Railway systems occurs on 31st December 1932, and to make recommendations that the report of the committee be submitted to this House by the beginning of the next session; and the number of members of the committee necessary to form quorum shall be six."

Mr. President: The motion was adopted.

The Indian Press (Emergency Powers) Bill (02.10.1931)

Mr. B. N. Misra: I would not have opened my mouth, but as we are proceeding I feel that the Government are bent upon suppressing and oppressing the Indian Press. If their only object is that incitement to murder must be stopped, we are all agreed to stop this incitement. If that was the only object, you do not want to a three days' discussion of this bill. Now, Sir, I ask, why do you find so many people against the Treasury Bench? We in these benches have cried ourselves hoarse and why should the time of the House be wasted like this? Really we feel that the Honourable the Home Member wants to institute a system of slavery. I think that most the Members of this House of our Magistracy. I have practiced in the in the courts for a quarter of a century, at least 27 or 28 years. I shall quote a specimen of a Magistrate in order to make my point clear. In the early part of 1904 or 1905, I appeared before a Magistrate of ten years standing. When I appeared in the first case, he had to acquit my clients and he then admired me. He said, "During my ten years of Magistracy I have never acquitted a man, especially if it was a police case." Even in private cases when there was a medical certificate held by the complainant, he always convicted the accused. In my case the complainant had a medical certificate and he had to acquit the accused. That is the mentality of the Magistrates. They take their orders from the superior officers like the District Magistrate or Police Superintendent. They are told they ought to have an elastic conscience. The District Magistrate's advice to him was that his conscience must permit of everything. He must carry out the orders of the District Magistrate. Even now a day the same thing is happening. If our Magistrates were really administering justice, there would not be any grievance at all. The Subordinate Magistrate simply has to obey the orders of the District Magistrate, which proceeds from the Commissioner of the Division or the Local Government or the India Government. That is the kind of mentality of our Magistrates. I do not know if the Honourable the Home Member has practiced in the law courts but he must have been a Magistrate in his younger days. All our fears are due to the mentality of our Magistrates. The law is not administered except according to the whim of the superior officers. I should say our Magistracy are not human beings. They are slaves who have to carry out the orders dinned into their years by the Police Superintendent or the Magistrate of the district. That is the mode of administration of justice by the Magistracy.

Now, Sir, I come to the motion of my friend, Sardar Sant Singh. Sir, my friend is asking that the Local Government should apply to the High Court. Now, where is the objection to that? If the Government are afraid that the High Court will be independent and administer impartial justice to people and, that is perhaps the only ground on which they can oppose giving them this power because they will be in difficulty. But illustrations like, "Oh, the house is burning", "the British Empire is dwindling" are more dreadful illustrations. But as a matter of fact I do not think, none of us believes, that the house is really burning, or that the British Empire is crumbling, and so forth. Sir, the house is not burning, and the British Government will continue for long. So that this kind of alarmist argument is unreasonable and simply sophistry. Sir, we have amongst ourselves what are called Astikas and what are called Nastikas, believers and unbelievers in God. The latter class do not believe in God in spite of all his manifestations on earth. They do not see the real state of things. Now, please consider, why there are so many people who differ from the Government Bench? If they think, Sir, that we are so many mad people, and they think that they are the only sane and wise people, then why not send us to the lunatic asylum (Laughter)? If, however, they think we have some sense, some reason, then I tell them that, after reconsideration, after thinking over our objections, they should not persist in the error of their ways. Their action, instead of suppressing murders or putting a stop to incitement to murder, will recoil on them tenfold, and there will be ten times as many murders as are is committed in the country to-day. (Hear, hear) (Laughter from Official Benches.) Sir, this is not the way! What is the real way? Sir, there was a time when the Europeans, were welcomed almost as Gods. I remember my old father saying half a century ago that he had implicit faith in these white people and that he had no faith in the dark people of this country, but, Sir, he had reasons for that, because that was the real state of things in those times, - I may tell you, that the Pandas of Jagannath even welcomed the Europeans and offered free into the temple. But now, Sir, their crookedness and their avarice have soared very, very high, and their behavior……….

The President: The Honourable Member must address the Chair.

Mr. B. N. Misra: Why do they put themselves in the position (An Honourable Member: "Look towards the Chair") of enemies? Do they think it is human thing to commit murders, is it natural that human beings should commit murders? I think you have experience and you know. (Laughter.) If a child cries, any one picks up the child out of sheer human sympathy? Sir, unless one's mind is abnormal or deranged, one never commits these murders. Then why do these people commit murders? I say, for their sins, for their actions: and they must think over their past karma, and their past actions.

Mr. President: The Honourable Member must address the Chair.

Mr. B. N. Misra: I am addressing the Treasury Benches through you, Sir. The Government officials must realize what their duty is; they must recall their own past actions and their own past deeds. Sir, somehow or other it is always beneficial to calculate our own actions, and to review our own sins and actions: I say those Government officials – who fall victim to these attacks. It must be due to their unreasonable and passionate actions and behavior. They must think of it and should take a lesson from the consequences of their actions. The position, then, is that the present amendment proposes that the Local Government should apply to High Court. That is an obviously reasonable motion, which I think the whole House ought to carry.

As usual like before, the British Treasury Benches prevailed and the motion was negatived.

Pay and Allowances of Staff of the Government of India Secretariat and Attached Offices (02.10.1931)
Mr. B. N. Misra:(a) Is it a fact that there is a difference in the pay and allowances of the staff of the Secretariat and attached subordinate offices?

(b) If so, will Government please state the reason for such difference?

The Honourable Sir James Crerar: (a) Yes.

(b) The reasons are stated in my reply to part (d) of the Honourable Member's question No. 938, on 24th September, 1931.

Demand for Supplementary Grants (03.10.1931)

The Honourable Sir George Schuster (Finance Member): Sir, I beg to move:

"That a supplementary sum not exceeding Rs. 2,63,000 be granted to the Governor General in Council to defray the charges which will come in course of payment during the year ending the 31st day of March, 1932, in respect of 'Expenditure in England under the Secretary of State for India'."

Mr. President: I should like to draw the attention of the Honourable Member, Mr. Misra, to the fact that he has included in his grievances two items, one relating to the Orissa Boundary Commission and the other to the Round Table Conference. There is no provision in this demand for any expenditure on the Boundary Commission for Orissa. Therefore, that grievance cannot be ventilated on the present occasion. I, therefore, call upon the Honourable Member to move his amendment only in regard to the non-representation of Oriyas on the Round Table Conference.

The Honourable Sir George Rainy: I think, Sir, my Honourable friends, Mr. B. Das and Mr. Misra will both recollect that we did discuss the non-representation of Orissa, and I certainly made a speech on the subject.

Mr. B. N. Misra: I had discussed only one part, but the other part I think was ruled out.

Mr. President: The Honourable Member's motion seems to be out of order on both grounds. Mr. Das moved item No. 4 on the first supplementary demand and ventilated the grievance of the non-representation of Orissa at the

Round Table Conference. I do not see any difference between the non-representation of Orissa and the non-representation of Oriyas (Laughter).

Mr. B. N. Misra: Sir, we have a grievance.

Mr. President: Very well, I want to hear the Honourable Member.

Mr. B. N. Misra: Sir, as regards Orissa Boundary Commission.........

Mr. President: I have already ruled that that is out of order.

Mr. B. N. Misra: As regards our non-representation at the Round Table Conference.

Mr. President: That has been already discussed.

Non-representation of Nationalist Muslims in the Round Table Conference (03.10.1931)

Mr. B. N. Misra: Sir, I beg to move:

"That the demand for supplementary grant of sum not exceeding Rs. 2,63,000 in respect of 'Expenditure in England – Secretary of State for India' be reduced by Rs. 100."

Sir, probably you will be wondering as to why of all people, I should come forward with a motion on behalf of nationalist Muslims. First of all, let me be not misunderstood that I have put this motion at the instance of my part or anybody. I have brought this motion forward because the nationalist Muslims go unrepresented in this House. Sir, it is not foreign to Hindu culture that we should consider it our duty to espouse an unrepresented cause. (Hear, hear.) You know, Sir, from Mahabharat that Vishma was a great hero, but he was a bachelor, he was issueless: and therefore, we Hindus, particularly I am now speaking of my Brahmin community, always offer shradh for him; it is incumbent, according to our Hindu ideas, that sons must offer pindas to their father. Of course if a Hindu has not a son, certainly the belief is that he must be given a son by somebody else; and therefore, Brahmins undertake it as their first duty to offer their first pinda to Vishma, who was a great hero but bachelor and issueless. Therefore, I move this motion on account of non-representation of the nationalist Muslims at the Round Table Conference. Sir, whatever may be said by others, probably you have been reading in the papers, and particularly we get messages from London, that the Round Table Conference cannot proceed further on account of the absence of Dr. Ansari, so well-known to the House and I think to you also, Sir. Sir, on account of the absence of the nationalist Muslims, that Conference cannot go on. Of course, when I say this I do not thereby cast any reflection on any others, but I say that the Government are well aware of this view, - and so the work is being delayed in London. I, therefore, request the Honourable Members of the Treasury Benches that they should not make it a party question or a Government question, and I would request my Honourable Mussalman friends of this House also not to oppose my motion; and I would request the Treasury Benches to leave the question to the free vote of the House, without themselves taking part in it; and then I think the House will agree to this motion.

Sir Muhammad Yakub: Sir, my Honourable friend, Mr. Misra has not done justice to the Mussalmans when he says that nationalist Muslims are not represented in the Round Table Conference or that the nationalist Muslims are represented in the House. Sir, I claim for myself and my other Muslim friends in this House that we are as much nationalist as any other nationalist in India. Sir, we are not an inch behind any person in this country in claiming the freedom of our country.

Mr. B. N. Misra: Then my Honourable friend cannot object to my motion at all.

Sir Muhammad Yakub: We in this House, as well as the Muslims outside the House, have always fought shoulder to shoulder with the other communities in this country for obtaining the freedom of our motherland. In the same way my friend is not right when he says that nationalist Muslims are not represented on the Round Table Conference. Can any one say that there can be a greater nationalist Muslim than Mr. Muhammad Ali Jinnah himself? .... So I say that it is a superfluous grievance to say that the nationalist Muslims are not represented, and for these reasons I am obliged to oppose the motion of my friend, Mr. Misra.

Mr. B. N. Misra: Sir, I was trying for the unity of India and if my Honourable friend says that there is no difference............

Mr. President: The Honourable Member cannot speak again unless he is withdrawing the motion.

Mr. B. N. Misra: Yes, Sir, I am withdrawing it after clearing the position. I think any one reading the papers will find that on account of the absence of Dr. Ansari............

Kunwar Hajee Ismail Ali Khan: Sir, on a point of order, when the Honourable Member has agreed to withdraw his motion what is the use of making a speech?

Mr. President: He is not in order in making a speech, but he can very briefly explain why he is withdrawing it.

Mr. B. N. Misra: Yes, Sir, I am not making a speech. I was speaking in the interest of the unity of India and of Muslims. It is no secret that there are communalists and nationalists. If my friend claims to be a nationalist Muslim, why should he object to another man going there? After all so many people have been included.............

Mr. President: The Honourable Member is again making a speech.

Mr. B. N. Misra: No, Sir, I will not make a speech but I beg leave of the House to withdraw the motion.

The motion was, by leave of the Assembly withdrawn.

The Unusual Difference of Salary between Higher Officers and Lower Grade Employees in India (19.11.1931)

Mr. B. N. Misra: Honourable Sir, I don't blame you for giving me the opportunity to speak so late. Before I speak on the reduction of the budget proposed or the trickery of the Income Tax Department, I would like to collect some information from the Honourable Finance Member. Hope, my act in this regard would not be treated as graceless.

I would like to know, if there is any country in the world, for example, Germany, United States, Canada or France, where the administration runs at such high cost in comparison to India? Is there an example of any country in the world with regard to the kind of disproportionate and unusual kind of high salary that is paid to the officers in India in comparison to the lower grade employees?

In United States, the salary that a lower grade clerk gets is equivalent to 3125 Indian rupees. The highest salaried Judiciary Officer or Administrative Officer there gets equivalent to 27,400 Indian rupees. In proportion it is calculated out to be 1 : 9. Is the administration in United States bad? In that same count, in Germany the lowest salary is equivalent to 1110 Indian rupees and the highest salary is 14,960 Indian rupees; which means the ratio is 1 : 12. Example of Canada is peremptory, as it is ruled directly by the United Kingdom and His Excellency, our Honourable Viceroy himself, has come from there. He himself can tell if the administration there is bad. As a matter of fact, Canada is a very well administered country. A clerk there, gets salary equivalent to 1650 Indian rupees and a high ranked officer gets salary equivalent to 17,400 Indian rupees; which means the ratio stands at the same 1 : 12. Now let us look into a poorer country like Japan. Here again the ratio is almost same, 650 : 8800, i.e., 1 : 13 almost. Now let us check into the country of the Honourable Finance Member, i.e., United Kingdom itself. Here the annual salary of a clerk is equivalent to 1266 Indian rupees and the salary of the highest ranked Administrative Officer is equivalent to 40,000 Indian rupees. The ratio stands at 1 : 32. Now I am coming to India where per head annual income is the lowest, a paltry 74 Indian rupees. It means, the monthly income is only 6 rupees. Here the clerk gets 360 rupees annually; which means monthly only 30 rupees, but the high ranked Administrative Officers do not get less than 48,000 rupees in any case. Interestingly, the ratio of lower salaried people and the higher salaried people painfully stand at 1 : 133 in this country.

In the matters of "cut" in the budget, the retrenchment of lower salaried employees would not help. If you need to retrench, retrench the high salaried employees so that you would get some financial benefit. If low-salaried employees are retrenched or get salary-cuts, it would not only hurt them badly; but the Government would also not get any visible surplus in the budget.

Those who are getting 6000 rupees, a cut of 600 rupees would not hurt them badly; but those who are getting only 30 rupees in salary, a cut of only 3 rupees would have a sky-fall effect on them. That apart, is a person getting 6000 rupees, genuinely 100 times better and more talented than a person getting only 60 rupees as salary? If the Treasury Benches are abiding by the British administrative principles, it is well and good. Then why such great difference in salary in India? If a clerk is getting 30 rupees salary here, then as per the British rules, a high-ranked officer should get 30 * 32 = 960 rupees. The excess amount he gets be deducted from his salary. It would be highly ethical and legal.

Chief Justices of High Courts (27.01.1932)

Mr. B. N. Misra: Sir, I had no intention to take part in this discussion, but the term "Chief Justice" as it is understood in the English language is known in Sanskrit Prad Bibek. That means in the widest sense a man whose knowledge has been sharpened to such an extent that he may be called a man possessing broad and independent views on any question, and not a man possessed of what is commonly known as the slave mentality of a public servant, or whose mentality has been framed throughout his service in the interest of public service. Prad Bibek or the Chief Justice is entrusted with the most onerous duties, that is the duty of maintaining the legal lore, and he should not be impeached in any way as regards his mentality or training. He is supposed to have held throughout his life independent and broad views, and it is only the profession that retains or gives a man that independence which service, whatever kind it may be, will never give. Sir, our main objection has been to the mentality of the civil service. There may be very good civil servants so far as their loyalty to their service or to their masters is concerned, but so far as their knowledge of men and things is concerned, so far as their legal knowledge is concerned, I doubt very much whether a man from civil service, barring perhaps a few rare and honourable exceptions, can be found to fill the post of Chief Justice of the High Courts in India. I do not mean to cast any reflection on the civil servants of India; they have rendered good service in their own way to their masters. My point is that to fill the post of Chief Justice only men from the legal profession who have their training at the Bar should be selected. This is invariably the case in England, in the Colonies and the Dominions, and there they never select a man from the service. It is our most sad experience that in this country, however eminent, however learned, however well versed in law they may be, no Indians have so far been selected to fill the post of Chief Justice of a High Court, and only white men have always been selected to fill that post. Why, Sir, there are any number of very brilliant and distinguished vakils, pleaders, advocates and barristers in the Indian Courts from whom a suitable selection can be made to fill the post of Chief Justice. Indians of proved merit and ability in the legal profession are not wanting who can distinguish themselves as Chief Justices of High Courts. We all know that Indians have filled very high and equally responsible positions with credit to themselves and advantage to the country in other spheres of life. I cannot say why for the position of Chief Justice suitable Indians who have had experience at the Bar should not be recruited, and why white men should be regarded as superior to Indians and chosen to occupy the posts of Chief Justices. Sir, in making the appointment of Chief Justice there should be no considerations of race, colour, because we want only pure and unalloyed justice and justice alone. Therefore, Sir, I appeal to all Members of this House without any distinction of caste or race to support this resolution.

The Hindu Widow's Right of Inheritance Bill (04.02.1932)

Mr. B. N. Misra:I rise to oppose this motion very strongly and very vehemently and with all the strength that I possess. I was ashamed to hear my Honourable friend Mr. Jadhav saying that Hindu widows become cooks. He said he did not like to wash any dirty linen in public but that is what he did indirectly. No sooner a child is born that the mother allows her breast to be sucked and feeds the child. Which woman does not do it? In which country, in which clime and in which age is this not done? If she allows her breasts to be sucked and she feeds the child and she feeds her grown up children and if she feeds other members of the family, what sin is there? What sin is there today if she can do it and if she does it? My friend, Diwan Bahadur Sarda, said that the position of a Hindu widow is bad. I have lived in this world nearly half a century, I do not know that a Hindu widow has a less respectable position in society than any other member of the family. She is called the "goddess" of the house, the Grihalakshmi. Even from the time of marriage a Kanya attains a position of great respect. From the time of Marriage she is allowed to walk in front and first and then the husband Bara has to follow (Hear, hear), as everyone who knows a Hindu marriage can testify. Even from the moment she is married as a child – and of course we have child marriages – she is accorded all respect in the House by everybody. Now it is said that Hindu widows are not given a share in the husband's property. But. Sir, supposing a family consists of only a husband and a wife and the husband dies. The widow gets the possession of the entire property for her maintenance, but she has to perform all her duties towards her dead husband. Supposing she is a mother when she becomes a widow, supposing she has three or four children, what is the position? Though according to Hindu law the sons are entitled to the property, still the mother is the legal guardian. Where then is her position inferior? She has the enjoyment of the entire property, and she brings up the children, and she looks after their education and so on. Supposing a woman has four or five children and becomes a widow at the age of 20 or 25. What happens? Now the situation arising out of the passage of this Bill will be that many people will try to introduce her to remarry. Supposing she gets remarried and gets a share in the property, and gets children by the second marriage what becomes the position of these children whom she gave birth to by first husband who become the children now of so and so. The only result will be a disruption in the family and gross neglect of the children, because in the absence of the mother who re-marries and possibly goes away and gets children by the second husband the uncles and others naturally will not care for them so much as if she had remained on as part and parcel of the family of her deceased husband. Even in the joint family, there are other brothers and still the widow is there to look after those children, but if she gets a share, then naturally the other members would not look after the children and what will be the condition of the latter? If therefore she remains in the family, her position is in no way inferior or bad, although she may not get a specific permanent share in the property, because the children are there and they get the property of the father, and when they grow up they look after the needs and wants of the mother. Supposing however, she has no children and becomes a widow, then even in that case the law allows her all necessary privileges, and she is entitled to maintenance, in fact to everything, and she is in no inferior condition. Of course if she has children, she at the same time gets exalted position of the mother and she commands additional respect. So, where is the worse condition attaching to the widow under the present system? Now this Hindu system has stood for no less than 5,000 years, and nowhere has any difficulty ever been felt. Of course, "spare the rod and spoil the child." If a person is not what she should be, if she is not behaving properly and her conduct is improper, certainly she deserves chastisement or punishment. That is what the Hindu law contemplates. The Hindu social system contemplates that there she does not follow the system of her religion, law and society, the maintenance cannot be continued. But in every case where she conforms to the rules and tenets of her religion, law and society, all her agnates or relations are supposed to maintain her. There is no torture or cruelty in this case. It all depends on her conduct whether she is liked or disliked. If she does something, which is forbidden and therefore disliked, she suffers. She has reason to complain justly. Innovations which were never contemplated by the Hindu Shastras and run counter to our religious principles are sought to be introduced by men who, after all, are only imitating and aping their neighours or other nationalities, but, Sir, Hindu society has stood all these centuries the onslaughts of Muhammadan and other invaders and onslaughts of social reformers. These onslaughts have become I regret to say more frequent in this Legislative Assembly, coming as they do from men imbued with the so-called reformed ideas. Nobody can say what is really beneficial to the society. Many minds think differently on the subject. There is a saying in my part of the country:

"Paraghara pitha dekhi rabei khabei, ghasi phadakare gooda madai chobaie".
" If you feel jealousy when your neighour makes cakes and you are anxious to eat cakes, do not take a piece of cow-dung and gnaw it with goor or sugar."
That is to say, one should not aspire to be what another is. For instance, the Christian society has a particular way

of living, while the Hindu widows remain inside the house and observe the purdah system. But if I were to live like an English gentleman and walked with my wife outside in the streets, what would be my position? The Europeans have been observing that kind of life from time immemorial and if we were to ape or imitate them, it would not be right for me, and I would be isolated. So I maintain that there is no need for any law on the subject because the condition of the existing Hindu society does not need it. May I ask the Diwan Bahadur Harbilas Sarda, who sponsored the early child marriage Bill, whether it is not a fact that his own brother did not invite him to the marriage of his daughter? His name may be known to the whole world as that of a great reformer, but let him go any village and find out how his law is being appreciated. I can only say that at the expense of Hindu society he is trying to get very cheap notoriety without spending a pie. Sir, if a man builds a temple or a mosque, he becomes famous; if a man does something wrong in the street, he also becomes notorious, and his name is tomtomed. Similarly, if a man makes water in the street, he also gains notoriety. Therefore, I maintain, that the Hindu society should not ape others at all. I appeal to my Hindu friends and all other Members of this House not to help the Diwan Bahadur in bringing disruption of the Hindu society but to allow the Hindu society to grow and develop as it has been doing for the last so many thousand years. Sir, with these words I oppose the Bill.

Party to the Post Master General, Madras, By the Managing Director of a Motor Mail Service (29.02.1932)

Sardar G. N. Mujumdar (On behalf of Mr. B. N. Misra):(a) With reference to the answer given to starred question No. 1075 of Sirdar Harbans Singh Brar on 29th September, 1931, are Government aware that "to bid farewell to Mr. H. M. Richardson, the outgoing Postmaster General, and to welcome Mr. C. D. Rae, the new Post Master General, Mr. C. Rajam, Managing Director, The Garage, Ltd., was "At Home" on the 1st February, 1932 "at India House, his residence" in Madras?

(b) Are Government aware that high officials of the Postal Department attended the function?

(c) Are Government aware that "after tea the guests moved to the drawing hall upstairs where they were entertained to a programme of dance by Srimati Ragini Devi, the famous oriental dancer" with instrumental music by her troupe of Patiala Court musicians?

(d) Is not the host, the Managing Director of the company, which is given a subsidy for Mail-Motor Service in Madras and in Calcutta?

(e) If answer to part (d) is in the affirmative, what is the amount of subsidy given for Madras and for Calcutta?

(f) if the answer to part (a) is in the affirmative, are Government prepared to stop these officials accepting these parties from Government contractors?

(g) If answer to (a) is in the negative, do Government propose to make enquiries and also see The Hindu of Madras, dated 2nd February, 1932?

The Honourable Sir Joseph Bhore: (a), (b), (c) and (d). Government have no information other than a report contained in the issue of The Hindu referred to by the Honourable Member in the last part of part (g) of this question.

(e) and (f). The Honourable Member's attention is invited to the answer to Sirdar Harbans Singh Brar referred to by him in part (a) of the question.

(g) Does not arise.

Office Hours in the Office of the Controller of Railway Accounts (01.03.1932)

Mr. S. C. Mitra (on behalf of Mr. B. N. Misra): Is it a fact that hours of office attendance have been altered only in the Controller of Railway Accounts Office from 10 A.M. to 5 P.M. whereas in the Railway Board the same hours continue?

Sir Alan Parsons: In the office of the Controller of Railway Accounts the office hours are 7 hours a day for 5 days in the week with a half hour recess making 6 1/2 hours net, and on Saturdays 4 hours, no recess being granted. In the office of the Railway Board the office hours are 6 hours a day for five days in the week and 3 ½ hours on Saturdays, no recess being granted.

Discharge of Temporary Staff in the Controller of Railway Accounts Office (01.03.1932)

Mr. S. C. Mitra (on behalf of Mr. B. N. Misra): (a) Is it a fact that some six temporary men out of the temporary staff of the Railway Board's Office were transferred along with the statistical work to the Controller of Railway Accounts Office and were given promises by the Deputy Secretary, Railway Board, that they would be confirmed against the six posts in class two that they were carrying with them?

(b) Is it a fact that only one man was confirmed and that was also because he was a member of the minority community? If so, why?

(c) Is it a fact that the temporary staff in the Railway Board's Office are being provided for while these temporary men are being thrown out? Is it a fact that some of them are far senior to those in the Railway Board's Office?

(d) Is it a fact that men with more than 25 years' service are being kept while young low-paid staff are being thrown out in the Controller of Railway Accounts' Office? Do Government propose to retain the young staff in place of those who have put in more than 25 years' service or those who are inefficient among the permanent staff?

Sir Alan Parsons: (a) The only assurance given to the 6 temporary men concerned was that they would not be adversely affected by the transfer.

(b) Only one man was confirmed because the efficiency and seniority of the other temporary men already working in the Controller of Railway Accounts Office had also to be considered.

(c) Owing to retrenchment the 5 remaining men in the Controller of Railway Accounts Office are being discharged. Temporary men in the Railway Accounts Office are also being discharged.

(d) I am informed that there is only one clerk with more than 25 years service in the Controller of Railway Accounts Office, but he is not approaching superannuation. The selection of discharges is being made strictly in accordance with the orders in the Railway Board's letter No. 683 – E. G. of the 3rd March, 1931, and Government see no reason to alter these orders.

Mr. S. C. Mitra (on behalf of Mr. B. N. Misra): (a) Is it a fact that when some eight posts on account of the transfer of the statistical work in the Controller of Railway Accounts Office were permanently and provisionally filled, seniority and efficiency of all the temporary clerks were considered and those who were not considered were either junior or inefficient?

(b) If the answer to the above is in the affirmative, why are junior men being given preference over those who are senior and were provisionally confirmed?

(c) Are Government prepared to investigate the matter and reconsider the case of the temporary clerks in the Controller, Railway Accounts' Office, if not, why not?

Sir Alan Parsons: (a) Yes, except for persons on deputation from other offices.

(b) No junior men have so far been given any preference, though, I understand, that one comparatively junior clerk is being considered for preferential treatment on account of his exceptionally good work.

(c) No. Government are satisfied that their orders on the subject are being carried out.

Railway Budget – List of Demands (03.03.1932)

Mr. B. N. Misra: I rise to support the motion of my friend Mr. Anwar-ul-azim. I am very doubtful whether the Railway Board functions as a Board at all, or whether it does any work except what really suits it, though it is not in accordance with the desire of the Assembly or in accordance with the needs of the country. Sir, I am reminded of a saying in Oriya "chaini (cheyeen) soithibaji (jie) taku uthaibakai (uthaiba kie)" which means that you can wake up a man who is really sleeping, but not one who merely pretends to sleep. That is the position of our Railway Board now. Do they exist in the interests of India and for the people of India? We have cried ourselves hoarse for so many years, and even this year today is the third day of our railway debate. Do the Railway Board care to do anything? The other day when I put a question about the percentage of Oriyas in Bengal Nagpur Railway, what was the reply of my Honourable friend Sir Alan Parsons? He said it was a communal question and he did not give a reply. Am I to teach him the meaning of the word "community" or "communal"? If Oriyas are a community, I think, it is very wrongly understood by him. We are hearing on the floor of this House so many answers relating to the Muslim community, the Sikh community, and so on. I include in the term Oriya all people resident in Orissa, whether they are Hindus, Muslims, Brahmins or Non-Brahmins, be they Christians, Jains or whoever they may be. They are all Oriyas. I have used the word as it is familiar. If I might coin new word, I might say Orissans instead of Oriyas. "Orissan" includes all the communities residing in Orissa, just as the word "Bengali" includes all the people residing in Bengal, whether Hindus, Muslims, Buddhists, Jains. Etc. (Mr. Lalchand Navalrai: We have got the word 'Sindhi'.") I am glad you have got one. I even include the domiciled Bengalis in the term Oriya, because they live in Orissa. I also include Telugus residents in Orissa Ganjam.

Mr. President: I hope the Honourable Member realizes that the motion on which he is making his speech relates to lack of supervision and control over Company-managed railways by the Railway Board.

Mr. B. N. Misra: I am only showing what control they

are exercising over Bengal Nagpur Railway. Only the other day we heard a lot about the grievances of the Muslim community against the Railway Board. Let me here tell them what is in the mind of the Railway Board or the Agents. I had a talk with an Agent of Railway one day. I asked him, "Why don't you employ Oriyas in you line?". Thevline goes through 800 miles of Orissa on all sides – on one side from Kharagpur to Jharsuguda and Sambalpur, and on the other side from Kharagpur to Naupada and other places in Ganjam district, then again from Vizianagram to Parvatipur, to Salur, Titlagarh, etc. Sir, you will be surprised to hear that they cannot point out even one per cent of Oriyas in their services. I asked them what the reason was, why they did not take in Oriyas? I was told that they are not available, but when applications are made, they are returned, saying that, there are no vacancies. Thousands of persons are employed every year in the several departments, such as Transport, Traffic, Audit, etc. They are getting such large number of Anglo-Indians, Europeans and others, and when they retire, their sons, and grandsons, are being employed in their places and no outsider ever gets a chance. I asked the Agent, "Why don't you like Hindu Kings and Muhammadan Emperors, give them dan, inam, jagirs and make the offices hereditary, so that they may descend from father to son"? Then we will understand the position. From the highest to the lowest offices you will not find any Oriyas worth counting. This is all due to the policy of favouritism which obtains in the railways and the Railway Board does not exercise any supervision over the company-managed railways. Outsiders never get a chance. This is gross negligence on the part of the Railway

Board, on account of which only the relations of existing employees have got a chance of employment. Now, Sir, the Orissa province is in the making. It is in the womb of the Boundary Commission. The Commission is laboring hard and we all hope that before long they will give birth to a new baby, the Orissa Province. Now, Sir, the Oriya speaking area comprises a vast tract of territory from Kharagpur to Jharsuguda, Bilaspur and Parlakimedi up to Vizianagram roughly. We have got 8 branch lines. The Bengal Nagpur Railway traverses about 800 miles of Oriya-speaking country, and yet there is not one per cent of Oriyas employed in the railways. Other communities are not satisfied with even 20 per cent. I shall be glad if there is at least 5 per cent of Oriyas employed.

Mr. Goswami M. R. Puri: On a point of order. The Honourable Member is speaking on Oriya representation in the railways, which is not relevant to this discussion.

Mr. Gaya Prasad Singh: He is showing that the lack of representation is due to the lack of supervision of the Railway Board.

Mr. President: The chair takes it that it is the Honourable Member's contention that the absence of Oriyas on Company-managed railways is due to lack of supervision of the Railway Board.

Mr. B. N. Misra: Yes, Sir, This is the trouble that the Oriyas have to undergo. A Commissioner of the Orissa Division, Mr. Phillip, as Member of the Advisory Board wrote a letter to Sir George Rainy or Mr. Hayman about an Oriya graduate. I hold the letter in my hand. This person has not been given any employment for about two years. There are many cases like this. Therefore I say you can awake one who is really asleep but you cannot awake one who pretends to sleep. It appears to me that the Railway Board is only an ornamental body. I have shown you the lack of supervision over the Bengal Nagpur Railway. No doubt other Members will be able to speak about other railways. The Railway Board is like a society, which is impervious and impenetrable. I had a talk with the Agent. He said that he got 1,200 applications. I asked Sir Alan Parsons how many Oriyas were taken in and he evaded the question by saying that it was a communal question. The Government find enough Oriyas cent per cent to man all offices, Collectorates, District Courts, etc., from Executive Councillor, Minister to District Collector, Principal, Lecturers, Teachers, Police Superintendent to Constables. But the Bengal Nagpur Railway cannot find even 5 per cent of the employees from amongst Oriyas! I may tell you, Sir, that from the point of view of economy also, it is more profitable to employ Oriyas. During the Christmas and Durga Puja holidays time, many employees get passes and they go to Madras, Punjab, Dacca and so on. All this expense in issuing passes could be saved if the local people, Oriyas, could be employed. They would not have wanted to travel long distances on passes. All this travelling expense could be saved to distant places like Madras, Dacca and the Punjab, etc. They want passes to visit their relations and their wives and what not, and children too. (Laughter.) Of course many people have got hosts of relations, whatever they might mean. Now passes are used not only on these two occasions, but on other occasion also. Sir, is it not a great loss the Bengal Nagpur Railway suffers, which they would not have suffered if they had taken the men from these Oriya tracts, in which I may say most of these stations lie? In that case they would not be required to spend enormous sums, especially in these days, on passes. Sir, therefore I have given a notice of cut and I shall place it before the House for consideration. (Laughter.) I see the whole Assembly is crying, and they are not listening to what I say. Sir, all this trouble is due to the policy of the Railway Board. That policy should be to take representatives of each province into confidence and see how the employment will go on equitably, smoothly and economically, what each province will require, what number of each community is fair. Sir, some of the representatives of the Assembly may form a better Board. What about these Advisory Committee Members.........

Mr. President: I have given the Honourable Member considerable latitude, but I cannot allow him to go on repeating himself in regard to the one issue which he has brought forward during the whole of this speech.

Mr. B. N. Misra: Sir, I would only suggest that this Railway Board should be abolished, and representatives from each province should be selected to form a Committee in order to consider the needs of each province, either communally or provincially, as necessary.

Employees of the Bengal Nagpur Railway (15.03.1932)
Mr. S. C. Mitra (on behalf of Mr. B. N. Misra): Will Government be pleased to state the number of employees in the Bengal Nagpur Railway drawing a salary of (a) Rs. 500 and above, (b) Rs. 50 to 499, and (c) Rs. 49 and below?

Mr. P. R. Rau: The information available will be found in Appendix F of Vol. I and Appendix C of Vol. II of the

Report by the Railway Board of Indian Railways for 1930-31, copies of which are in the Library of the House.

Passes issued during Holidays on the Bengal Nagpur railway (15.03.1932)

Mr. S. C. Mitra (on behalf of Mr. B. N. Misra): (a) Will Government be pleased to state the number of passes issued by the Bengal Nagpur Railway in 1931:

  (i) during the Durga Puja holidays,

  (ii) during the Christmas Holidays.

General Budget – List of Demands (19.03.1932)

Mr. B. N. Misra: Sir, with regard to this controversy, I have to say a few words. Much has been said about the subvention to the North-West Frontier Province and about Orissa. I am not speaking in a spirit of envy because the Frontier Province got it, but in a different spirit. Probably, Sir, you know the custom in Indian dinners of Bhojansabha, where you don't ask for food yourself directly, but you ask that it should be brought to your neighbor-guest so that you may be served. That is the spirit in which I speak now and not in a spirit of opposition because a subvention has been given to the North-West Frontier Province. Much has been said about that province. It has been said that that province protects India from foreign invasion. Sir, our own memory is very treacherous and it is our greatest enemy. It may not be known to all, that my province of Orissa is the Middle Eastern Frontier Province. Before Christ, about 200 B. C., it was King Kharabela and King Raktabahu of Orissa that saved our country, India, when there was as an Ionian invasion from the seaside, and prevented them from entering the country. Sir, I think I can claim with greater force that if there is a frontier province which has saved India from foreign invasion it is my province of Orissa, which prevented the entry of foreigners through the sea. My Honourable friend Mr. Yamin Khan spoke of the North-West Frontier as the guardian angel and all that. The fact remains that all the Muhammadan invasions and other invasions were made through that country, which allowed invaders to come from that side. But it is my province which protected India from all the invasions and attacks from the seaside. Even very recently during the German War the German battle ship "Emden" came and shelled Madras and when it came to Puri it was stopped. Of course people who are superstitious say that it was the Lord Jagannath who is not the god of any single province or community but the Lord of the Universe, that stopped it, but the fact remains that its further progress was stopped near the Puri coast. So even very recently foreign invasion was prevented. Therefore I say that Orissa should be treated as a frontier province, - the Middle Eastern Frontier as I call it. It is that province that requires protection, but the attention; which has been paid to that province is well known to all. Sir, the Government deserve our thanks for they have appointed a Committee for the formation of a province. But, Sir, they have done it in a very half-hearted manner. Sir, mark the wording of the reference to the Committee, "If an Oriya province is to be formed what will be the boundaries of the province and what will be its effect on other provinces". Sir, mark the small word "If". If the Government have not after 30 years of struggle decided to have a province, what is the use of finding all this about boundaries and so on? Was it done in the case of the formation of the Provinces of Bihar and Orissa and Sind, etc.? This is a step-motherly treatment to Orissa and shows that Government have appointed this Committee with great reluctance as a show. Sir, if they have not made up their mind why have they brought a man from 6000 miles away as a member, and one gentleman fro Assam, and a millionaire from Bombay? When they have to make a province, they should do it well, not in this half-hearted manner. Say definitely without "If".

Mr.President: Order, order. The Honourable Member is speaking on the Foreign and Political Department and he is hardly in order in discussing the formation of Orissa Province.

Mr. B. N. Misra: Sir, I am talking of the middle Eastern frontier and it deserves attention. The other day His Excellency the Viceroy in addressing us spoke as follows:

"The course suggested is the grant of a central subvention to the North-West Frontier Province. The need for such a subvention and its probable amount are under inquiry of my Government. It is our intention to consult the Indian Legislature when the details have been worked out."

Sir, I am speaking about the Government's attitude. His Excellency did not speak a word about Orissa, and the Foreign and Political Department have not treated the case of Orissa with as much attention as they should have done. I think when my turn comes, I shall speak about that also; but I say they have not paid as much attention to the middle Eastern frontier, though they have paid a great deal of attention to the North-West Frontier. I think the middle Eastern frontier deserves more attention from other parts of India and other parts of India must remember that my province has done more than North-West Frontier has ever done. I began by saying that memory is treacherous; the past is always forgotten; people deal with present; but I hope my friends will remember when the claim of Orissa is pressed.

Several Honourable Members; The question may now be put.

Mr. President: I accept the closure. The question is that the question be now put.

The motion was adopted.

Number of Clerks in the Office of the Superintendent of Education, Delhi, Ajmer-Merwara and Central India (31.03.1932)

Mr. S. C. Mitra (on behalf of Mr. B. N. Misra): (a) Will Government be pleased to state the number of clerks working in the office of the Superintendent of Education, Delhi, Ajmer-Merwara and Central India and how many of them are Hindus, Muslims and others?

(b) Is it a fact that the son of the Head Clerk of that office is also working under his father?

Sir Frank Noyce: (a) There are ten clerks in the Office of the Superintendent of Education, Delhi, Ajmer-Merwara and Central India, of whom seven are Muslims and three Hindus.

(b) Yes.

Departmental Punishment of Government Servants (31.03.1932)

Mr. S. C. Mitra (on behalf of Mr. B. N. Misra): Will

Government please state if it is a fact that no departmental punishment is permissible under rules in the following areas:

(a) If a Government servant merely attends a political meeting and takes no part in the proceedings thereof;

(b) if a Government servant is honourably acquitted or discharged after full enquiry by a court of law on the charge of bribery or any other allegation amounting to turpitude such as misappropriation of Government money, etc., and

(c) if a Government servant, though handed over to the police, is not ultimately challaned by the authority for want of evidence against him?

The Honourable Sir James Crerar:(a) The attention of the Honourable Member is invited to rules 22 and 23 of the Government Servants Conduct Rules, a copy of which is in the Library.

(b) and (c). An order of acquittal or discharge by a court of law is not necessarily a bar to the institution of departmental proceedings. Nor would the inability of the police to pursue an investigation into the conduct of a Government servant always prevent such conduct being the subject of departmental proceedings.

The Tea Districts Emigrant Labour Bill (05.04.1932)

The Honourable Sir Joseph Bhore:
Sir, I beg to move:

"That the Bill, to amend the law relating to emigrant labourers in the tea district of Assam, be referred to a Select Committee consisting of Sir Cowasji Jehangir, Mr. K. Ahmed, Mr. C. C. Biswas, Mr. Abdul Matin Chowdhury, Mr. A. G. Clow, Mr. Tin Tut. Mr. H. B. Fox, Mr. N. M. Joshi, Mr. B. N. Misra, Mr. H. P. Mody, Mr. G. Morgan, Mr. T. R. Phookun, Mr. Gaya Prasad Singh, Mr. K. P. Thampan, Mr. Muhammad Yamin Khan, Sir Frank Noyce, Mr. S. G. Jog and the Mover, and that the number of members whose presence shall be necessary to constitute a meeting of the Committee shall be five."

The Child Marriage Restraint (Amendment) Bill (13.09.1932)

Mr. B. N. Misra: About a quarter of an hour, Mr. President, I would not have at all stood up, were it not for the utterance of the Honourable the Home Member and the attitude of the Government. Sir, I may be wrong, but I was always under the impression that the policy of the Government was not to interfere in social affairs, particularly with regard to the marriage as it is known in India amongst the Hindus whose number is 30 crores with so many castes and sub-castes. Whatever might have been said by Pandit Satyendra Sen and others about the shastric laws, I would say that certainly in India there are many kinds of marriages. That was in the very olden days. All that is forgotten now. Perhaps none of the Honourable Members will agree that a woman could be carried away now a days by force following the Rakshasa form of marriage. All people will regret that course. None of the people follow the Rakshasa or the Paisacha form of marriage now. There are many other things amongst the ancient customs, which we do not adopt now. In the matter of marriage each caste and each community follows its own custom. I would ask my Hounourable friends whether before 1929 that is before the passing of the Sarda Act, they could point out any legislation undertaken for prescribing the age of marriage anywhere. They can go back to three thousand years and yet they can never find any legislation prohibiting marriage below a certain age. I stand upon this fact that each society was managing its own affairs. No Government interfered in the religious practices of any community. Marriage practices never formed the subject of legislation at any time. All these bills that you find in the agenda would not have come in against the Sarda Act, but for the fact that people believe that their religious practices have been interfered with. Some of the people who call themselves progressive have come forward with this legislation against early marriage. I do not know who these progressives are, I do not know how can I define the word 'progressive'. Is it arithmetical progression or geometrical progression or what? You find there are so many castes and so many classes in the country, but you do not find any class classed the progressive. They might have formed a new religion and if so, you would have found a classification called progressive in the census list. If I remember aright, Mr. Gokhale when he was introducing the Free Compulsory Primary Education Bill complained that the literate men in India comprised only 4 per cent out of 30 crores. Now, if I make a calculation, how many out of these literate people of 4 per cent are progressives like my Honourable friend. I say there is no definition of this word 'progressive'. If I may say so, they are the most autocratic people, who want their personal views to be imposed upon others. Where was the necessity of the Sarda Act? Did we ever get any complaint that the system of marriage then in vogue was bad? There was no complaint at all. Why should these social reformers thrust their views upon the public. I was pained to hear the Honourable the Home member say that Government would support the Sarda Act. I was all along defending the Government and I never thought that the Government would be so unreasonable as to interfere in the social and religious matters. The Honourable the Home Member said that he would oppose this Bill and I would submit that for the first time the Government is laying down a new principle in social and religious matters, namely one interference.

The Honourable Mr. H. G. Haig: Government are only adopting the same attitude which they adopted in 1929.

Mr. B. N. Misra: That was a wrong attitude, namely interference in social and religious matters. If his predecessor did some wrong, he need not repeat the same mistake. I would submit that Queen Victoria in her memorable proclamation assured the people of India of strict religious neutrality and non-interference in all social and religious matters. I hope the government should always remember that declaration of that great Queen. India was allowed to pass into the hands of the Crown only on that assurance. Otherwise many more sepoy mutinies would have been enacted. It is because the Government never interfered in the religious and social matters of the people that they have been ruling these two centuries. If the Government should interfere in the religious matters, then the feelings of the people will be estranged and the people will soon lose their confidence in the Government. As my Honourable friend Pandit Sen pointed out these orthodox people are very loyal to the

Government and they have full faith in the Government. I was also under the same impression till now, but now I find I was wrong in my impression.

Now, to come to the real fact of child marriage, what do we find? According to the Ramayana and Mahabharata, there were eight systems of marriages, called the Rakshasa, Paisacha, Gandharva, etc., marriages. No one would support those systems of marriages now. Rakshasa form is carrying by force a woman or following the kukkuta and kukkuti form that is a cock catching hold of a hen. In ancient times we also heard Swayamvara form of marriages. All these are not in vogue now. According to our customs we are following the system of Prajapatya invariably, sometimes Daiba or Arsh marriages now. Supposing a woman above 15 years is taken in marriage into a family, what happens? She will not agree with the ways and customs of the house into which she enters into family alliance. It is purely from the domestic point of view, we want to take young girls in marriage. When a girl between 7 and 12 is taken in marriage into a family, she becomes part and parcel of the new family and she gets herself accustomed to the new surrounding much sooner than she would have been had she come into a family later on, say after 15 years of age. There are two stages up to which even the Indian Penal Code exempts any person even if he or she commits a crime, because it is not the age of discretion. Section 83 of Indian Penal Code says that nothing is an offence which is done by a child above 7 years and under 12 years, because he has not attained sufficient maturity of understanding to judge the nature of offence. That is the age when they are supposed to acquire some understanding in the affairs of the world. That is also the age we impart education and train them. The ages between 7 and 12 are the best for a girl to get herself married. Afterwards she might form independent views and assert her own independence. That is how we can have a happy home and a happy domestic life. This age between 6 and 12 is the best age for a girl to come to a stranger's family because she can adopt their manners and customs and their views.

The great poet Bisnusarma says:

"Yannabe bhajanelagnah Sanskaronanyatha bhabet."

"An impress on a new clay pot lasts long."

After that she will have her own views and principles and she will not care for the views of her husband's father or mother. S from the common sense point of view, apart from, apart from shastric injunctions, that is the best age when you can take a wife who will be docile and follow your manners and ways. The opponents of child marriage say that on account of this marriage there are many widows. Sir, I am shocked to hear that. Did the girl become a widow through her own fault? She became a widow because it was an accident that the man died. She may also become a widow in her 15th or 16th or 20th year, and nobody can help it. So I think this argument has no foundation and no legs to stand upon. Moreover, the law provides for widow re-marriage and my Honourable friends know that among many castes there is widow remarriage. Only among the Brahmins there is some restriction. So this argument about child marriage increasing the number of widows is absolutely unfounded. Another advantage of early marriage is that there are many poor families in the country and if a girl is married at an early age, the husband's family can take care of the girl. Among these poor people girls after a certain age cannot go out lest there should be cases of abduction and kidnapping. But no man will ever cast an evil eye on a girl of 7 or 9 or try to kidnap or abduct her. So this is one advantage that once you give your daughter in marriage you are relieved of all burden. And it is a relief for the poor people who form the majority of this country's population. Sir, in our society and also in Muslim society there are many things which assume religious importance and you have noticed that they also resent the Sarda Act and against any interference by the Assembly or by Government in their social matters. On the ground, Sir, I support this motion and I condemn the attitude of Government in opposing this motion.

Several Honourable Members gave their views in the same line, which was probably considered right for the conservative Indian society of the time.

Construction of Mahanady Canal in Orissa (21.09.1932)

Mr. B. N. Misra: Will Government be pleased to state:

(a) the name of the company which began construction of the Orissa Canal (Mahanady Canal) system;

(b) the year when construction began as also the year when it ended;

(c) the total amount invested by the said company;

(d) the reason why Government purchased the above canal system from the company;

(e) the total capital outlay thereon on its completion and

the rate of interest on the capital outlay on the said canal system;

(f) whether the people desired it; and

(g) the reason why it was claimed as a protective work?

The Honourable Sir Frank Noyace: (a), (b), (c) and (d). The Honourable Member is referred to pages 51 – 54 and 208 of the Triennial Review of Irrigation in India, 1918 – 1921, copies of which are in the Library of the House.

(e) The total capital outlay on the completion of the project was Rs. 2,60,27,000. The rate of interest during 1930 – 31 was about 3.3252 per cent in respect of capital outlay to the end of the year 1916 – 17 and 6.11 per cent on the subsequent outlay.

(f) I regret that no information on this point is now available.

(g) The project was not classified as a protective work. It is, however, of the greatest value from a purely protective point of view as explained on page 54 of the Review referred to in reply to the earlier parts of the question.

Mr. B. N. MIsra: What is the length of this canal in Orissa Division at present?

The Honourable Sir Frank Noyce: I am afraid I shall have to ask for notice of that question.

Construction of the Rusikulya and the Ganjam Gopalpur Canal Systems (21.09.1932)

Mr. B. N. Misra: Will Government be pleased to state:

(a) the dates when the Rushikulya canal system and the Ganjam Gopalpur canal were constructed;

(b) the capital outlay on each of these two works separately;

(c) the rate of interest per cent payable on the capital outlay on each of these two works; and

(d) the object for which the Ganjam Gopalpur canal was constructed?

The Honourable Sir Frank Noyce: (a) The Rushikulya canal system was completed in 1901 and the Ganjam Gopalpur canal in 1893.

(b) The capital outlay to the end of the year 1930-31 was Rs. 54,00,731 on the Rushikulya system and Rs. 1,55,493 on the Ganjam Gopalpur canal.

(c) The rate of interest during 1930-31 is 3.3252 per cent on outlay to the end of 1916-17 and 5.44 per cent on the subsequent outlay.

(d) The object for which the construction of the canal was undertaken was to complete the water communication between the country bordering the Chilka Lake and Gopalpur, then the port of the Ganjam district, and to provide a link in the system of inland water communication with Calcutta if in the future through communication should be established.

Contribution by the Government of India to certain Provincial Governments for Construction of Government Buildings (21.09.1932)

Mr. B. N. Misra: Will Government be pleased to state:

(a) The amount of money that they have contributed to the Government of Bihar and Orissa for the construction of their buildings at the headquarters of Patna and Ranchi, including the Government houses, Secretariat buildings and such other allied buildings; and

(b) the amount of money that they sanctioned for the

construction of such buildings in Assam after 1913 up-to-date?

The Honourable Sir Frank Noyce: (a) and (b). The information is being collected and such information as is found to be available will be laid on the table of the House in due course.

Delimitation of the Oriya Tracts in Madras (21.09.1932)

Mr. B. N. Misra: Will Government be pleased to state:

(a) whether they have asked the Government of Madras to take the opinion of the Local Legislative Assembly (where the number of Oriya members is less than three per cent) under Section 52A of the Government of India Act, regarding the delimitation of the Oriya tracts in Madras Province proposed by the (O'Donnel) Committee?

(b) If the answer is in the affirmative, the reasons therefore; and

(c) whether they will be pleased to lay on the table :

(i) the letter of the Government of Madras containing its views regarding the delimitation of the Oriya tracts in Madras Province as proposed by the Boundary Committee;

(ii) the proceedings of the Madras Legislative Council of 2nd, 3rd and 4th August, 1932, relating to the same; and

(iii) the percentage of Oriya members and their number in Madras Legislative Council?

The Honourable Sir C. P. Ramaswami Aiyar: (a) and (b). No reference was made under section 52-A of the Government of India Act, 1919. The Local Governments were asked to report how the recommendations of the Orissa Boundary Committee had been received; and discussion in the Legislative Council is one obvious means of ventilating such a matter.

(c)   (i) The whole question is under examination and Government do not propose to lay on the table the views of the Local Government.

(ii) The proceedings of the Madras Legislative Council are received in the Library of the House and the Honourable Member may see them there.

(iii) I have no information but observe that the Honourable Member seems to be already in possession of the facts.

Formation of a Special Agency Division out of Ganjam and Vizagpatam District Agency Treacts (21.09.1932)

Mr. B. N. Misra: Will government be pleased to state:
(a) the date and the year when the Government of Madras submitted proposals to the Government of India for the formation of a special agency division in 1919-20 out of the Ganjam and Vizagapatam District Agency Tracts;
(b) the estimated cost of expenditure for the administration of the special agency division and also the schemes of development proposed along with the said proposal for the creation of the special agency division; and
(c) whether these expenses were taken into consideration when the Madras Government claimed to be relieved of its contributions to the Government of India?
The Honourable Mr. H. G. Haig: (a) 27th February, 1920.

(b) The initial non-recurring expenditure was roughly estimated at ten lakhs and the recurring expenditure was estimated to be about the same sum. The policy of the Government was the general development of these backward areas in almost the entire field of general administration.

(c) Yes.

Refusal by Madras government to furnish Figures to the Accounts Officer attached to the Orissa Committee (22.09.1932)

Mr. B. N. Misra: Will Government be pleased to state:

(a) if they are aware that the Madras Government did not at first furnish figures to Mr. Balvali, the Accounts Officer attached to the Orissa Committee, and that Mr. Balvali had to stay in Madras without work for a number of days on that account; and

(b) the number of days Mr. Balvali toured round the District of Ganjam and Vizagapatam to compile and verify the information?

The Honourable Sir Frank Noyce (on behalf of The Honourable Sir C. P. Ramaswami Aiyar): (a) I am not aware of any refusal or omission by the Madras Government to furnish figures. There was a slight misunderstanding touching procedure, but this was subsequently cleared up.

(b) I have no information.

Mr. B. Das: Is it not a fact, Sir, that Mr. Balvali had to wait for nearly a month in Madras and the Madras Government did not furnish him with any information until the Finance Member from Delhi telegraphed to the Finance Member in Madras to supply the information which was wanted, and then the Government of Madras gave Mr. Balvali the information within three or four days?

The Honourable Sir Frank Noyce: The Honourable member will, I am sure, not expect me to furnish detailed information in reply to that question, but I understand that the delay was only a question of a few days.

Mr. B. Das: Was it not partly due to the reticence of the Madras government to supply the information as that may lead to the parting away of the northern districts of the Madras Presidency to Orissa?

The Honourable Sir Frank Noyce: I do not think so.

Mr. B. N. Misra: Will the Honourable Member kindly inquire whether as a matter of fact Mr. Balvali had to wait in Madras and then tour through Vizagapatam and Ganjam for about ten days, as no information was given to him by the Madras Government?

The Honourable Sir Frank Noyce: I can see no necessity for inquiries into what is now past history.

Comparative Statements of Revenue and Expenditure of the Ganjam District (22.09.1932)

Mr. B. N. Misra: Will Government be pleased to lay on the table a comparative statement of Revenue and Expenditure of the Ganjam District furnished by the Government of Madras to the Simon Commission, the figures compiled by Mr. Balvali for the Orissa Boundary Committee and the figures accepted by the Attlee Sub-Committee after due verification?

The Honourable Sir Frank Noyce (on behalf of The Honourable Sir C. P. Ramaswami Aiyar): The Madras Government submitted no such statement to the Statutory Commission.

For a statement of the Revenue and Expenditure of the Ganjam District the Honourable Member is referred to pages 602-603 of the Memoranda submitted by the Government of India to Indian Statutory Commission. For the Orissa Committee's figures I would refer the Honourable Member to Appendices I and II of its report. A summary of the report of the Attlee Sub-Committee is given on pages 50-51 of Volume II of the report of Indian Statutory Commission but I have no information of any detailed verification of figures by this Committee.

Mr. B. N. Misra: Is it not a fact, Sir, that the Madras Government also claimed relief from the contribution, which the Government of India were giving?

The Honourable Sir Frank Noyce: I would suggest to the Honourable Member that he should put down a question on that subject.

Boundaries of the Proposed Oriya Province (22.09.1932)

Mr. B. N. Misra:(a) Will Government be pleased to state Whether they are aware of (i) the proposal of the late Lord Curzon's Government to unite Oriya-speaking tracts in 1903, (ii) the representations made by the Oriyas to the Montague-Chelmsford Enquiry in 1918-19, (iii) the Resolution of the Bihar and Orissa Legislative Council regarding the union of Oriya tracts in 1922-23, and (iv) the report of the Phillip-Duff Commission in 1924?

(b) Will Government be pleased to state when they are going to give their final decision about the boundaries of the Oriya Province?

(c) Will it be at any rate before the inauguration of the new reforms?

The Honourable Sir Frank Noyce (on behalf of the Honourable Sir C. P. Ramaswami Aiyar): (a) Yes.

(b) and (c). The whole question is under consideration and Government are unable to make any statement at present.

Average Annual Income and Expenditure of Angul District and Ganjam and Vizagapatam Agencies (22.09.1932)

Mr. B. N. Misra: Will Government be pleased to state the average annual income and expenditure in 1927-28, 1928-29 and 1929-30 of (a) Angul district in Bihar and Orissa, (b) Ganjam Agency in Madras, and (c) Vizagapatam Agency in Madras ?

The Honourable Sir Frank Noyce (on behalf of the Honourable Sir C. P. Ramaswami Aiyar): I am unable to supply the information asked for by the Honourable Member as I am Not in possession of the figures. A statement of expenditure of the Angul district in Bihar and Orissa is given in the Bihar and Orissa Budget estimates.

Oriya and Non–Oriya Speaking Population of Angul (22.09.1932)

Mr. B. N. Misra: Will Government be pleased to state:

(a) the total population of Sadr Sub-Division in Angul,

(b) the number of Oriya-speaking population in Angul, and

(c) the number of Non-Oriya-speaking population

in Angul?

Absence of Waiting Rooms at Mancheswar, Bengal Nagpur Railway (22.09.1932)

Mr. B. N. Misra: (a) Are Government aware:

(i) that there is no waiting room for the first, second, intermediate or third class passengers at Mancheswar, Bengal Nagpur Railway; and

(ii) that much hardship is experienced by the passengers?

(b) if the answer to part (a) is in the affirmative, are Government prepared to advise the Bengal Nagpur Railway to remove such grievances?

Mr. P. R. Rau: With your permission, Sir, I propose to reply to this and question No. 661 together. Government have no information as to whether there are waiting rooms at the station referred to. But I am sending a copy of the Honourable Member's questions and of this reply to the Agent, Bengal Nagpur Railway, for such action, as he may consider necessary.

Absence of Intermediate Class and Third Class Waiting Rooms at Certain Important Stations of the Bengal Nagpur Railway (22.09.1932)

Mr. B. N. Misra: (a) Are Government aware that there are no waiting rooms either for intermediate or third class passengers in railway stations at such big commercial places and junctions as Vizianagram and Parvatipur, Bengal Nagpur Railway, on account of which, much hardship is experienced by the passengers?

(b) If the answer to part (a) be in the negative, are Government prepared to advise the Bengal Nagpur Railway to remove such a grievance?

Reduction in the Number of Letter-Box Peons in Cuttack (22.09.1932)

Mr. B. N. Misra: (a) Are Government aware that there were three letter-box peons for Cuttack Sadar formerly and that the reduction of the number to two causes much inconvenience to the public and hardship to the peons?

(b) If, so, do Government propose to make enquiries and remove the difficulties?

Mr. T. Ryan: (a) and (b). Government have no information on this subject, but a copy of the question is being sent to the Postmaster General, Bihar and Orissa, who is fully competent to deal with the matter.

Electric Connection for Post Offices in Cuttack (22.09.1932)

Mr. B. N. Misra: (a) Are Government aware that since the installation of electricity in Cuttack Town all Government offices have got electric connections except the Post Offices located there such as Chandnichouk, Choudhury Bazar, etc.?

(b) Do Government propose to make enquiries and to provide all Post Offices with electric connection?

Mr. T. Ryan: (a) Government have no information on this point.

(b) The matter is within the competence of the Postmaster General, Bihar and Orissa Circle, to whom a copy of the question is being sent.

Appointments in the Upper Division of the Finance Department (23.09.1932)

Mr. B. N. Misra: (a) Will Government please state the names of persons appointed to the Upper Division of the Finance Department since 1923, otherwise than by direct recruitment?

(b) How was the seniority of each person determined? Was any special concession in the matter of seniority given to any individual? Was any credit for past service given to these persons for purpose of determining their seniority?

(c) Is it a fact that persons promoted to the Subordinate Accounts Service and Audit and Accounts Service are given credit for some of their past service for purpose of determining seniority?

(d) Do Government contemplate reviewing the cases of all the persons appointed to the Finance Department Upper Division otherwise than by direct recruitment, with a view to fixing their seniority afresh by allowing them credit for part of past service?

(e) How was the pay of the person fixed? Was any uniform principle observed? Is it not a fact that in one case more than treble the pay in the substantive appointment was given and that two other cases special increases were sanctioned? Do Government propose to review all these cases?

(f) How many of the individuals were promoted within the Finance Department itself?

The Honourable Sir Alan Parsons: I am unable to put my depleted office to the labour of collecting all these details. If any individual has a grievance with regard to seniority and pay, there is always a channel by which he can get his grievance investigated?

Appointments in the Upper Division of the Finance Department (23.09.1932)

Mr. B. N. Misra: (a) Is it a fact that 50 per cent of the vacancies in the First Division are to be filled by promotion from the Second Division? How long has the rule been in force? How many promotions have been made in the Finance Department?

(b) Do Government contemplate making up the deficiency in the number of Second Division men promoted to First Division by giving all appointments occurring in future to deserving Second Division clerks?

(c) Do Government propose to take similar action regarding promotions from Third to Second Division?

The Honourable Sir Alan Parsons: (a) The rule which issued on the 8th December, 1928, is as stated by the Honourable Member, provided suitably qualified persons are available for promotion. Since that date, no permanent promotions have been given, though there have been officiating promotions on three occasions.

(b) and (c). No.

Distribution of Duties among the Ministerial Staff of the Finance Department (23.09.1932)

Mr. B. N. Misra: (a) Is it a fact that some Superintendents in the Finance Department do not do any case work themselves?

(b) Is it also a fact that number of senior second Division men are employed on Third Division duties in that Department?

(c) Is it a fact that Third Division men are employed on Second Division duties in the Issue and other Branches of Finance Department?

The Honourable Sir Alan Parsons: (a) and (c). No.

(b) The question whether the work now performed by some clerks in the Second Division is of a character which would permit of its being done by Third Division clerks is under consideration.

Duplication of work in Various Branches of the Finance Department (23.09.1932)

Mr. B. N. Misra: Are Government aware that there is duplication of work amongst the various branches of the Finance Department? Do Government contemplate a detailed inquiry (on which members of the staff are represented) with a view to ensuring a scientific distribution of work?

The Honourable Sir Alan Parsons: The answer to both parts of the question is in the negative.

Promotion of Military Sub-Assistant Surgeons to the Rank of King's Commission (30.09.1932)

Mr. B. N. Misra: (a) Is it a fact that while considering the question of promotion to the rank of Honorary King's Commission during the last three or four years only length of service has been taken into consideration and no importance was attached to the field of meritorious services of the Military Sub-Assistant Surgeons as also their seniority in the army list?

(b) Is it a fact that during the Great war fair chances were given to all the Military Sub-Assistant Surgeons to show their merits and win supernumerary promotion (vide paragraph 10, Appendix 27, Regulations for the Army India) but now such supernumerary promotions won under very trying circumstances in the field have been ignored for further promotion? If so, why?

(c) Is it not a fact that in all other departments of the Government of India special promotions to the rank of Honorary King's Commission are made by selection and not by length of service? D Government propose to take necessary action to see that in future such promotions are made in accordance with the seniority in the Army list?

(d) Is it a fact that Military Sub-Assistant Surgeons were given the benefit of their war service by way of accelerated promotions? Is it a fact that such accelerated promotion is not taken into account when promoting that personnel to the King's Commission? If not, why not? Are Government aware that as a result of this their established seniority is virtually turned into juniority at the time of promotion to the King's Commission?

Mr. G. R. F. Tottenham: (a) No.

(b) and (d). The answer to the first two portions of part (d) is in the affirmative. Sub-Assistant Surgeons who receive special promotion are borne as supernumerary in the new grade until they are absorbed by promotion in the ordinary course. When they are considered for further promotion, their seniority is reckoned from the date of their admission to the Department. Special promotion is a reward in itself and it is not the policy necessarily to prolong the effects of that reward throughout the remainder of man's service.

(c) The answer to the first part is in the affirmative. The fact that an officer has received accelerated promotion in the past is naturally taken into account in making further promotions, but his seniority is reckoned in the manner described in the answer to parts (b) and (d).

Non-Retirement of Military Sub-Assistant Surgeons holding the Rank Subedar Major (30.09.1932)

Mr. B. N. Misra: (a) How many Military Sub-Assistant Surgeons have completed five years service in the rank of Subedar Major or have earned the full pension of their rank?

(b) Is it a fact that in the army as a whole Subedar Majors on completion of five years service are compulsorily retired? If so, will Government be pleased to state why this rule is not applied in the case of Military Sub-Assistant Surgeon?

Mr. G. R. F Tottenham: (a) No Subedar Major of the Indian Medical Department has served for five years in the rank. Four have earned the full pension of a Subedar Major, but none has so far earned the double rate admissible to an officer of that rank who has held Honorary King's Commissioned rank for three years.

(b) Yes. Last year the question of limiting the tenure of appointment of Subedar Majors and Honorary King's Commissioned officers of the Indian Medical Department was considered and dropped on account of the extra expenditure involved.

Communities of Retrenched Military Sub-assistant

Surgeons (30.09.1932)

Mr. B. N. Misra: Is it a fact that 150 Military Sub-Assistant Surgeons have been retrenched? If so, will Government please state the number of Hindus, Muhammadans, Sikhs and Christians and the period of their service?

Mr. G. R. F. Tottenham: It has been decided to reduce the cadre of Sub-Assistant Surgeons by 150, but so far only 74 Sub-Assistant Surgeons have actually been retrenched. Of these, 41 are Hindus, 15 Sikhs, 11 Muslims and seven Indian Christians. 29 of them had less than ten years' of service, 25 between 10 and 20 years' service, 13 between 20 and 30 years', and seven over 30 years' service.

Retrenchment of Military Assistant Surgeons (30.09.1932)

Mr. B. N. Misra: Will Government please state what, if any, retrenchment is being made in the list of Military Assistant Surgeons?

Mr. G. R. F. Tottenham: The cadre of Military Assistant Surgeons has been reduced by 10.

Trade Agreement Signed at Ottawa (08.11.1932)

Mr. B. N. Misra: Sir, yesterday you allowed us to discuss this issue on political, economic and other grounds. Sir, politics is a very vast subject and what appears to be very important in your opinion may not be so in the opinion of others and what may appear to be very important to a constituency or to a Member may not be so from the viewpoint of another. In the present issue before us about the Ottawa Agreement, I have been always thinking the viewpoint of the Government. Sir, whenever

India is concerned, e.g., for the Geneva Conference, for the League of Nations, she has been pointed out as one of the most prominent Members of the League and Indian delegates go there to sign as if they are really the representatives of India. What we find in practice, however, is that they are only the nominees of Government or favourites of Government and are not the favourites of the people or the representatives of the people of India. As was observed yesterday, probably the British Government dictates and the Indian Government dittoes it. That is how the representatives go forward from India to sign these agreements, which are thrust on us. There are also other matters, which have been discussed for the last so many years, such as the question of central responsibility. This question has not yet been settled and it has not been taken serious notice of. Other things, such as the formation of the new Orissa Province for which we, in Orissa, have been agitating for over 30 or 40 years, have not been taken notice of and settled promptly. When such important questions remain to be settled, this Ottawa Agreement has been thrust on the Assembly for consideration. No time is allowed for us to consider the full implications of this Ottawa Agreement. We do not know whether it is beneficial to India or Great Britain. As is well known, India is purely an agricultural country and we have enormous quantities of raw materials, such as linseed, groundnut, cotton, jute, castor seed and so many other things, which are exported from India to other countries. We not only export to England, but also to other countries. The quantity that is exported to Great Britain is much less than what we export to other countries like Japan, America and Germany. I find from a report that we export linseed to the value of 451 lakhs to all other countries, whereas we export to Great Britain linseed valued at 110 lakhs. The export of groundnut to all other countries is worth 1,713 lakhs, whereas to England only 103 lakhs. Mark the proportion, Sir. If we give Imperial Preference only to England, what will be the fate of all our exports to other countries? (Hear, hear.) This aspect of the question has not at all been considered in Ottawa Agreement. The same is case with castor seeds. The same is the case with castor seeds. To all other countries, the export is worth 289 lakhs whereas to the United Kingdom, it is worth only 59 lakhs.

You will see from the items that I have just quoted that we are trading not only with Great Britain, but with other countries as well. Great Britain wants now preference. Of course if there is anything advantageous to her, she always grasps, at it wants preference. If there is anything advantageous to India, we are not allowed to enjoy that advantage. After she gets the raw produce from India, Great Britain makes them into finished articles, and exports them to India. India gets no advantage in the bargain; probably India has to pay 10 or 15 times more for the manufactured goods from Great Britain. This aspect of the matter has not been considered at all in the Ottawa Agreement. India being mostly an agricultural country, we have now to consider seriously whether we should not manufacture finished products out of the raw produce that we have got so much in abundance. Why should we at all export these raw products to England and get them manufactured into finished products there? Why should we not finish these in our own country? Then it will be beneficial to us. In considering the Ottawa Agreement, that should be our main consideration, namely, whether India could not get more benefit by retaining all the raw produce here and manufacturing them into finished articles here. We have all along been fighting for the right to manage our own affairs in the way most advantageous to India. For over 100 years and more, England has been taking all the best of our country and we were getting the worst. We are probably paying in some cases 30 or 40 times out of the same raw materials that are being sent by us. We are just now lifting our head and we are just now trying to become a manufacturing country. We have established a few mills in India, and, with the advent of the new constitution, if we are given power to manage our own affairs in the way most advantageous to us, then we can become a great manufacturing country. They are now sitting at the Third Round Table Conference hammering out a constitution for India. We must know what kind of constitution we are going to get. We must know what powers we are going to get under the new constitution, whether we will be given a chance to manage our affairs.

The Honourable Sir Joseph Bhore should, in fairness, give us more time to study this Ottawa Agreement. He has been in the Government of India Studying this problem for the past so many years, and we as laymen ought to be given more time to consult experts. This Ottawa Agreement has been placed in our hands only for the past fortnight and, in fairness, we ought to be given more time to consult business men and experts and see how this Agreement is going to affect India. It is not right that the Government should, on the very day of the commencement of the session, ask the House to pass a

Resolution ratifying the Agreement without seriously considering its implications on the future well being of India. The Honourable Sir Joseph Bhore has very thoroughly considered this problem with the help of so many experts in the Government of India and I wish that, in fairness, he should allow us more time to consider this question. Of course with the vast power vested in Government, they can easily hoodwink any Member and win over any Member to the side of the Government and they will run to the Government lobby and will cast their vote for Government. But what will be the fate of the dumb voiceless millions, 30 crores of them. What will be their fate if this Ottawa Agreement is ratified by this Assembly? We must have enough time to consider whether the Agreement will be beneficial to the masses of India? As far as I have studied this problem, I have come to the conclusion that the ratification of this Ottawa Agreement will not be beneficial at all to India, but it will be beneficial to England. If the Honourable the Commerce Member, who is an Indian, is true to the salt that he eats at the expense of the poor Indian taxpayer, he will do only that which is beneficial to India and he will not think of the British Government or the Britisher. He is paid by the Indian taxpayer and I hope he will not think of injuring the source from which he is paid, and where he gets his bread from. I mean no personal reflection against my Honourable friend. It is very unfair on his part to have asked the House on the very commencement of the session to ratify an Agreement, which bristles with so many complicated matters. I will only say in conclusion that the concluding of such an Agreement and enacting legislation thereon at a critical period at this juncture when the horizon is cast with political turmoil and when the question of transferring of powers to Indians is looming large would not be proper and desirable. I would urge Government to postpone the consideration of this question till the new revised constitution comes into force and India obtains a chance of expressing its clear opinion under the National Movement. I trust that Government will postpone the ratification of the Agreement in this session of the Assembly with support of the official and nominated block and prevent the strong suspicion that has already been created in the public mind in respect of the economic motives of the United Kingdom in dealing with India in a one-sided manner. The following analysis of the Indian Agreement recently disclosed by the President of the Board of Trade, in the House of Commons, evidently shows how Great Britain will benefit at the cost of Indian Industries and trade:

"The value of the Indian Agreement would mean an enormous increase in the activities of our houses exporting to India with a corresponding effect on the manufacturing centres in the United Kingdom."

From the Indian point of view the gain of the United Kingdom will doubtless be the loss to the Indian industries and a further reduction of the purchasing power of the Indian masses. Sir, in this view of the case I shall appeal to all Honourable Members to remember that while proceeding to one or other of the lobbies, the entire blame will lie upon them if they hastily come to a decision without considering this matter thoroughly and clearly. I personally support the amendment of Dr. Ziauddin Ahmad that it must be referred to a Committee.

Realisation of Terminal Tax on Passenger Tickets to Puri, Bhubaneswar and Sakhigopal (09.11.1932)

Mr. B. N. Misra: (a) Will Government be pleased to state:

(1) from what year they have been realizing terminal tax on passenger tickets to (i) Puri, (ii) Bhubaneswar, (iii) Sakhigopal; and

(2) the amount collected on the same account for each of the stations separately?

(b) Will Government be pleased to state if they have spent any amount for any purpose at any of those places mentioned above?

(C) If so, will Government be pleased to lay on the table a statement showing the amount collected under terminal tax for (i) Puri, (ii) Bhubaneswar, and (iii) Sakhigopal and the amount spent at the above places separately?

Mr. P. R. Rau: (a) (1) From 1921.

(2) The tax is at the rate of 1 anna for third class passengers, 1½ annas for intermediate class passengers, 2 annas for second class passengers and 6 annas for first class passengers and is levied on all passengers arriving at and departing from Puri, Malatipatpur, Sakhigopal, Delang, Khurda Road, and Bhubaneswar.

(b) The amounts collected are not retained by the Government of India, but handed over to the local authorities for expenditure on local purposes. The tax was imposed in order to provide funds for the improvement of the sanitary condition of Puri.

(c) Government consider that the collection of this information will entail the expenditure of labour in commensurate with its value and regret that they cannot comply with this request.

Preponderance of Muslim Postal Officials at Jhelum (14.11.1932)

Mr. B. N. Misra: (a) Is it a fact that the Postal administration at Jhelum is entirely in the hands of Muslim officers, viz., the Superintendent, Post Offices, the Head Clerk to Superintendent, Post Offices, the Inspector of Post offices, Jhelum Sub-Division, the Postmaster and Deputy Postmaster, Jhelum, and the Head Deputy Postmaster, Jhelum, the Town Inspector, Jhelum, and the Head Correspondence Clerk, Jhelum Head Office, are all Muslims?

(b) If the reply to part (a) be in the affirmative, will Government please state why no action has been taken to remove this overwhelming preponderance of Muslim officers at one station?

The Honourable Sir Frank Noyce: (a) Except that the Deputy Postmaster, Jhelum, is a Hindu, the facts are as stated by the Honourable Member.

(b) Government do not propose to interfere in the matter which is within the competence of the Postmaster General, to whom a copy of the question has been sent.

Mr. B. N. Misra: Are Government aware that the Inspector is a resident of Jhelum District?

The Honourable Sir Frank Noyce: I was not aware of that.

Mr. Muhammad Anwar-ul-Azim: Will the Honourable Member kindly tell us what is the position of the post offices at Puri and Cuttack, in view of the reply just given to Mr. Misra?

The Honourable Sir Frank Noyce: I am afraid I must ask for notice of that question.

Mr. Lalchand Navalrai: Will the Honourable Member be pleased to state what is the communal policy of Government in keeping Muhammadans or Hindus in one post?

The Honourable Sir Frank Noyce: As a rule postings are made without reference to communal considerations.

Criminal Law Amendment Bill (15.11.1932)

Mr. B. N. Misra: Sir, I was not willing to intervene in this debate but for the neighbor on my left side. The, bill, as it has emerged from the Select Committee has, as its object, to stop the civil obedience movement. If that is so, I would like to put the same questions to the Honourable the Home Member. This movement is not one of one day and it is not only India; probably this has been thought of for generations by people who are armless and helpless. Such people have always used this. In India we have such a thing as sitting dhurna or praying to God or some such means of peaceful persuasion. These are the only methods followed by peaceful and armless people. Of course we have no arms and no other means; and this movement now is not a small movement. I think the Honourable the Home Member and the Treasury Benches realize that this is a great movement. So I shall ask him some questions for which I do not think he will require six or ten days' notice at all: neither will he have to search for any departmental files. He can give a reply if he chooses from his own common sense and from his own knowledge. He and the other occupants of the Treasury Benches are probably thinking that they are going to stop this movement. I think all of us know more or less that Jesus Christ was crucified. He preached and went on preaching; but with his crucification, did Christianity die? I ask the Home Member to answer that question. Christianity never died: on the other hand, it spread and from that little country it has gone out all over the world. So this movement will never die. I want the Honourable the Home Member to answer me whether Christianity died or if any other movement has died in this way as a result of persecution against it. Mahatma Gandhi is in prison today; Pundit Jawaharlal Nehru or Mr. Subhas Chandra Bose or any other man may be put in jail and persecuted; but will all these persecutions stop the movement? That is what I am asking. No sooner Mahatma Gandhi came from London last year from the Round Table Conference than he was arrested and imprisoned. Perhaps Mr. Sen-Gupta was arrested on board the steamer. Whatever that may be, has this movement died during this whole year? That is the question I want to ask. Sometime or other it was given out in the papers that the movement was dead; but still we read in the papers every day of so many arrests and imprisonments. I say, this movement will never die, because this is a righteous movement and the people believe in it, they may be right or they may be wrong, but still they believe in it. There is a saying in Sanskrit "No – Vishnu preethibee patee" which means this. It has two meanings, which I shall explain. One is that our king or sovereign power is our God. Sir, there is another meaning, that is to say, one who is A – Vishnu or who is not God-like, protector-like, preserver-like, is not our sovereign. But as we have to respect the sovereign power, it should be in purity and sympathy that it should command the respect of the subjects. That is the whole essence. But, what do we find in India? The sovereign power is most unsympathetic to the people of India. They do not care for the poverty-ridden people; that is why, the people are against the Government, that is why, the civil disobedience movement has started.

The British administration began in this country about 150 years ago. When the Great and Good Queen Victoria assumed charge, I think she declared in the preamble that she assumed charge "For the Better Government of India." If she had known then that the power would be so mercilessly abused as is done in India today, perhaps she would not have lent her name, which was a household word, to be abused in this manner. Such a good name should not be abused in this manner. The Britishers today are no longer God-like and they do not deserve our respect. They have now become A-Vishnu. Vishnu is the God. He is the preserver or protector. Our British people do not care to protect our interests. Those Honourable Members who sit on the Treasury Benches are there merely to protect the British peoples' interests and not to protect India's interests. We had the Ottawa Agreement, and still it is being discussed. Our interests are never identical; our interests are never protected by the British Government; the British Government want to protect the interests of their own people. That is why people in this country are so much against the Government today. It is said that by means of these ordinances and Bills you will kill the civil disobedience movement or any similar movement. I say, you will not be able to kill it. You may imprison some 33,000 people or three times more that number. India is not such a small country like the British Isles. India has got several crores of population. Sir, I am asking this question very seriously - do the Government really think that by this Bill they can kill terrorism or kill the civil disobedience movement?

Now, coming to the Bill itself, it is really a very repugnant measure. In the first or second clause, it is stated that its life will only be for three years. I was always thinking that very likely this Third Round Table Conference will perhaps decide matters in such a way as to bring about conciliation in all quarters and there will be no necessity for such measures as these, there will be no place for such obnoxious measures like these. I think the Honourable the Home Member or the Law Member, whoever is responsible for it, has, I must say, committed a great blunder in trying to fix the life of the Bill at three years. They could have put 3,333 or any number of threes in the Bill if they thought that there would be no conciliation or satisfactory result from the third Round Table Conference. Let them put any number of threes, and they can be multiplied, and we shall be constantly living like this; the country will not be happy and nobody will be happy. I would, therefore appeal to the Treasury Benches to adopt the conciliatory method. They are the advisors to His Excellency the Viceroy, but I should mostly blame his advisers if they do not give the best piece of advice to His Excellency, to adopt a conciliatory policy in this matter. You may put, as I said before, 30,000 people in jail; there are already a large number of jails; they do not care for your laws; they have no respect for your laws, because they do not plead guilty, and you may be sure of it that, by passing not only this Bill, but hundreds of such bills, nothing will daunt the people. Nobody will be afraid of this or any other similar measure. If we are alive, we shall see that, with the spread of the movement, all the jails will still be full, and nobody will be afraid of your jails. Now, what will bring about peace and happiness or contentment in the country? Goodwill alone will satisfy the people. Be preserver-like, be God-like, and protect the interests of Indians. No sooner you begin to protect the interests of Indians, without showing any bias against Indians, you will yourself feel the change. Sir, this movement will never stop; it will go on.

Now a word about the punishment of parents for the faults of their boys. I think Honourable Members opposite, who have drafted this provision, have children. I think the Honourable the Law Member has boys – I do not know. Supposing his son, who may be studying in Calcutta or elsewhere, does something or joins the Congresswallas, is the Law Member who is sitting here to be punished or fined? (Laughter.) Sir, I am asking this question in all seriousness, and I am appealing to him to consider the unreasonableness of the provision. If my son goes as a Congresswalla, how can you fine me for it? I am sitting here. My son might go with some Congresswala. I cannot keep him in a box. (Laughter.) Am I to be punished for it? It is really silly that parents should be punished for the faults of their sons. If you think that parents encourage their boys to join the movement and if there is prima facie evidence against the parents, then, by all means, punish them; but to fine the parents merely for the faults of their boys is, I must say, lawless law. How can you punish the parents for the fault of their boys? I think one can go on condemning the provision for any length of time, but I do not want to prolong the debate. (Several Honourable Members: "Please go on.") Sir, the whole Bill is defective from top to bottom. It looks as if the whole Bill has been drafted without a conscience, it looks as if there was not even a grain of common sense left anywhere. I am sorry to find that the Honourable Sir Brojendra Mitter, who is drawing only Rs. 6,000 a month and is earning so little, should have lent his name to the Bill. He was earning much more in Calcutta, and I do not know why he should put himself in this awkward position by subscribing his name to this Bill for the paltry sum of Rs. 6,000. (Laughter.) The whole Bill should be condemned from every quarter. It does not deserve any support. For my part, I would like that it should be circulated again, and I support my friend, Shaikh Sadiq Hasan.

Expending Powers accruing to Provinces according to the Report of the Financial Relations Committee (22.11.1932)

Mr. D. K. Lahiri Chaudhury (on behalf of Mr. B. N. Misra): Will Government be pleased to lay on the table:

(a) a copy of an estimate of the expending power which will accrue to each Province according to paragraphs 16 and 17 of the Financial Relations Committee's Report;

(b) the memorandum of then Madras Government with its estimates with the existing and proposed expenditure in putting forth its financial position as laid down in paragraphs 16 and 17 of the Meston Report or Award; and

(c) whether the sum of about Rs. 8 1/2 lakhs payble by the Government of Bihar and Orissa as interest on the capital outlay on the Orissa Canal System was taken into account in the ordinary estimates of income and expenditure of the Government of Bihar and Orissa as stated in paragraphs 16 and 17 referred to above?

The Honourable Sir George Schuster: (a) and (b). Government do not consider that any useful purpose would be served by having these papers; which are now 12 years out of date, reprinted, but if the Honourable Member has any particular points on which he desires information, I will endeavor to enlighten him.

(c) Yes.

Terminal Tax on Passengers going to Bhubaneswar, Sakhigopal and Puri (22.11.1932)

Kumar Gupteswar Prasad Singh (on behalf of Mr. B. N. Misra): (a) Will Government please state the object of the terminal tax on passengers going to (10 Bhubaneswar, (2) Sakhigopal and (3) Puri?

(b) in what year was it first imposed?

(c) What Railways are authorized to collect the same and from what year respectively?

(d) Will Government please state the total collection under this head till March, 1932, by each Railway?

(e) If the figures are not available, will Government please make inquiry and lay on the table a statement showing the collections by each Railway for (1) Puri, (2) Sakhigopal, and (3) Bhubaneswar, respectively?

Indian Medical Department Assistant Surgeons employed on the North Western Railway (22.11.1932)

Kumar Gupteswar Prasad Singh (on behalf of Mr. B. N. Misra): Will Government please state:

(a) The total number of Indian Medical Department Assistant Surgeons employed on the North Western Railway;

(b) the total number of men of the Indian Medical Department allotted by the Railway Board for the North Western Railway; and

(c) if the number of men of the Indian Medical Department is in excess of the number allotted, what steps have been taken to reduce them?

Mr. P. R. Rau: Information is being collected and a reply will be laid on the table in due course.

The Criminal Law Amendment Bill - contd. (23.11.1932)

Mr. B. N. Misra: Sir, of the several clauses in this Bill, the present clause, which is now under discussion seems to be the most imaginary. As my friend, Mr. Mitra, pointed out there may be 20,000 or more public servants in India, I am putting a most moderate number....

Mr. S. C. Mitra: The Railway Administration itself has got several lakhs of people.

Mr. B. N. Misra: All right, there may be some lakhs, but can the Honourable Home Member point out even a hundred cases of public servants who have failed to discharge their duties either in pursuance of the Congress movement or any other movement? This is like the Sanskrit saying...."Siro nasti kutah byatha?", which means "you have no head, but wherefrom are you getting headache?" (Laughter.) I want to know from the Honourable the Home Member whether he can cite any cases in which the public servants have failed in their duties? Can my friend point out, out of the several lakhs of public servants in the country, at least 1,000, 500, 100, or even 10 cases, which have come to his notice, of public servants who have failed in their duties? Can he say that even one per cent of the total number has failed? As has been said, the whole Bill is directed against the Congress movement. It happens to me, Sir, as I said in the beginning of my remarks, that this is most imaginary case. Supposing a cook fails to prepare food at a proper time and he delays to prepare the food by, say, 20 minutes, then certainly he will come under this definition (Laughter), because the cook has not prepared the food by a certain time and, therefore, the master, a public servant, has failed in his duties and so he must be punished with one year's imprisonment. I appeal to the Honourable the home Member to consider the effect of this vague clause. Of course, Magistrates will be ready to hear such cases and award punishments. It reminds me of a talk I had with a Magistrate who, in a particular case, had gone wrong in his judgment. He said: "Well, our superior advisers have said we must have an elastic conscience, i.e., a conscience that will not feel pricks and so we should also have no conscience. The biting of conscience must be like a foot ball; it will come and go, but it will not affect our conscience." So, perhaps, this Legislature is now played like a football; anything can be carried in this House. I am sure; the Government will carry even this vague motion. I appeal to all Honourable Members not to agree to such an absurd clause as this. The question is: are there many cases at all to justify the introduction of such a clause like this?

Major Nawab Ahmad Nawaz Khan: There have been many such cases.

Mr. B. N. Misra: I am asking the Honourable the Home

Member to tell me how many such cases there are.

Mr. M. Masood Ahmad: Were those cases in North-West Frontier Province?

Mr. B. N. Misra: Sir, this clause ought not to be on the Statutes book at all without sufficient justification. Now, what is the meaning of this phrase "induces or attempts to induce a public servant?" Suppose a child has a fall, and if the doctor is late by half an hour, if the wife asks the husband to stay, she comes under this definition, because he fails in his duties. The motive must be taken into consideration, but nothing is said about the motive. Supposing a boy is ill, and his mother tells the father to take care of the boy for just half an hour, but if the father happens to stay away owing perhaps to more pressing or urgent work, can she be punished? I appeal to the Home Member that, before he hears any further speeches, he should at once agree to withdraw this clause. Of course, as an Englishman he is equipped with a better command of the English language than I can claim to possess and he will be able to give a proper explanation. The whole clause is absolutely vague and meaningless. Suppose when a carriage passes along the road, a dog barks and the carriage tumbles down, will the dog come under the purview of this clause? (Laughter.) What is the motive behind all this, I for one cannot understand. Sir, I therefore, whole-heartedly support the motion that the clause be omitted.

Manufacture of Salt on the Orissa Coast (12.12.1932)
Sardar G. N. Mujumdar (on behalf of Mr. B. N. Misra): (a) Are government aware that in 1822 the revenue from salt duty in Orissa coast was Rs. 18 lakhs as stated in

Toynbie's History?

(b) If the answer to part (a) be in the affirmative, will Government please state when and how salt manufacture on the Orissa coast was stopped?

The Honourable Sir George Schuster: (a) It is stated on page 70 of Toynbie's Sketch of the History of Orissa from 1803 to 1828, on the authority of Mr. Sterling that at some unspecified period that salt monopoly in Orissa yielded a net revenue of little less than 18 lakhs of sicca rupees, I presume annually. 15 sicca rupees were equivalent to 16 Company's rupees.

(b) Manufacture by the "Panga" method ceased in 1889. (Panga method means evaporation by artificial heat of salt earth dissolved in water.) This was due to a variety of causes. The extinction of jungles from which firewood had been obtained, the heavy fees demanded by zamindars for the excavation of salt earth and for the extraction of fuel from the forests and the gradual dying out of the prejudice against the use of imported salt.

Manufacture by the "Karkatch" method ceased in 1897-98. (Karkatch means evaporation of sea brine by solar heat.) This method, though cheaper, was handicapped by the weakness of the brine, and the unsettled weather that is apt to prevail on that part of the coast during the manufacturing season. It succumbed on the opening of the East Coast Railway to the competition of Madras and foreign salts.

Manufacture of Salt at Huma, Sordo and Naupada in the Ganjam District (12.12.1932)
Sardar G. N. Mujumdar (on behalf of Mr. B. N. Misra): (a) What quantity of salt is being manufactured at

(i) Humma, (ii) Sordo, (iii) Naupada (in the Ganjam District) annually during the last ten years respectively?

(b) If the information to the above question is not available, will Government please enquire and place the reply on the table of this House?

The Honourable Sir George Schuster: (a) and (b). I am obtaining the information asked for and will lay it on the table in due course.

Manufacture of Salt at Parikud, Mealud and other places on the Orissa Coast (12.12.1932)

Sardar G. N.Mujumdar (on behalf of Mr. B. N. Misra): (a) Will Government please state if they have taken any action to encourage salt manufacture in (i) Parikud, (ii) Mealud and (iii) other places on the Orissa coast?

(b) What is the distance between Huma and Parikud?

The Honourable Sir George Schuster:(a) Not directly. The development of local industries is a matter of the Local Government.

(b) The distance is 25 miles over Ganjam Road or train to Balugaon and 12 miles over Chilka Lake.

Rules for Determining Seniority in the Office of the Controller of Railway Accounts (12.12.1932)

Sardar G. N. Mujumdar (on behalf of Mr. B. N. Misra): (a) Is it a fact that the rules for determining the relative seniority of non-gazetted staff of the Controller of Railway Accounts' Office lay down that the seniority shall be fixed with reference to substantive pay?

(b) If so, will Government please state what objections

there are to fixing the seniority of clerks in lower class according to the length of their continuous service? Is it a fact that Auditor General in India, at the time of introducing the time scale of pay in 1922, had held that pay was not the criterion for purpose of seniority and that this rule still holds good in the Posts and Telegraphs and Civil Accounts Offices and the Office of the Director of Railway Audit and is generally applicable to the Staff of the Railway Board also?

(c) Is it a fact that while determining the relative seniority of the staff transferred from the office of the Secretary, Indian Railway Conference Association, due consideration was paid not only to their previous service but also to the initial starting pay which was higher than the minimum pay of the grade?

(d) If the reply to part (c) above be in the affirmative, will Government please state why the continuous service of clerks taken over from the late Accountant General Railways' Office and other departments is not considered a deciding factor for fixing seniority?

(e) Is it a fact that, to complete the strength of the office of the Controller of Railway Accounts, clerks were permanently taken over not only from the late Accountant General Railways' Office but also, time after time, from the Railway Board, Indian Railway Conference Association, old Chief Auditor's Offices, other departments and offices on special duty?

(f) If the reply to part (e) above be in the affirmative, will Government please state whether their grades of pay were different? Is it a fact that the staff attached to officers on special duty, were given higher pay than they would have drawn in the ordinary course, and which they were allowed to draw even after transfer to the office of the Controller of Railway Accounts?

Mr. P. R. Rau: (a) and (b). I would refer the Honourable Member to the rules for determining the relative seniority of non-gazetted staff in State Railway Accounts Offices, a copy of which is in the Library of the House. These apply to non-gazetted staff of the office of the Controller of Railway Accounts as well. They were framed last year after full consideration and Government see no reason to alter them.

(c) and (d). I am informed that the seniority of the clerks in the office of the Controller of Railway Accounts was fixed strictly in accordance with these rules after taking into account all relevant factors, such as, pay, length and character of service. It may, however, be mentioned that promotion depends on merit and suitability and not primarily on the position in the seniority list.

(e) It is a fact that the office of the Controller of Railway Accounts, when it was constituted in 1929 was recruited from various sources.

(f) The answer to both parts of the question is in the affirmative. The pay of staff transferred to this office was paid in each case after taking all circumstances into consideration, including the pay they were in receipt of before such transfer.

Orissa Committee Report (12.12.1932)

Mr. B. N. Misra:(a) Will Government be pleased to state whether they have despatched their views on the Orissa committee Report?

(b) If the reply to the above question be in the negative, will Government be pleased to state when they are going to send their final views on the Orissa Committee's Report to the Secretary of State for India?

(c) Do Government think that the matter will not come up before the third Round Table Conference?

(d) If the reply to part (a) be in the affirmative, will Government be pleased to inform the house what were the views expressed by them in their dispatch?

The Honourable Sir Brojendra Mitter: Sir, with your permission, I shall reply to questions Nos. 1622, 1623 and 1624 together.

The Government of India have obtained from the Local Governments concerned their views on the Orissa Committee's report and have addressed the Secretary of State in the matter. The whole question is under consideration and I am not in a position to state the views either of Local Governments or of the Government of India at this stage.

2. As regards the discussion of the question at the Round Table Conference and the representation of Orissa thereon, I would invite the Honourable Member's attention to the reply given by my Honourable colleague, the Home Member, to Mr. Bhupat Sing's short notice question on 22nd November last.

Orissa Committee Report (12.12. 1932)

Mr. B. N. Misra:(a) Will Government be pleased to state the dates on which they requisitioned and received the opinions on the Orissa Committee Report from Local governments of (i) Bihar and Orissa and (ii) Madras?

(b) Will Government be pleased to state the opinion of the Bihar and Orissa Government with regard to the separation of Orissa?

(c) Will government be pleased to state the opinion of the Madras Government with regard to the separation of Orissa?

Placing of the Orissa separation Case before the Third Round Table Conference (12.12.1932)

Mr. B. N. Misra:(a) Will Government be pleased to state the reasons why they have not sent an Orissa delegate to the Third Round Table Conference?

(b) Will Government be pleased to state whether they have arranged to put the Orissa separation case before the Third Round Table Conference and in what manner?

(c) If not, do they propose to place it before the Joint Parliamentary Committee?

Statements Laid on the Table

The Honourable Sir Harry Haig: Sir, I lay on the table the information promised in reply to starred question No. 1679 asked by Mr. B. N. Misra on the 14th December, 1932.

Starred Question 1679: Dealings of Pathan Money-lenders with their Debtors employed in the Imperial Secretariat.

The reply was: The Senior Superintendent of police, Delhi, has so far received two complaints of molestation by Pathan moneylenders. In both cases the complainants did not desire the Police to take any action against the Pathans concerned, who were nevertheless warned not to molest them.

The Indian Limitation (Amendment) Bill (09.02.1933)

Mr. B. N. Misra: Sir, I strongly oppose this measure. If you want to make lazy people more lazy, I think you have to pass this Bill. The position is, the debtor is always in a very unhappy position; he has to repay when he borrows money, and it is his duty to do so. We have many duties to discharge, and so to pay up a debt is also a great duty devolved upon a debtor. Now, if you extend the period of limitation, what will be the consequence? Sir, I remember a case in which the pro-note was executed for Rs. 200. At the end of three years, the amount doubled to Rs. 400, and in eight years, it probably came to Rs. 800, because the rate of interest specified was 25 per cent or so. Then, after few years, it was found that the total amount came up to Rs. 1600 or so, whereas the money originally taken was only Rs. 200, because every three years the pro-note was renewed for an enhanced sum including the interest. Therefore, by extending the period of limitation, you place a temptation in the way of a lazy man to renew the pro-note and avoid payment in due time; he sleeps over the matter.

I think, Sir, the period of limitation is very healthy, and the shorter the period, the better it is to all concerned, because, as pointed out just now, a sum of Rs. 200, which was first taken as a loan, accumulated to Rs. 1,600 in eight years by renewing the pro-note every three years. If the law was stringent, this man would have paid back his debt in time and would have saved his land and property. My opinion is that it will do good to nobody if the period of limitation is extended. If a debt is to be paid within a certain period, it must be paid by that time. Therefore, considering all facts, I oppose extending the period of limitation.

Demotion of certain Inspectors of Crews on the East Indian Railway (06.03.1933)

Mr. B. N. Misra: (a) Is it a fact that the following staff were appointed as Inspectors of Crews (Ticket Checking Staff) in the grades of Rs. 150 – 10 - 200 in the Operating Department of the East Indian Railway, before the 1st June, 1931, the date of introduction of the present Moody-Ward scheme of ticket checking:

Messrs. M. Azam, K. M. Asgar, M.L. Takru, M. V. Bhavnani. G. P. Dass, J. W. Workman, M. A. H. Shirazi, Kartarsingh, A. L. Deefholts?

(b) If so, will Government please state (i) under what circumstances were they demoted to grades Rs. 110 – 5 – 140 and Rs. 70 – 5 – 95 since 1st June, 1931; (ii) whether the posts held by them were temporary, but they were confirmed in their appointments; and (iii) whether Fundamental Rule 23 is applicable to them?

(c) Is it a fact that the nature of duties assigned to these Inspectors of Crews in these demoted grades are almost the same after 1st June, 1931, as before 1st June, 1931, in the old Crew system?

(d) Is it a fact that their services have been confirmed since 1st June, 1931, in these reduced grades?

(e) Is it a fact that their services have been considered as continuous since the dates of their appointments? If so, why have they not been admitted to the benefits of Provident Fund since the dates of their appointments?

(f) Will Government state whether the Railway Board letter No. 683-EG. Of 3rd March, 1931, pertaining to the main principles of retrenchment or reduction or demotion is applicable to these Inspectors of Crews? If so, how was their case not considered along with the ticket checking staff of the permanent establishment, when these Inspectors held temporary appointments for periods exceeding 12 months' continuous service?

(g) Is it a fact that the old pays and grades of the ticket checking staff of the permanent establishment have since been restored to them? If so, under what circumstances have these privileges been denied to these Inspectors of Crews?

Mr. P. R. Rau:I have called for the information and will lay reply on the table in due course.

Consolidated Allowance of Inspector of Crews on the East Indian Railway (06.03.1933)

Mr. B. N. Misra:(a) Is it a fact that the old T. T. Is. Of the Accounts Department of the East Indian Railway have been given consolidated allowances at the following rates as a compensation for the mileage allowances they used to draw before 1st June, 1931?

Restored Pay	Consolidated allowances
Up to Rs. 100	Rs. 35
From Rs. 101 to Rs. 190	Rs. 50
From Rs. 191 and above	Rs. 65

(b) Is it a fact that these Inspectors of Crews used to draw travelling allowance at Rs. 2-8-0 per diem before 1st June, 1931 and that after this date those of them who have been demoted as T. T. Es. In grades Rs. 70 – 5 – 95 are given only Rs. 20 as consolidated allowance? If so, why?

Mr. P. R. Rau: (a) Yes.

(b) I have called for the information and will lay a reply on the table in due course.

Age Limit for the Ministerial Service Examination of the Public Service Commission (27.03.1933)

Bhai Parma Nand (on behalf of Mr. B. N. Misra): (a) Will Government please state the age-limit fixed for the candidates sitting in the examination held by Public Service Commission to fill up clerical vacancies in the various grades in the Government of India offices;

(b) Will Government please state whether in the case of permanent incumbents in lower grades who desire to qualify for higher ones this age limit has been relaxed as is done in the case of other competitive examinations like the Indian Audit and accounts Service examination; if not, why not?

(c) Are Government aware that the permanent Government employees in lower grades labour under serious disadvantages as they are not only debarred from sitting in competitive examinations to qualify for higher grades of service but also are not given an opportunity to improve their lot by taking departmental examinations as there are none such held?

(d) Are Government prepared to remedy this situation by raising the age-limit for permanent Government servants in the open competitive examinations held by the Public Service Commission or by holding departmental examinations at fixed intervals? If not, why not?

The Honourable Sir Harry Haig: (a) The general rule is that to be eligible to appear at examination for the first and second divisions, candidates must be over 20 and under 24 years of age and as that for the typist and routine grade, over 17 and under 24. The Public Service Commission, who conduct those examinations, are empowered to modify these limits as they think proper.

(b) Yes, in some of the previous examinations.

(c) and (d). I would refer the Honourable Member to the reply givenon the 5th September, 1932, to unstarred question No 16. I would also point out that unqualified departmental candidates are eligible for promotion to higher grades up to a certain limit on grounds of merit.

Periodical Examination of Ticket-Checking Staff of the East Indian Railway (27.03.1933)

Bhai Parma Nand (on behalf of Mr. B. N. Misra):(a) Is it a fact that the ticket-checking staff (T.T.Es. and T.Cs.) are examined periodically?

(b) If so, what interest has the administration in examining them?

(c) Are subordinates ever 45 years of age exempted from the courses at Rail Schools? If so, why is not such an exemption provided for in this examination?

(d) How many examinations in knowledge of the rules and orders are a subordinate required to undergo during his 30 years of service?

(e) Is an entrance examination to service not sufficient?

(f) Are officers and subordinates other than the ticket checking staff in the East Indian Railway examined for accuracy, powers, and knowledge of the rules and orders periodically; if so, with what result?

Mr. P. R. Rau:(a) Yes.

(b) The examinations are intended to see whether the staff have a thorough knowledge of the rules by which they are expected to be guided in the course of their work.

(c) Government have no information, but I am sending a copy of this question to the Agent, East Indian Railway, to consider whether any exemption is desirable.

(d) Government have no information. These rules are prescribed by the Administrations.

(e) No.

(f) I have no doubt that the East Indian Railway Administration examines its staff as often as it considers necessary.

Periodical Examination of Ticket-Checking Staff of the East Indian Railway (27.03.1933)

Bhai Parma Nand (on behalf of Mr. B. N. Misra):(a) Is it a fact that the ticket checking staff on the East Indian Railway with long service are required to undergo periodical tests in thorough knowledge? If so, has the knowledge of subordinates other than the ticket checking staff coming in constant touch with the public (like Goods, Parcel Booking, Guards, Station Masters and Assistants, Divisional Superintendents, Commercial Inspectors and Superintendents, etc.), ever been tested? If not, why not?

(b) Will Government be pleased to lay a statement on the table showing the number of ticket checking staff out of a total strength found ignorant of the rules and knowledge of the orders comparing the same with the other officers and staff on the East Indian Railway for the last five years with the length of service of each?

Mr. P. R. Rau:(a) The ticket checking staff are required to undergo tests in the knowledge of the rules by which they are to be guided. Government have no information as regards other subordinates.

(b) I am afraid the collection of the information required, will involve an undue expense of labour with no commensurate result.

Denial of the Privilege of Further Contribution to the Provident Fund to the Subordinates on the East Indian Railway (27.03.1933)

Bhai Parma Nand (on behalf of Mr. B. N. Misra): Is it a fact that subordinates on the East Indian Railway contributing to the Provident Fund for over five years have been denied the privilege of further contribution on the plea that they are daily-rated staff? If not, what is the correct interpretation of the Agent, East Indian Railway's circular, No. P.I/41-7813 of the 30th August, 1932?

Mr. P. R. Rau: The answer to the first part of the question is in the negative. I am informed that the circular referred to in the second part was issued under a misapprehension and has been since cancelled.

Sanction of Free Passages to Subordinates of Non-Asiatic Domicile on the East Indian Railway (27.03.1933)

Bhai Parma Nand (on behalf of Mr. B. N. Misra): (a) Is it a fact that a certificate is required in the case of non-superior officers of non-Asiatic domicile before they become eligible for free passages to the effect that had they not been appointed, no Anglo-Indian in India would have been taken on in the post? If so, was such a condition made known to them before they were taken on in service on their discharges from the British forces?

(b) Will Government state whether the orders passed by the Agent, East Indian Railway, in case No. 12/207/29 during 1929 cover the cases of subordinates eligible for free passages as sanctioned from 1930? If so, how and why?

Mr. P. R. Rau:(a) Under the rules issued in 1930 for passages for non-superior officers of non-Asiatic domicile, it is necessary that before such an officer is admitted to the passages, a certificate that if, at the time of appointment, he had not been available, no Indian, Anglo Indian or a statutory native of India would have been appointed, is required from the Agent. I am not sure that I understand the second part of the question, but if my Honourable friend is referring to such persons as had served in the Army before they were taken into railway service, who may be among these non-superior officers, the answer is in the negative.

(b) I am unable to understand what my Honourable friend is referring to, but it is obvious that orders passed in 1929 cannot apply to concessions introduced for the first time in 1930.

LEGISLATIVE ASSEMBLY

(28.03.1933)

QUESTIONS AND ANSWERS

Denial of Hill Allowance to the Railway Staff stationed at Dehra Dun (28.03.1933)
Mr. B. N. Misra: Is it a fact that the staff at Dehra Dun have been denied the privilege of the hill allowance

sanctioned on the Hardwar Dehra Dun Railway which is only paid to the staff up to Harawalla? If so, why? Is not Dehra Dun on a higher elevation than Harrawala?

Mr. P. R. Rau: I have called for the information from the Agent, East Indian Railway, and I shall lay a statement on the table in due course.

Classification of certain Assistant Station Masters with Station Masters (28.03.1933)

Mr. B. N. Misra: Is it a fact that Assistant Station Masters, classes "C" and "D" are classified along with Station Masters, Class "A" only on the Oudh and Rohilkand section of the East Indian Railway? If so, why? Does such classification exist on the East Indian Railway proper and other Railways? What are the emoluments of the different classes? Will Government state whether an Assistant Station Master, Class "C" drawing Rs. 95 on promotion to Station Master, Class "A", is eligible to draw Rs. 75? If so, why? Is it a promotion or demotion? Will Government state whether such a discrimination exists amongst the Assistant Station Masters, Class "F:, on promotion to Station Master, Class "E"? If so, why?

Mr. P. R. Rau: Government have no information in this matter. A copy of the question is being sent to the Agent, East Indian Railway, to rectify any anomalies that may exist and which require rectification. All the matters dealt with are within the competence of the Agent to decide and Government do not propose to intervene in this matter.

Non-Recognition of Services rendered during the Great War on the East Indian Railway (28.03.1933)

Mr. B. N. Misra: (a) Is it a fact that on the East Indian Railway no recognition of services rendered during the Great War of 1914-19, by way of counting them towards length of service or seniority, is accorded to loyal persons? If so, why?

(b) Do Government propose to recognize the loyal services of persons abroad during the Great War, who, on demobilization after an interval of an year or less , joined the Railways in India with a view to enabling them to retire earlier?

Mr. P. R. Rau: I have called for certain information and will lay a reply on the table in due course.

Grievances of the Guards of the East Indian Railway (28.03.1933)

Mr. B. N. Misra: (a) Is it a fact that Guards on the North-Western Railway are given 24 hours uninterrupted rest after working for six days irrespective of the hours of employment? If so, why are the Guards on the East Indian Railway denied this privilege?

(b) Is the strength of Guards on the East Indian Railway such that they never get leave in time for want of relief? If not, what was their strength in 1930 and 1932, respectively, in each Division – (Reserve should be stated separately) - , and what number availed themselves of the leave on average pay, casual and medical leave, respectively, during 1930 and 1932?

Mr. P. R. Rau: Government have no information but are sending a copy of the question to the Agent, East Indian Railway for consideration of the points raised. I may add, however, that running staff are at present outside the scope of the Indian Railways (Amendment) Act, 1930.

Charge of Political Agentship of States in Orissa (01.04.1933)

Kumar Gupteswar Prasad Singh (on behalf of Mr. B. N. Misra): Do Government contemplate to give the charge of the Political Agentship into the hands of Governor in the new province of Orissa?

Mr. H. A. F. Metcalfe: No, Sir.

Headquarters of the Political Agent of States in Orissa (01.04.1933)

Kumar Gupteswar Prasad Singh (on behalf of Mr. B. N. Misra): Is it a fact that the number of the states of Orissa is more than that of the Central Provinces? If so, are Government prepared to consider whether the headquarters of the Agent's office should not be somewhere in the future Orissa Province in a place like Cuttack or Puri?

Mr. H. A. F. Metcalfe: Yes. Ranchi has been chosen temporarily as the headquarters of the combined Agency both in view of its geographical situation as almost all the States are comparatively easily accessible from it, and also because accommodation was available for the office and Agency staff at economical rates. At the present time the Honourable Member is doubtless aware that Government would be entirely unjustified in embarking upon Schemes involving heavy additional expenditure, and it has been possible to inaugurate the new Scheme at a cost less than the previously incurred when the States were in relation with the Local Governments. The question of change of headquarters from Ranchi to any other station will depend upon experience of actual working.

Creation of New Office of the political Agent for the States of Orissa and the Central Provinces (01.04.1933)
Mr. B. N. Misra: Will Government be pleased to state:

(i) whether a new office of the Political Agent for the States of Orissa and Central Provinces is going to be started with effect from the 1st April, 1933;

(ii) what is the total number of the States that will come within the jurisdiction of this office from Orissa and the Central Provinces , respectively;

(iii) how many Oriya speaking States there are in the Central Provinces which are claimed to be Oriya States;

(iv) what is the population of Oriyas in these States, viz.; Bastar, Jaspur, etc.;

(v) what is the proportion of percentage of population of the people speaking the languages of:

        (a) Oriya,

        (b) Bengalee,

        (c) Hindustani, and

(d) other non- Oriya languages,

(vi) what is the proportion of the percentage of people of following different communities :

        (a) Oriyas,

        (b) Bengalees,

        (c) Hindustanis,

        (d) other non-Oriyas, other than

        (e) Aboriginals;

(vii) how many clerks, typists and what other staff will be taken for the new office;

(viii) what is the percentage of Oriya representation in proportion to the non-Oriyas in the new office;

(ix) whether Government contemplate taking into this office any of the clerks from Political Agent's office of

Sambalpur?

Mr. H. A. F. Metcalfe: (i) The Honourable Member has, doubtless, seen the Press Communiqué of the 20th March, but I may take this opportunity of explaining the proposed arrangements. The Agent to the Governor General of the new Eastern States Agency, which will comprise the States of Bihar and Orissa and Central Provinces (excluding Makrai) will have, as from the 1st of April, 1933, his temporary headquarters at Ranchi. His staff will include a Secretary, and at Sambalpur another Secretary and Political Agent.

(ii) 26 states from Bihar and Orissa and 14 excluding Makrai from Central Provinces.

(iii) to (vi). The collection of the information, for which Honourable Member asks, would entail considerable time and labour and the statistics can no doubt be obtained from books of reference such as Census Reports and Gazetteers, which are available to the public.

(vii) It is proposed to entertain the following staff for the new office:

1 Agent to the Governor General, Eastern States.

1 Secretary to the Agent to Governor General, Eastern States at Ranchi.

1 Secretary to the Agent to the Governor General, Eastern States, and Political Agent, Sambalpur.

1 Assistant Secretary.

1 Superintendent.

8 Head Assistants.

8 Assistants.

18 Clerks and typists.

Complaints about Adulteration in Country Liquor Bottles in Delhi (05.04.1933)

Mr. B. N. Misra: (a) Are Government aware that there is a general complaint of the Delhi public about the adulteration up to 25 per cent in country liquor bottles at the retail sale shops? If not, do Government propose to order an open enquiry into the matter?

(b) Are Government aware that when the public do not get real wine in Delhi, they are obliged to get their requirements at much trouble from the rural shops near Delhi, such as Sonipat, Bahadurgarh, Palwal, Gohana, etc., in the Rohtak and Gurgaon districts of the Punjab Province?

The Honourable Sir George Schuster: Enquiries are being made and the information asked for by the Honourable Member will be laid on the table in due course.

Duty on Country Liquor (05. 04.1933)

Mr. B. N. Misra:(a) Is it a fact that reduction was made in 1932 in Delhi in the duty on country liquor and that the auction of country liquor shops was let off at higher bids in license fees than in previous years?

(b) Is it a fact that Government again reduced the duty on country liquor in Delhi province this year and that in the auction of 1933 of country liquor shops in Delhi the license fee has actually decreased instead of going up?

(c) Are Government in a position to account for the fall in license fees in the auction of 1933 of country liquor shops in Delhi?

(d) Is it a fact that the retail sale merchants of country liquor purchase bottles at Rs. 1-7-0 per bottle from the distillery and sell at Rs. 3-2-0 per bottle?

The Honourable Sir George Schuster: The information

asked for by the Honourable Member is being collected and will be laid on the table in due course.

Denial to Railway Subordinates of Moradabad of the Privilege of Seeing Officers at Calcutta (10.04.1933)

Mr. B. N. Misra: (a) Is it a fact that the subordinates of Moradabad are denied the privilege of seeing officers at Calcutta?

(b) If not, under what circumstances did Mr. L. E. Vining address the following on the 9th June, 1932:

"You will not be given permission to see anyone in Calcutta. You have got to realize without further delay that my orders are to be carried out and I shall have to take serious view of your attitude which is bordering an insubordination which I am not prepared to tolerate?"

Mr. P. R. Rau: With your permission, Sir, I propose to reply to questions Nos. 1182, 1183, and 1184 together. I have called for certain information and will lay a reply on the table in due course.

Punishment given to the Subordinates of the Moradabad Division, East Indian Railway (10.04.1933)

Mr. B. N. Misra: Is it a fact that the subordinates of the Moradabad Division on the East Indian Railway are punished in anticipation of their explanations? If not, will Government be pleased to lay on the table a copy of the Divisional Superintendent, Moradabad, letter No. 112/99/27-E., of the 4th July. 1932, and what action do Government propose to take to punish the officers concerned?

Suspension of certain Subordinates of the Moradabad Division, East Indian Railway (10.04.1933)

Mr. B. N. Misra:(a) Is it a fact that the subordinates of the Moradabad Division were suspended by Mr. L. E. Vining and Mr. C. Pearce, and were paid during the period of suspension the subsistence allowance, but never received any punishment for the offence which could not be established? If so, why are they paid quarter pay in the absence of punishment?

(b) Will Government be pleased to lay on the table the following letters issued by the Divisional Superintendent, Moradabad: (1) L./489 of 3rd December, 1932; (2) 3/32-E. of 5th December 1932; (3) E-29/32 of 6th December, 1932; (4) E.-Control of 12th October, 1932; (5) C. C. - 11/ M. B. – 10 of 12th October, 1932; (6) C. C. 17/ M. B. -24 of 12th October, 1932; (7) C. C. – 19/M. B. – 32 of 17th October, 1932; (8) E. T. -3 /32-R. A. S. M of 24th October, 1932; (9) E. T. -3/32-R. A. S. M. of 1st November, 1932, and (10) E. T. – 3/32- R. A. S. M. of 29th/30th November, 1932, with supporting documents?

Muslim Police Officers in Delhi (10.04.1933)

Mr. B. N. MIsra: (a) Is it a fact that the Deputy superintendent   of   Police,   Kotwali,   the   deputy superintendent, C.I.D., and the Deputy Superintendent on Special Duty at Delhi are Muhammadans?

(b) Is it also a fact that the Circle inspector and the Sub-Inspector- in-charge of Kotwali are also Muhammadans?

(c) Are Government aware of their general policy to avoid preponderance of one community in a department and also at a particular station?

(d) Are government also aware that the population of

Delhi and its suburbs mostly consists of Hindus, and the Muhammadans are much less in number?

(e) Is it a fact that in spite of there being already two Muslim Deputy Superintendents of Police and many other Muslim Police Officers in Delhi, another Muslim Deputy Superintendent of Police has very recently been brought in place of the only Hindu Deputy Superintendent of Police?

(f) If the reply to part (e) be in the affirmative, was a Hindu or non-Muslim particularly asked for from the Punjab Government? If not, why not?

The Honourable Sir Harry Haig: (a) and (b). The replies are in the affirmative.

(c) to (f). I would refer the Honourable Member to the reply given by me to parts (c), (d) and (e) of Sardar Sant Singh's unstarred question No. 180 on the 5th April, 1933.

Meetings of Qadianis held in the House of the Deputy Superintendent, Criminal Investigation Department, Delhi (10.04.1933)

Mr. B. N. Misra: Are Government aware that meetings of Qadians are held almost on every Friday and Sunday in the house of the Deputy Superintendent of Police, C. I. D., Delhi, who himself belongs to that sect and that all other religions are openly criticized in those meetings? If so, under what rule are these meetings allowed to be held in the house of a responsible police officer who is the custodian of law and order?

The Honourable Sir Harry Haig: The Deputy Superintendent of Police, C. I. D., is a member of the Anjuman-i-Ahmadiya, Lahore. No meetings of the kind described are held in his house.

Non-Political Cases investigated by the Delhi Criminal Investigation Department (10.04.1933)

Mr. B. N. Misra: (a) Will Government be pleased to state the non-political cases investigated by Delhi C.I.D. during the last three years?

(b) If the reply be in the negative or if there was a negligible number, how do Government justify the retention of a post of Deputy Superintendent in the Delhi C. I. D.? Is it a fact that a criminal agency has recently been created exclusively to deal with the non-political cases?

The Honourable Sir Harry Haig:(a) The information is not easily available.

(b) Though the Delhi C. I. D. has investigated some non-political cases during the last three years, its primary function is the watching and investigation of political, communal and revolutionary movements of crime. No separate staff has been sanctioned for the investigation of non-political crime. The Central Investigating Agency referred to in the question as the "Criminal Agency", is merely a local rearrangement of Police Station investigating staff and has no connection with the Delhi C. I. D.

Duties of the Deputy Superintendent of Police, Criminal Investigation Department, Delhi (10.04.1933)

Mr. B. N. Misra:(a) Is it a fact that the Deputy Superintendent of Police, C. I. D., is merely an intermediary between the Superintendent of Police, C. I. D. and the Inspectors, C. I. D.? What work does he actually do?

(b) Is it a fact that this appointment was particularly created in order to deal with criminal cases and also to relieve the Superintendent of Police of C. I. D. during his short leave, etc., when there was only one Deputy Superintendent of Police in Delhi?

(c) Is it a fact that since then a post of Deputy Superintendent of Police, Headquarters, has permanently been created and separate C. I. Agency has been established? If so, how do Government justify the retention of this post during the present days of financial stringency?

The Honourable Sir Henry Haig:(a) and (c). The answer to the first part is in the negative. As regards the second part, I would refer the Honourable Member to the reply I have just given to his question No. 1187. The work done by the Deputy Superintendent is of exacting nature requiring the whole-time attention of a Gazetted Officer.(b) No, Sir.

Local and Conveyance Allowances given to the Gazetted Police Officers in Delhi (10.04.1933)

Mr. B. N. Misra:(a) How much local and conveyance allowances are given to the gazetted police officers in Delhi and when and why were these sanctioned?

(b) Have these allowances ever been revised and overhauled? If not, why not? If so, when and with what effect?

(c) Are government prepared to revise the grant of conveyance allowance given to the Deputy Superintendent of Police, C. I. D., Delhi, and reduce its scale?

The Honourable Sir Harry Haig:(a) I lay on the table a statement showing the local and conveyance allowances at present drawn by a Gazetted Police Officers in Delhi. These allowances were sanctioned when the posts were created, with the exception of conveyance allowance of the Deputy Superintendent of Police, C. I. D. This was first sanctioned as a temporary measure for a period of six months from 1st August, 1930, in recognition of the fact that he was expected to supervise work in a large area, in which he did not draw travelling allowance. The local and conveyance allowances drawn by other Gazetted Officers were sanctioned in view of the fact that Delhi is an expensive centre and because the duties of these officers at headquarters necessitate the keeping of a motor car.

(b) The sanctioned local and conveyance allowances except those which were in existence before the 1st January, 1919, and have not been enhanced since that date have been subjected to emergency cuts varying from 10 per cent to 20 per cent since March, 1931.

(c) Government do not consider that the conveyance allowance drawn by the Deputy Superintendent, C. I. D., is excessive, and are not, therefore, prepared to take the action suggested.

Statement

Designation of Gazetted Officers   Local Allowance   Conveyance Allowance

Rs.   Rs.

1. Senior Superintendent of Police 150

2. Superintendent of Police, C. I. D. 129

3. Assistant Superintendent of Police 90   109

4. Deputy Superintendent of Police City . . . .

.   75   87/8
5. Deputy Superintendent of Police Headquarters .
.   75   87/8
6. Deputy Superintendent of Police, C. I. D. . . . .
.   75   87/8

Motor Drivers of Police Officers in Delhi (10.04.1933)

Mr. B. N. Misra: Are government aware that none of the police officers in Delhi has got his private motor driver, but, that the police constables detailed as their orderlies or gunmen are being utilized as motor drivers? If so, why and under what orders?

The Honourable Sir Harry Haig:I am making enquiries from the Chief Commissioner, Delhi, and will lay a reply on the table in due course.

Reservation of a Compartment in every Railway Train for an Ice Vendor (12.04.1933)

Mr. B. N. Misra: Is it a fact that a compartment is reserved in every train for an ice vendor? If so, is it meant for the exclusive use of the ice vendor or for the use of persons connected with Government Railway Police travelling with or without permits?

Mr. P. R. Rau: Government have no information, but it is believed that a compartment is reserved during the summer months for the ice vendor on all trains. Whether any other passengers are allowed to travel in that compartment is for the local authorities to determine.

Travelling of a Police Constable in the Compartment reserved for the Ice Vendor between Moradabad and Delhi on the East Indian Railway (12.04.1933)

Mr. B. N. Misra: Is it a fact that on the 30th March, 1933, a constable in uniform with two persons in plain clothes travelled by the 5 Moradabad–Delhi train between Moradabad and Delhi on the East Indian Railway in a compartment reserved for the ice vendor? If so, why and under what circumstances are persons holding tickets and who have paid the fare not permitted to travel in order to avoid congestion and over crowding?

Mr. P. R. Rau: Government have no information, but a copy of this question is being sent to the Agent, East Indian Railway, for disposal.

Re-organisation of the Railway School at Chandausi, East Indian Railway (12.04.1933)

Mr. B. N. Misra: (a) Is it a fact that the Railway administration are contemplating a re-organization of the railway school at Chandausi, East Indian Railway? If so, (i) will there be any reduction of staff, (ii) do Government, as per recommendation of the court of inquiry, propose to consult the recognized unions in respect of retrenchment, and (iii) what provision of leave and service will be made in respect of the staff contemplated to be reduced?

(b) Is it a fact that at the railway school, Chandausi, East Indian Railway, there are four office clerks? If so, will Government please state whether they intend to revert the clerks who belong to other administrations than the East Indian Railway to their parent railways?

(c) Is it a fact that the present Superintendent of the railway school, Chandausi, never had experience of the management of a school? If it is not so, where and in what capacity did he have such experience?

Mr. P. R. Rau:(a) and (c). I am making inquiries and will lay a reply on the table in due course.

(b) This is a matter within the competence of the Agent, East Indian Railway, to whom a copy of this question has been sent.

Discussion of Individual Cases with the Representatives of Recognized Unions on the East Indian Railway (12.04.1933)

Mr. B. N. Misra:(a) Is it a fact that Divisional Superintendents on the East Indian Railway do, according to their discretion, refuse to receive representations from recognized trade unions on behalf of individual members in respect of individual grievances, etc.? If so, why and what are the rules and orders in respect of the individual's case represented by his union? Are unions debarred from representing individual cases?

(b) Do the Railway Board desire to issue instructions in accordance with the recommendations of Royal Commission on Labour that heads of departments and divisions should receive and discuss individual cases with the representatives of recognized unions so as to avoid unnecessary delay and labour?

(c) Will the Railway Board please lay on the table a list of unions recognized by railway administrations?

P. R. Rau:(a) Government are not aware what the exact practice followed by Divisional Superintendents on the East Indian Railway is. The attitude of the Railway Board was expressed in the memorandum furnished by them to the Royal Commission on Labour, viz., that the representation of individual grievances by Unions is not encouraged since it is considered that adequate machinery for dealing with these exists, individuals having the recognized official channels through which they can seek redress.

(b) I have not been able to trace a recommendation in the report of the Royal Commission on labour that Heads of Departments and Divisions should receive and discuss individual cases with the representatives of recognized unions. The Royal Commission on labour have recommended that a recognized union should have the right to negotiate with the employer in respect of matters affecting the individual interests of members. This is still under consideration by the Railway Board and the Government of India.

(c) I am calling for up-to-date information and lay a reply on the table in due course.

State Prisoners in Custody (22.08.1933)

Mr. B. N. Misra: Will government be pleased to state:

(a) the total number State Prisoners in custody

       (i) under Regulation III of 1818, and

       (ii) the Bengal Ordinance; and

(b)   (i) the total number of State Prisoners getting no allowance at all for their families and dependents;

       (ii) the total number of prisoners getting upto Rs. 600 per annum;

       (iii) the total number of State Prisoners getting Rs. 600 to Rs. 1,000 per annum for the upkeep of their families and their dependents;

(iv) the total number of prisoners getting Rs. 1,000 to Rs. 2,400 per annum for the upkeep of their families and their dependents; and

(v) the total number getting more than Rs. 2,400 per annum?

The Honourable Sir Harry Haig: (a) (i) 36.

(ii) The Honourable Member presumably refers to Bengal Criminal Law Amendment Act, 1930. The number of persons detained under the Act was 1,439 on the 31st July.

(b)   (i) 16. One case is under consideration.

      (ii) 9.

      (iii) 4.

      (iv) 3.

      (v) 3.

The figures relate to State Prisoners under Regulation III of 1818. I regret I am unable to give similar information regarding the family allowances of detenus whose cases are dealt with by the Government of Bengal under provisions of Bengal Criminal Law Amendment Act.

Separate Museum for Orissa (22. 08.1933)

Mr. B. N. Misra: (a) Will Government be pleased to state:

      (i)   the amount of money set apart for archaeological work in the various provinces of India;

      (ii) the amount set apart for Bihar and Orissa; and

(iii) the amount spent every year in Orissa?

(b) Has the amount spent in Orissa been found sufficient for the purposes of the archaeological findings in Orissa?

(c) Will Government be pleased to state the place in Orissa where the Archaeological Department has worked?

(d) Do Government propose to institute a separate museum for Orissa, which is going to have a separate Province of its own?

Mr. G. S. Bajpai:(a) and (b). If the Honourable Member will kindly indicate the years for which the information is required, I shall endeavor to obtain it for him.

(c) The principal monuments where special repairs have been carried out are the Black Pagoda at Konarak, Rock Edicts of Ashoka at Dhauli, Raja Rani and other temples at Bhuvanesvara, the caves of Khandagiri and Udaigiri, etc.

(d) 'Museums' are a provincial subject under Devolution Rules, and it will be for the new Provincial Government of Orissa to consider whether or not to establish a museum.

Dissatisfaction of Oriyas on Account of Non-Inclusion of certain Areas in the Proposed Orissa Province (22.08.1933)

Mr. B. N. Misra:(a) Are government aware of the dissatisfaction of the Oriyas on account of the non-inclusion of (i) the Singbhum District (Bihar and Orissa), (ii) the southern portion of Midnapur (Hijli District in Bengal), Parlakhimedi, Tarla, Mandasa, Tekkali of Ganjam District, (iv) the Jaipur Agency of the Vizagapatam District, and (v) Fuljhar of the Central Provinces?

(b) Will Government be pleased to state the number of meetings that have communicated to Government the dissatisfaction felt by the Oriyas?

(c) Are Government aware that there is a very influential section among the Oriyas who say that unless all the areas demanded by the Oriyas are included they will not accept the province?

The Honourable Sir Joseph Bhore:(a) and (b). Up to the 31st July, 1933, the Government of India have received 87 representations protesting against the omission from the proposed Orissa province of all or some of the areas referred to by the Honourable Member. Not all these representations purport to be the outcome of meetings held; some are from individuals and others from local associations or bodies. 80 out of 87 representations received deal with Ganjam areas.

(c) Government are not aware of such attitude on the part of any influential section among the Oriyas.

On this question of **Mr. B. N. Misra**, a lot of reactions had come from several Members; which are delineated below for the perusal of the readers.

Mr. Maswood Ahmad: Is it a fact that the separation of the Orissa province has affected four provinces, that is, Madras, Bengal, Central Provinces and Bihar?

The Honourable Sir Joseph Bhore:I think that is quite correct.

Mr. Maswood Ahmad: Was there any Muslim Member on the Orissa Boundary Committee?

The Honourable Sir Joseph Bhore: My Honourable friend has put a question on that point. When I come to it, I will give him a reply.

Mr. M. Maswood Ahmad: What step was taken by Government to know the Muslim point of view about the boundary of Orissa?

The Honourable Sir Joseph Bhore:I have no doubt that the Committee appointed conducted a very complete inquiry and received representations from individuals interested.

Mr. Gaya Prasad Singh: Are Government aware that the claim of the Oriyas to the inclusion of Singbhum in their new province is quite unjustified?

(No answer)

Mr. Gaya Prasad Singh: Are Government aware that the Committees, which were appointed in this connection, have unanimously rejected the claim of the Oriyas for the inclusion of Singbhum in their new province?

The Honourable Sir Joseph Bhore: My Honourable friend may refer to the reports of Committees concerned.

Mr. Amar Nath Dutt: May I put a question to the questioner himself? May I know the grounds on which the Oriyas have asked for the inclusion of the southern portion of Midnapore in the province of Orissa? Is it on the ground of conquest or what else?

The Honourable Sir Joseph Bhore: The question is not addressed to me, Sir.

Mr. Amar Nath Dutt: If it is not on the ground of conquest, will he kindly state whether he will claim up to the northern portion of Burdwan, that is, Katwa?

Mr. Gaya Prasad Singh: Is it not a fact that on ethnological, historical, linguistic and racial grounds Singbhum cannot be included in the new province of Oriyas?

The President (The Honourable Sir Sanmukham Chetty): To whom is the question addressed?

Mr. Gaya Prasad Singh: Anybody can answer it -- either the questioner himself, or the Government Member.

Maulvi Muhammad Shafee Daoodi: May I know whether the protest made by Oriyas includes Singbhum definitely?

The Honourable Sir Joseph Bhore:I think so, but I am not quite definite upon that point.

Mr. S. C. Mitra: Are not Government aware that the people of Midnapore district strongly protested against their inclusion in the newly created province of Orissa?

The Honourable Sir Joseph Bhore:I take my Honourable friend's word for that.

Mr. Gaya Prasad Gingh: Is it not a fact that the people of Singbhum also protested against the proposed inclusion of Singbhum in the Oriya province?

The Honourable Sir Joseph Bhore: It is likely.

Allegations against a Clerk in the Office of the Controller of Railway Accounts (24.08.1933)

Mr. B. N. Misra:(a) Is it a fact that there is a bogus clerk in the office of the Controller of Railway accounts, actually working in the name of his ten years old son, as an agent of the Bombay Life Insurance Company, monopolizing all the offices of the Government of India Departments for his profession and thus deliberately defying the Government Servants' Conduct Rules?

(b) Is it a fact that in December, 1926, a report to this effect was made against that clerk to the officers by Superintendent of his section but the matter was hushed up by intervention of Rai Bahadur B. D. Puri, the then Deputy Director of Finance in the Railway Board, who got that clerk transferred temporarily to the Railway Board's office on 20 per cent more pay than that which he was getting in the office of the Accountant General, Railways?

(c) Is it a fact that after his re-transfer from the Railway Board's office the said clerk continued and still continues the insurance work?

(d) Is it a fact that in April, 1932, Mr. I. S. Puri, the then Deputy Controller of Railway Accounts, stopped the increment of the said clerk on account of his inefficiency and passed on his increment papers very adverse remarks?

(e) Are Government aware that soon after the transfer of Mr. I. S. Puri from the Controller of Accounts and on arrival of Mr. P. G. Shaw in that office, the papers containing the adverse remarks mentioned in part (d) above were destroyed by the said clerk and a fresh increment slip was prepared and sanction for the same was obtained by the mediation and help of superintendents? If so, what steps have Government taken as to a complete inquiry into the case?

(f) Are Government prepared to issue instructions to all the clerks of the Government of India and attached offices to desist from doing any kind of insurance work either in their own names or in the names of their relatives?

Mr. P. R. Rau:(a), (b), & (c). I am informed that there is a clerk in the office of the controller of Railway accounts whose father and minor son jointly hold the agency in question, and that he used to assist his father outside office hours. In 1926 a report was received against him and he was warned that he should not engage in any private business without sanction. It is understood that he is now not doing any insurance work either directly or indirectly. The clerk in question was employed under the Railway Board temporarily for four months in 1926-27.

(d) & (e). The original increment slip was lost but the question whether an increment should be granted was carefully considered in its merits before it was sanctioned.

(f) The instructions contained in the Government Servant's Conduct Rules are considered to be sufficient.

Inequality in the Distribution of Higher Posts in the Railway Clearing accounts office (07.09.1933)

Mr. B. N. Misra:(a) Is it a fact that in the Railway catering Accounts Office the staff transferred from the North Western Railway are having a lion's share in the upper grade posts at the cost of the staff transferred from other Railways, and, if so, will Government be pleased to state the reasons for the same?

(b) Are Government aware that this inequality in the distribution of higher posts was clearly brought to the notice of the committee appointed by the Railway Board to fix the seniority of the staff of the Railway Clearing Accounts Office, and that committee recommended that in case of future promotions, at least, special consideration should be given to the non-North Western Railway men, even if these men are not technically the senior most?

(c) Will Government be pleased to state whether any action has been taken on the above recommendation and if not, why not?

(d) Will Government be pleased to lay on the table a comparative statement showing the position of all sub-heads and class I clerks transferred from the railways as on 1st April, 1929, when the office was made permanent, and at present?

(e) Are Government prepared to take any action that may be necessary to see that the above inequality is set right in future?

Mr. P. R. Rau:I am making enquiries and shall lay a reply on the table in due course.

Resolution Re Admissions to the Military Academy (07.09.1933)

Mr. B. N. Misra: Sir, I beg to move the following Resolution that stands in my name:

"That this Assembly recommends to the Governor General in Council:

(1) that steps be taken to increase the number of admissions to the Military Academy both by direct examination as well as by selection from the ranks;

(2) that if this be found not practicable at present, steps be taken to increase the number of admissions by selection from the ranks and especially from the 'Y' cadets before they pass the age limit."

Sir, my object in putting this Resolution before the House is to draw its attention to the unsatisfactory and slow pace we are going on with the Indianisation of the army. Honourable Members know that at present we are taking 60 cadets a year by both direct examinations and selection from the ranks and, if the annual recruitment of Commissioned Ranks in the Indian Army be approximately 120, we can ultimately only aspire to a 50 per cent ratio of Indians to British Officers at the most and that in not less than a period of 25 years. This is quite simple arithmetic. Now, Sir, I ask the House to consider this position fully. I maintain that unless the pace of Indianisation is more than 50 per cent of annual recruitment, it is absolutely impossible to achieve our object, namely, the Indianisation of the Indian Army within a reasonable distance of time. If the objective before all of us is to achieve the status of a Dominion, any scheme of Indianisation of the army, which we are working, at present, or which may be drawn up in the future, must have a direct relationship to that objective. To be frank, I want to know whether the present pace of Indianisation, which leads us only to 50 per cent after a period of about a quarter of a century from now, satisfies the legitimate wishes of the people of India. Unless more vigorous steps are taken, it will remain pious hope. We, as responsible public men, do urge upon the Government that a scheme must be prepared so that public opinion may be satisfied that there is a reasonable chance of the Indian Army being Indianised within a reasonable distance of time and the responsibility of self-defence being made over to the Indian Parliament at some time or other in the near future.

Sir, the question, therefore is that the number of admissions to the Indian Military Academy be increased to more than half the number of vacancies that occur every year, so that the objective, namely, the Indianisation of the Indian Army be achieved within a reasonable distance of time. I do not want to limit the qualification of the Indian cadets. You can put them through a test. I do not desire the efficiency of the Army to be in the slightest degree impaired, because we shall be putting in their hands the property and lives of 35 crores of men. I am for very rigorous and strict tests of their capacity. But, what I cannot understand is tat, with ample material and heroic history behind us, it is thought that we cannot produce 120 boys per year from amongst nearly one quarter of the world's population who will be able to stand the most rigorous and strictest test of efficiency before they are granted King's Commissions. Sir, the lessons of the Great War are not yet forgotten nor will they be ever forgotten. Our soldiers stood the horrors and the gravest consequences of the War as well as any other nation of the world and they proved their mettle. You can have no better test of endurance and heroism.

I wish to refer to the scheme adopted by the Government of India in 1922, which contemplated complete Indianisation of the Indian army within 30 years. Turning to Appendix I of that report, the number of commissions to be granted during the first 14 years according to that scheme annually averaged 81.4. The number to be granted during the second period averaged annually 182 and the number to be granted annually during the third period averaged 227 on an increasing scale. In this way the scheme contemplated complete Indianisation of the Indian Army in 30 years. Sir, I hold that there is no reason to think that the conditions, which existed in 1922 have undergone such a material change that the same principle cannot be adopted now. With the development of new political structure in India, the defence of India must to an increasing extent be the concern of the Indian people and not of the British Government alone and, in order to give practical effect to the principle, the rate of Indianisation in Indian Army should be commensurate with the main object in view, having regard to all relevant considerations such as the maintenance of the requisite standard of efficiency. We must have more Indians in the Army. Our sole concern must be to have an increasing number of Indians in the Army. For so many years, only Europeans have been employed in the Army. Indians have not at all been encouraged. If they have been engaged, it is only as sepoys and not as officers. What I plead before you is that Indians must be officers in the Army. With these words, I move my resolution.

Mr. President (The Honourable Sir Sanmukham Chetty): Motion moved:
"That this Assembly recommends to the Governor General in Council;
(1)   that steps be taken to increase the number of admissions to the Military Academy both by direct examination as well as by selection from the ranks;
(2)   that if this be not found practicable at present, steps be taken to increase the number of admissions by selection from the ranks and especially from 'Y' cadets before they pass the age-limit."

Prosecution of certain Officials of the Central Telegraph Office, Calcutta, for Divulging the Contents of Telegrams regarding Races (12.09.1933)

Mr. B. N. Misra:(a) Has the attention of Government been drawn to remarks at page 155 of the Telegraph Review for April, 1933, under caption of "Gambling"?
(b) Is it a fact that some years back certain officials of the Central Telegraph Office, Calcutta, were prosecuted for divulging the contents of telegrams regarding horse races?
(c) If the answers to parts (a) and (b) be in the affirmative, what steps have Government taken, or propose to take as a preventive measure?
(d) Will government please lay on the table a statement

showing the number of Telegraph employees (by designation) employed on this work in different offices in each Circle and how many of them are Indians and Anglo-Indians?

Honourable Sir Frank Noyce:(a) Government have seen the article.

(b) Government are aware of only one case of the kind to which the Honourable Member refers.

(c) The article refers to a matter of discipline in the Calcutta Telegraph Office and shows that the Chief Superintendent who is fully competent to deal with the matter has already taken such steps as he considers appropriate; Government do not, therefore, propose to interfere.

(d) I regret I am unable to answer the Honourable Member's question, as it is not clear what particular work the Honourable Member means by the expression "this work".

Permission to the Telegraph Employees to Work in the Race Course (12.09.1933)

Mr. B. N. Misra:(a) Is it a fact that the Government Servants' Conduct Rules preclude the departmental employees from receiving remuneration from other firms or agents?

(b) Is it a fact that permission is granted to the employees in the Telegraph Department to work in the racecourse due to economic depression?

(c) Is it a fact that arrangements are made by the Department to give them off or reshuffle their duties in such a way as to enable them to work in the racecourse on every Saturday?

(d) Will Government please state if any complaint has ever been received from any head of office for sparing these men at the appointed time on the fixed dates regularly? If so, from which offices and on how many occasions?

(e) Will Government please state if there was any occasion in any office to refuse this permission? If so, when and where?

(f) Is it a fact that many of these workers are granted permission to perform night duties permanently? If so, why?

(g) Will Government please lay on the table a statement showing the names of other departmental offices in which such permission is granted and the number of men thus employed and how many of them are Indians and Anglo-Indians?

The Honourable Sir Frank Noyce:(a) Yes, except with the previous sanction of the proper authority.

(b) Such permission is of long standing and was granted before the economic depression.

(c), (e) and (f). Government have no information. The arrangement of duties in Telegraph office is carried out by the officer-in-charge.

(d) Government have not been able to trace any such complaint.

(g) I regret that I am unable to answer the Honourable Member's question, as it is not clear what offices he means by the expression "other departmental offices".

Duty System of Telegraphists and Signal Room Clerks (12.09.1933)

Mr. B. N. Misra: With reference to answer given to unstarred question No. 100, dated 13th March, 1933, by Mr. Rameswar Prasad Bagla:

(a) has the attention of Government been drawn to page 369 of the Telegraph Review, November, 1932, where a representation to the Director General appeared under heading "Frequent night duties"?

(b are Government prepared to order a departmental enquiry into the duty system prevalent in signal offices?

The Honourable Sir Frank Noyce:(a) Yes, the representation, which is reproduced on the page mentioned, was duly replied to by the Director General.

(b) No, Government do not consider that there is any necessity for such inquiry.

Report of the Varma Committee (12.09.1933)

Mr. B. N. Misra:(a) Has the attention of the Government been to question No. 5 under section H – Supplementary Questionnaire of the Varma Committee?

(b) Is it a fact the investigation conducted has not been embodied in the Report?

(c) Will government please lay on the table the whole correspondence on the subject with reasons for omission of their findings on the subject in this Report of the Committee?

(d) With reference to paragraph 30 of the Varma Committee Report, will Government please lay on the table the whole correspondence and evidence on the duty chart and daily absence list, which are essential for the computation of telegraph staff?

The Honourable Sir Frank Noyce:(a) and (d). Government have not yet taken the report of the Varma Committee into consideration and I, therefore, regret that I am unable to reply to the Honourable Member's questions.

Meal Relief in Post Offices (12.09.1933)

Mr. B. N. Misra:(a) Will Government please state what are the differences in the conditions of service in the Indian and continental signal offices in respect of meal relief, which preclude the Government to accept the standard of 45 minutes' relief?

(b) Will Government please state the result of the enquiry regarding meal relief in British Post Offices?

The Honourable Sir Frank Noyce:(a) and (b). For the reasons explained in the reply to part (h) of Mr. Rameswar Prasad Bagla's unstarred question No. 100 in this House on the 13th March, 1933, Government do not propose to take any action in the matter of comparison between the Indian and British and Continental signal offices in respect of the period of meal relief.

Insolvent Employees in certain Government Departments (12.09.1933)

Mr. B. N. Misra: With reference to starred question No. 850, dated the 21st March, 1933, by Mr. Lalchand Navalrai, will Government be pleased to state how many insolvents are still in the active service in the Telegraph side of the Posts and Telegraphs Department in gazetted ranks in (i) Railway, (ii) Posts, and (iii) Telegraph Departments separately?

The Honourable Sir frank Noyce: Government regret that the information is not readily available and could not be obtained without an expenditure of time and labour, which would be unjustifiable.

Indebtedness of Gazetted Officers in the Telegraph Department (12.09.1933)

Mr. B. N. Misra: (a) Are Government aware that many gazetted officers in the Telegraph Department are hopelessly encumbered with debt taken from private individuals?

(b) Will Government please lay on the table a statement showing the number of employees still in service in the Telegraph Department among the (i) subordinate and (ii) gazetted ranks whose pay has been attached by the Court?

(c) Is it a fact that Government is considering the desirability of amending Rule 16 of the Government Servants' Conduct Rules with a view to make dismissal a compulsory condition for those Government servants who have been adjudged insolvents?

(d) Will Government please state the number of employees during the last 10 years in the Telegraph Department whose services have been dispensed with for misappropriating the public money or for abetting or falsification of Government accounts?

The Honourable Sir Frank Noyce: (a) Although Government are aware that certain of the gazetted officers in the Telegraph branch of the Posts and Telegraphs Department are financially embarrassed, they have no reason to suppose that the number is large.

(b) and (d). Government regret that the required information is not readily available and cannot be obtained without an undue expenditure of time and labour.

(c) No.

Alleged Falsification of Accounts by a Clerk of the Office of the Director, Telegraph Engineering, Eastern Circle (12.09.1933)

Mr. B. N. Misra: (a) Is it a fact that the services of a clerk who was attached to the office of the Director, Telegraph Engineering, Eastern Circle (now amalgamated with the Postmaster-General's Office, Calcutta), were dispensed with for alleged falsification of accounts and misappropriation on the judgment of the Presidency Magistrate during the time when Mr. Fox was Personal Assistant?

(b) Is it a fact that the trying Magistrate passed severe strictures on the conduct of some responsible officers?

(c) Will Government please lay on the table the full copy of the judgment? If not, why not?

 (d) Is it a fact that the officers whose conduct was criticised are still in service?

The Honourable Sir frank Noyce: (a) The clerk was dismissed from service on the charges referred to not in connection with the cases in which he was acquitted by the Presidency Magistrate but in connection with other cases of falsification of accounts and misappropriation of Government money, brought to light as a result of departmental investigations after his acquittal by the Magistrate.

(b) So far as Government are aware, the trying Magistrate made adverse comments on the conduct of one officer only.

(c) Government regret that they are unable to comply with the Honourable Member's request as the dismissal of the clerk referred to in part (a) of this question was not in connection with the cases forming the subject of the judgment and the officer referred to in my reply to part (b) above has since died.

(d) The Honourable Member is referred to the reply to parts (b) and (c) above.

Unauthorised Appointments in the Postal Department (12.09.1933)

Mr. B. N. Misra: (a) Has the attention of Government been drawn to Chapter XIV of the Report of the Telegraph Establishment Enquiry Committee and to pages 353, 390 of the Telegraph Review of November and December, 1932, on the subjects of certain unauthorized appointments?

(b) Have Government undertaken any enquiry? If so, with what results? If not, why not?

(c) Is it a fact that all these appointments are being carried on for years with the full knowledge of the Circle Heads?

The Honourable Sir Frank Noyce: (a) As regards the first part of the question, Government have not yet considered the Report of the Committee. As regards the second part, Government have seen the article in question.

(b) Government have made no enquiries as the matter is one with which the Head of the Circle is competent to deal.

(c) Government have no information.

Decentralisation of the Administration of the Posts and Telegraphs Department (12.09.1933)

Mr. B. N. Misra: (a) Is it a fact that the administration of the Posts and Telegraph Department is being gradually decentralized like other Government Departments?

(b) Have Government taken any disciplinary action against the responsible officers where they have flouted the orders of the Director General? If so, will Government be pleased to state the number of such officers and the nature of punishment awarded?

The Honourable Sir Frank Noyce : (a) Yes, so far as is practicable.

(b) Government are not aware of the orders of the Director General being flouted by responsible officers. Occasionally orders may be disregarded; such cases when they come to notice are dealt with according to the circumstances. The Department has been so long in existence that it would be an impossible task to compile a statement of such cases.

Rules for Recognition of Government Servants' Organisations (12.09.1933)

Mr. B. N. Misra: (a) Has the attention of Government been drawn to the two editorials in the Telegraph Review for December, 1932 and June 1933 on the subject of Rules of Recognition of Government servants' organizations?

(b) Is it not a fact that the editorial under caption "A bone of contention" in the June, 1933, issue is based on the recommendations of the Whitley Commission?

(c) Is it a fact that under the existing rules of recognition, service organizations cannot represent the grievances of individual members?

(d) Is it not a fact that on many occasions Government ask for individual concrete instances from the organizations whenever common grievances are represented?

(e) In view of the recommendations of the Royal

Commission on Labour in India, are Government prepared to consider the modification of the existing rules of recognition of Government servants' organisations? If not, why not? If so, when?

The Honourable Sir Frank Noyce:(a) Government have seen the article

(b) The article refers to certain passages in the Report of the Commission.

(c) Yes, representations must be confined to matters, which are, or raise questions; which are, of common interest to the class represented by the Association.

(d) Such occasions may rise, but are not frequent.

(e) Government have under consideration revision of the Recognition Rules in their application to industrial workers.

Inspection of Combined Post and Telegraph Offices (12.09.1933)

Mr. B. N. Misra:(a) Is it a fact that the inspection of combined post and telegraph offices has been transferred from the duty of a Superintendent of Telegraph Traffic to that of a Postal Inspector and Superintendent?

(b) Is it a fact that under the existing rules Postal clerks are eligible for the posts of telegraphists after training?

(c) Is it a fact that the majority of 228 telegraphists surplus to requirements have been transferred to the post offices and the occasion for such transfers are too frequent?

(d) Will Government please state whether suitable telegraphists and clerks in the Telegraph Department are eligible for promotions to the grades of Postmasters, Postal Inspectors and Superintendents provided they possess the required qualifications? If not, why not? Will

Government please state whether they are prepared to consider the question now?

The Honourable Sir Frank Noyce:(a) and (b). The replies are in the affirmative.

(c) No, only 68 telegraphists have been so transferred.

(d) The reply to the first part is in the negative. As regards the second part, the duties of telegraphists or clerks in telegraph offices are quite different from those of officials in the grades of Postmasters, Postal Inspectors or Superintendents of Post Offices and the experience gained by them in their own grades would be of no value in the grades named by the Honourable Member. The reply to the last part is in the negative.

Non-Grant of Leave to the Inferior Servants of the Telegraph Department (12.09.1933)

Mr. B. N. Misra:(a) Are Government aware that there are no provisions for leave reserves staff for the inferior servants of the Telegraph Department and consequently leave on average pay granted to superior establishment is denied to this class of employees?

(b) If answer to part (a) be in the affirmative, are Government aware of the hardship caused to the servants of Government?

(c) If answer to part (b) be in the affirmative, do Government propose to make necessary provision for their leave reserve and grant them average pay for privilege leave? If not, why not?

The Honourable Sir Frank Noyce:(a) Yes.

(b) and (c). The existing rules do not provide for the grant of leave on average pay to inferior Government servants generally and Government do not propose to make an exception in respect of the inferior staff of the Telegraph Department.

Grievances of the Telegraph Staff (12.09.1933)

Mr. B. N. Misra:(a) Are Government aware of the fact that in the May and July, 1933, issues of the Telegraph Review on pages 180-190 and 255-256, three articles appeared under the captions (i) " Who is it to blame", (ii) "Legitimate Claims" and (iii) "Viceroy's Camp"?

(b) Will Government be pleased to state whether the facts on which the articles have appeared are substantially correct? If so, what action have Government since taken or propose to take to redress the grievances of the staff?

The Honourable Sir Frank Noyce:(a) Yes.

(b) As regards the first part of the question, the reply is in the affirmative.

Of the cases referred to, the claim for enhanced overtime allowance made by certain telephone operators, Dacca and Narayanganj, was not admitted, on the ground that it was a very belated one when it reached the Director General. I have however given instructions that the claim should be re-examined.

The claim of certain task work messengers for overtime allowance for duty performed in 1930, in the Viceroy's camp office at Calcutta, was not referred to the Director General by the Postmaster-General, Bengal and Assam, who apparently disposed of it under his own powers.

Realisation of Subscription of Members of Service Organisations through the Salary Bills of the Staff. (12.09.1933)

Mr. B. N. Misra:(a) Is it a fact that recoveries of cooperative credit societies, clubs, etc., attached to different Government offices are made through the salary bills of the staff?

(b) If the reply to the above question be in the affirmative, do Government propose to grant the same facilities to service organisations recognised by Government in respect of realisation of subscriptions of members through their salary bills? If not, why not?

The Honourable Sir George Schuster:(a) and (b). There are no cases where deductions for such purposes are made through salary bills in the same way, for instance, as a subscription to a Provident Fund. In certain cases however an arrangement was introduced as a concession whereby sums due from members of co-operative societies in the Posts and Telegraphs Department could be realized through the assistance of departmental officials. The practice is limited to certain cases and it is considered undesirable to extend it.

Retrenchment in the United Provinces Postal Circle (12.09.1933)

Mr. B. N. Misra:(a) Is it not a fact that promotions and discharge of officials under the retrenchment scheme in United Provinces Circle of the Posts and Telegraphs Department are being done on the grounds of communalism?

(b) Will Government be pleased to state if they have received any appeals from the staff of the United Provinces Circle on the grounds mentioned in part (a)?

(c) Are Government prepared to make sifting enquiries into this matter and take such steps as would stop these practices?

The Honourable Sir Frank Noyce:(a) As has been often stated in the House, promotions are not made on communal grounds. In carrying out retrenchment, however, the communal ratios existing before the beginning of the retrenchment campaign have been maintained as nearly as circumstances allowed.

(b) No such appeals have been traced.

(c) In the absence of any reason to suppose that their orders are not being carried out in the United Provinces Circle, Government do not propose to initiate enquiries.

Teaching Staff of the Royal Indian Military College, Dehra Dun (12.09.1933)

Mr. B. N. Misra:(a) Will Government be pleased to state (i) the number of members of the senior staff of the Royal Indian Military College at Dehra Dun, (ii) their academic qualifications, (iii) the classes in which they obtained their degrees, if any, (iv) their ages and dates of appointment, (v) the salaries on which they started and their present salaries, (vi) their extra allowances and the duties for which they are given, and (vii) other privileges, like free bungalows with their rental values, etc.?

(b) Are there any Indians on senior staff of this college, or has any Indian been appointed on the senior teaching staff? If not, why not?

(c) If the answer to part (b) be in the negative, were there no Indians available with these or better qualifications? Why have no Indians been appointed, keeping in view the Government declared policy of Indianising a certain proportion of the military services?

(d) Is it a fact that this college has nothing to do with

military training? If so, have Government considered whether they can obtain more efficient Indians on lower salaries for it?

Mr. G. R. F. Tottenham:(a) I lay a statement on the table giving the information desired by the Honourable Member so far as available.

(b) and (c). No Indian has been appointed permanently to the senior teaching staff because the object of the college is to give a Public School education on British lines and British masters are considered essential if this object is to be fulfilled.

(d) Apart from simple drill and physical training no military training is imparted at the college. For the reason given in the reply to parts (b) and (c) the answer to the second part of this question is in the negative.

Teaching Staff of the Indian Military Academy, Dehra Dun (12.09.1933)

Mr. B. N. Misra:(a) Will Government be pleased to state if there are any Indians on the teaching staff of the Indian Military Academy, Dehra Dun? If not, why not?

(b) Why are military officers only appointed for the teaching of such subjects as Elementary Mathematics, Geography, Law, Drawing, Higher Mathematics, Economics, Science, etc.?

(c) If the answer to the latter part of (b) above be in the affirmative, are Government prepared to take the necessary action to replace the military officers with Indians with proper qualifications?

(d) Will Government please state the number of officers in the Military Academy getting (i) Rs. 300 and upwards and (ii) below that?

(e) How many (i) Europeans, (ii) Indians are there in the cadre above Rs. 300?

Mr. G. R. F. Tottenham:(a), (b) and (c). The attention of the Honourable Member is invited to the answer to starred question No.759 asked on the 13th March last.

(d) (i). 15.

   (ii). 2.

(e) (i). 15.

   (ii). None.

Election of Members to the Salt Industry Committee (16.09.1933)

Mr. President (The Honourable Sir Sanmukham Chetty): I have to inform the Assembly that the following Members have been elected to the Salt Industry Committee, namely:

(1) Mr. E. Studd,

(2) Mr. Lalchand Navalrai, and

(3) **Mr. B. N. Misra**

DEATH OF MR. B. N. MISRA (20.09.1933)

A special session of the Central Legislative Assembly was held on 20th September 1933 on account of the sad and sudden demise of **Mr. B. N. Misra**the previous day, i.e., on 19th September 1933.

The Honourable Sir Joseph Bhore (Leader of the House): Sir, death has again removed with tragic suddenness yet another sitting Member of this Assembly. Mr. B. N. Misra was, I believe, a Member of the first Assembly and also of the third Assembly. I personally will remember him best for his ardent advocacy of the claims of Orissa, his own home. Unhappily he has not been spared to see what we hope will be the fruition of his desires. It will be unnecessary for me to say much about one who was in such recent touch with us all. I need only say that his quiet unassuming presence made him liked by every one with whom he came in contact. May I ask you, Sir, to convey to his relatives our deep sympathy with them in their bereavement?

Sir Cowasji Jehangir(Bombay City: Non-Muhammadan Urban) : Mr. President, on behalf of myself and my party, I rise to associate ourselves with the words that have fallen from the Leader of the House. Mr. Misra was one of those quiet unassuming Members in this Honourable House who had not a single enemy amongst us. His great mission was fulfilled, namely, the separation of Orissa; but most unfortunately he did not live to see a Governor and Council in his own province. Mr. Misra, I believe, was writing the history of his province, which perhaps we may be privileged to read in the future – whatever he left on paper. Mr. Misra was attached to his province and came here to represent faithfully the views of his constituency, and he never missed an occasion to do so. We regret – most of us – that we were not able to be present yesterday at his funeral, which we should have certainly done had we been informed in time. May I also suggest that you, Sir, should convey to the family of the deceased our sincere sympathy with them in their bereavement?

Mr. C. S. Ranga Iyer(Rohilkund and Kumaon Divisions: Non-Muhammadan Rural): Sir, I rise to associate myself and my Party with all the sentiments that have fallen from the lips of the Honourable the Leaders of the House and of the Independent Party. When Mr. Misra came to my room in the Cecil Hotel a week ago, with the manuscript of his new book, "The History of Ancient Utkal", which he wanted me to revise, I little knew that I would be standing on the floor of the House to speak out my feelings about the passing away of a good man and true, or that I would have been going yesterday to Sanjauli to stand by the funeral pyre amidst pouring rain. He was one of those good men who pleased those with whom he came in contact. His good manners, his sweet temper and his great sense of humour always made him very likeable, always made him the best friend in politics in which friends are few. He was one of the pioneers of the new Orissa movement, and, as the Leader of the House has truly said, the great tragedy in his passing away at this time lies in the fact that he did not have the privilege of enjoying the fruit of his labours. Sir, we express our deep regrets here and our deepest sympathies for the bereaved family.

Mr. Jagan Nath Aggarwal(Jullundur Division: Non-Muhammadan): Sir, on behalf of my friends in this part of the House I wish to associate myself with all that has fallen from the previous speakers. It is matter of great regret that Mr. Misra, whose last appearance we all remember in this House on the non-official day when he moved the Resolution relating to the Military Academy, was suffering from blood pressure. We all remember the painful experience we had that day. It was with great difficulty and simply out of a sense of duty that he did not flinch from moving that Resolution – it was with difficulty indeed that he could manage to carry out his wish and we all felt that there was really something wrong with him; but he stuck to his duty to the last and it is with deep regret that we learnt rather late in the day yesterday that he had passed away. In fact this last event in his life has proved what we all knew so well during the years we had been in contact with him, that he cared much for his duty rather than his own comfort or convenience. As has been truly said by the Leader of the House, he did not live long enough to see the fruition of his endeavours in the creation of an independent Orissa province. He was, as we all know, a kind and unassuming figure who made more friends than enemies, and there is hardly a man in this House or outside who can say that on any occasion Mr. Misra had spoken ill of anybody or had done harm to any one. We will all miss him, and I would request you, Sir, to convey to his family the sentiments of all of us that we share their loss and to express our deep sense of sorrow and regret at his tragic death on this occasion.

Mr. N. N. Ankalesaria(Bombay Northern Division: Non-Muhammadan Rural): Mr. President, it is a great pity that at the very fag end the even tenor of this Session should have been marred by the tragedy of Mr. Misra's death. To every one of us death must come sooner or later; to Mr. Misra death has come in somewhat painful circumstances, removed as he was far away from his home and family and from his community of which he was a very prominent and very honoured member. To most Members of this House, who did not know Mr. Misra well, he might have appeared a somewhat perplexing personality; but to those who knew Mr. Misra intimately, as I claim to have done, Mr. Misra was possessed of very good qualities of head and heart. He was a thoroughly good natured man, simple hearted, almost like a child, pleased with everybody and almost incapable of being displeased with anybody. He was well versed in Hindu philosophy and Hindu religion, and it may be of interest to know that he was actually engaged in writing a work on the comparative History of Religions at the time of his death. He was a barrister, and that he was held in high esteem by his community and his province is shown by the fact that he was an elected Member in the first Assembly and that he lost the election in the second Assembly against the Swarajist candidate only by one vote. Sir, in spite of his conservatism in religious matters, he had very progressive ideas, and he was the first man in his community to cross black waters. I have nothing to add except to say that I join in the tribute of respect for our departed colleague and in the request to you to convey our sympathy and condolence to his bereaved family.

Sir Leslie Hudson(Bombay: European): Sir, on behalf of myself and my party, I wish to add my tribute to the memory of our late fellow Member, Mr. Misra, and to associate myself with the remarks which have fallen from the Honourable the Leader of the House and other Honourable Members in regard to the regret which we all feel that he has not been spared to see the fulfilment of his life's labours and desire in the separation of Orissa. By his kindly disposition, he had endeared himself to every one of us in the House, and we shall all miss him.

Nawab Major Malik Talib Mehdi Khan(North Punjab: Muhammadan): Sir, I associate myself on my own and my party's behalf with what has been said by previous speakers. I well remember the day when I first came to this House, Mr. Misra asked me to help him in his scheme for the separation of Orissa and I promised to do so. He had a very quiet and unassuming nature and his qualities of head and heart were very great. Again, sir, after he made his last speech the other day, on Indianisation of Army, he came out of the House and told me that he could not very well render his speech on account of illness which was afflicting him that day. It is pity that he has not been spared to see his pet scheme of separation of Orissa fructifying and to take part in the new order of things to be brought about by it. Sir, we all mourn the loss of a friend who was a jewel covered with slugged stone. Sir, I also request you to convey our sympathy and condolence to his bereaved family.

Mr. Gaya Prasad Singh(Muzaffarpur cum Champaran: Non-Muhammadan): Sir, as one coming from the province of Bihar and Orissa, I should like to associate myself with all that has been said by the Honourable the Leader of the House, by other Honourable Members. I remember very well the last illness of Mr. Misra, and when he was suffering from high blood pressure I told him repeatedly to leave Simla and to go down. I even asked my friend, Dr. Dalal, to give him the advice to leave Simla, which Dr. Dalal did; but his consciousness of duty kept him in Simla and has died practically in harness. Sir, Mr. Misra was a man of very amiable disposition and of loving nature; he was very regular in attendance at the meetings, a lesson which many of us might learn. I would request you, Sir, to convey to the members of the bereaved family an expression of our sincere sorrow and regret at his death under circumstances under which it has taken place in Simla far away from his family members.

Maulavi Muhammad Shafee Daoodi(Tirhut Division : Muhammadan): Sir, it is a really irreparable loss that Orissa has suffered. I know how the people of Orissa had confidence in Mr. Misra and his labours to bring about the separation of Orissa. He did his very best, and it is a pity that he has not been spared to see fruition of his labours. I feel very much that I was not able to be present at the funeral pyre, for, had I known about his death a little earlier yesterday, I would have tried to be present in spite of my indisposition. Sir, I wish to associate myself with every word that has fallen from the previous speakers.

Mr. Bhupat Sing(Bihar and Orissa; Landholders): Sir, being a representative of Bihar and Orissa, I beg to associate myself with all the remarks which have fallen from the previous speakers. Sir, Mr. Misra comes from a very respectable Brahmin family of Orissa, and the people of the new proposed province of Orissa owe a deep debt of gratitude to him for all that he has done for the creation of a separate Province. He was a very noble soul, and a typical Brahmin with the ideals of plain living and high thinking. I sincerely feel sorry that he could not see the fruition of his work, which he had almost completed on ancient history and culture of Orissa; which dates many centuries back and which was his life's ambition. He was also a master of Oriya language. Sir, I express my heartfelt condolence to Mrs. Misra and the bereaved family.

Mr. President (The Honourable Sir Sanmukham Chetty): I wish to associate the Chair with the tribute that has been paid to the memory of our late colleague, Mr. B. N. Misra, who was so well loved by all parts of the House. His devotion to duty, of which his regular attendance in this House was an ample proof, may serve as an example to all of us. It shall be my duty to convey to the members of the bereaved family our sense of loss and sympathy on this occasion.

END OF AN ERA

Passing Away of Barrister Biswanath Misra

September 19 1933. It was the auspicious day of "Mahalaya." Ailing and going through both mental and physical stress and strain for some times past, a disturbed Biswanath went for his showers to the bathroom in the morning and fell down dead with a massive cardiac infarction in distant Shimla, far away from his home at Cuttack and far away from his near and dear ones.

The sad and sudden demise of the great patriot and passionate Orissa-lover was a great shock to the country, as a whole and to the policy makers in England too.

The same evening his cremation was held at the Sanjauli Crematorium of Shimla. Some of the eminent persons of the time attended to the funeral ceremony, despite heavy downpours. The nationally known personalities who attended the funeral were Kumar Gupteswar Prasad, Bhai Paramanand Bahadur, D. Dutt, Tarak Paul, Abdul Matin Chaudhury, Dr. Ziauddin, and many others.

Obituaries Published

Obituaries were published in abundance in almost all the newspapers of the country. A few of them have been included here for perusal.

The Oriya Daily "ASHA," 25. 09. 1933

"Srijukta Barrister Biswanath Misra is no more. He has lost his life on last 19th morning at Shimla due to a massive cardiac arrest. Srijukta Misra, a few days back, had gone in a deputation with the problem of Orissa to meet the Viceroy. He had joined the separate Orissa movement since long. In his sad demise, we join in condolence with the bereaved family and extend our deepest grief to the surviving members.

"New Orissa" 21. 09. 1933

In the editorial of this magazine brought out from Berhampur, it was published under the title:

Utkal's Loss

"It is with feelings of profound sorrow that we record the death in Simla of Mr. Biswanath Misra, Bar-at-Law, one of the two representatives of Orissa in the Indian Legislative Assembly. The news of this sudden demise of heart failure has come as a shock to Utkal as a whole and to us in particularly. It was only last month, prior to his departure for Simla that he was with us and with his usual geniality was discussing the problems of Orissa and India. He was hale and hearty then. He was so even the day before the actual end. Hence the shock was greater. The Late Mr. Misra belonged to an older school of politicians, who thoroughly national in his outlook, was yet not a congressman. But he did not stint support to congress activities of a constructive nature. In the Assembly he was always on the popular side and never stood for reactionarism. He was very popular with the people of Orissa and to that fact he owed his election to the Assembly more than once. He was one of the pioneers and prominent leaders, who agitated for the creation of the separate province for Orissa, which unfortunately he has not lived to see formed. He had completed a History of Orissa and was planning its publication, when death suddenly cut him off from his labour of love. It speaks volumes for his sense of duty that he died in harness. His death is great loss to Utkal and it is not exaggeration to say that people of Orissa have lost a genuine friend in him. We extend our sincere sympathy to his big family on their sudden and unexpected bereavement. May his soul rest in peace."

"The Statesman" 21. 09. 1933

Pioneer of Oriya Movement Mr. B. N. Misra Dead

Simla

– September – 19

Mr. B. N. Misra, a Member of the Assembly representing an Orissa non mohammadan constituency, died of heart failure at the Hindu Hotel this morning. He was in his seat at yesterday's sitting of the Assembly.

Mr. Misra was a Barrister of Gray's Inn and Pioneer of the movement for the creation of a separate province of Orissa. In his early days in England he devoted much time and patience to studying in British Museum the History of Oriya people and their present territory and the results of this prolonged researches are embodied in a book, 'A Short HIstory of Ancient Utkal' which he was hotting to publish very soon.

As a Barrister he practiced successively in Calcutta, Patna and Cuttack but for the past two or three years, the complaint, which brought about his death compelled him to stay away from the courts. His home was in Cuttack where he leaves his widow, five sons and four daughters.

He entered the Assembly when he won the seat vacated by Pandit Nilakantha Das, the congress man in 1930. At first he was a frequent and humorous Speaker, but ill health had dogged him for sometimes before his death.

"Advance" 21. 09. 1933

The "Advance" from Calcutta published through United Press, "Mr. Misra was ailing with hyper tension since last few days; but his end would come so suddenly, nobody had ever expected. Even he had attended to the functions of Central Legislative Assembly yesterday and this morning too, he had interacted with some of his friends."

Apart from the above newspapers and magazines, many others in different languages of the country had published their obituaries with grand eulogies about Barrister Misra on his sudden and untimely demise.

EPILOGUE

Barrister Misra was a person with a great ego; ego with regard to Oriya pride, Oriya language and Orissa as a separate state; but at the same time he was a strong nationalist in heart. On September 12, 1933 Barrister Biswanath Misra had raised the Indian Military Academy issue in the Assembly. At the time he was undergoing wrenching heartache. The reasons were many. He was extremely perturbed because of the political turmoil the country was going through then. Amidst that, the problems of unification of the segregated Oriya tracts and formation of a separate Orissa state were torturing him mentally and physically to the core. He was further disconcerted because of the differences existing amongst some of the power-loving Oriya leaders who were more concerned about their future roles in the separate state of Orissa rather than its real formation and boundary determination.

In matters of the Indian Military Academy, he could foresee the uncanny scheme of the Britishers. Despite, their negating, Barrister Biswanath's clairvoyance could tell him that sooner than later the Indian Government would pass an ordinance and differentiate the white British officers by putting them in a separate cadre. As a result of it, Indian officers would not be able to command the white soldiers. Even in spite of seniority, an Indian military officer would not be allowed to be promoted above a white British Officer.

Because of his apprehensions, despite malaise and severe heart conditions, he was forced to stand up and raise the issue on the floor of the Assembly. It was vehemently denied then by the Government spokespersons; but interestingly, ten months after the death of Barrister Biswanath, in July-August session of 1934, the British Indian Government brought out a bill in that regard and got it passed in the Indian Legislative Assembly amidst loud protests and furore.

Barrister Misra's nationalistic character could clearly be observed from his commitment to Mahatma Gandhi in noncooperation movement, Salt Taxation Bill protest, his actions in the Legislative Assembly in matters of hanging of Bhagat Singh, the Ottawa Agreement, the illogical disparity of salary between the lower ranked and the higher ranked employees of British Government in India, the irrational travelling allowances and facilities claimed by the British Indian Officials, misuse of the term "Yours Obediently", Indian Press Bill, Appointment of Chief Justices of High Courts, Bengal Suppression of Terrorists Outrages Act, 1932, etc., and finally, the Indian Military Academy Bill.

His love for Orissa and Oriya language needs no reiteration. It was just unfathomable and unparalleled. No wonder, he was "Mr. Orissa". His active participation in the conventions of Utkal Sammilani to arouse the Oriya pride in the populace across the Oriya speaking tracts needs no mention. His tremendous efforts to raise the level of higher education in Orissa are undoubtedly mention-worthy. The contributions he has made to bring engineering, and above all, law education to Orissa can never be forgotten. The activities he carried out all his life for the unification of segregated Oriya-speaking tracts and formation of a separate Orissa state probably bear no parallel in the history of Orissa. Going through the obituary memorials offered in the Central Legislative Assembly after his sad and untimely demise, this claim can be safely vouched for. His articles in those regards, published in the various national and local dailies, speak volumes for his dedication, devotion and commitment towards the cause of Orissa. His involvement in the creation of Phillip-Duff Committee for earmarking the boundary of Orissa basing on the opinions of the estranged Oriya-speaking people living in the sequestered tracts was a path-breaking event for the time. His comment "Divide et Impera" on the floor of the Central Legislative Assembly accusing the Government in context with the O'Donnel Committee Report for inclusion of different places and areas in the new state of Orissa had created a lot of outcry at the time. He was recklessly courageous to pass extremely unpleasant comments on the British rule and rulers without fear or phobia. The most critical act he had undertaken during the period was meeting Lord Simon of Simon Commission, the most despised character of the time nationally, to apprise him of the desirability of a separate state for Orissa, of which Simon was convinced to some extent and had given a favorable view in his report.

GALLERY

BARRISTER BISWANATH MISRA1

MEETING KING GEORGE V ASKING'S COUNSEL2

CENTRAL LEGISLATIVE ASSEMBLY MEMBERBARRISTER BISWANATH MISRA 3

BISWANATH WITH WIFE KAMALA DEVI4

Sitting (Left to right) : 1. Mr. R.N. Misra, 2. Mr. L. Panigrahi, 3. Raja of Madhupur, 4. Raja of Parala Khemundi, 5. Mr. B. Das, 6. Mr. M.S. Panigrahi, 7. Mr. B.N. Misra (Barrister). Standing (Left to Right) : 1. Mr. G.B. Dutta, 2. Mr. S.S. Gantayat, 3. Mr. J.N. Acharya, 4. Mr. L.N. Sahoo, 5. Mr. G.C. Samantaray. Oriya Deputation - Simla Date 17.9.1932

ORIYA DEPUTATION TO MEET THE VICEROY5

BARRISTER BISWANATH ALONG WITH MEMBERS OF 4THCENTRAL LEGISLATIVE ASSEMBLY ON MARCH 17th, 19326

DOCUMENTS

Aug. 10   FRANK HILL GASKELL, formerly a commissioned officer and lately a solicitor, of 17 How
          Gardens, Cardiff, (31), second son of Joseph G., of Penhill, Cardiff, Glam., manage
          public companies. Called 17 Nov., 1910.

     22   JOHN EVERARD HOME MYLNE, undergraduate of Queen's College, Oxford, of Woodf
          Bristol Road, Weston-super-Mare, (10), eldest and only son of William John Home M.
          Weston-super-Mare, Somerset, M.A., of Queen's College, Oxford, gent. Called 24 J
          1914.

Sep. 28   MAUNG KYA GAING, pleader, of 113 Sutherland Avenue, W., (29), eldest son of U Y
          of Ohne, Pegu district, Burma, merchant. Called 4 June, 1913.

     29   ISHWAR SINGH, of Kohat, N.W.F. Province, India, and of 42 Sinclair Road, W. Kensing
          (29½), youngest son of Bhai Kaka S., of Kohat, India, cloth merchant, decd. Ca
          4 June, 1913.

Oct. 5   TSZ FUNG LAM, of Hong Kong, and of 40 Portland Place, W., (32), first son of Pak Ping
          of Hong Kong, gent. Called 17 Nov., 1915.

     14   SYED MOHOMMAD AHMAD, of Takeya, district Rae Bareli, India, and of 23 Calthorpe St
          Gray's Inn Road, W.C., (22), only son of Syed Mohommad Aminuddin, of Takeya,
          Bareli, Oudh, India, landholder. Called 28 April, 1915.

     ,,   BANSI DHAR KAPOOR, of Meerut, United Provinces and Oudh, India, and of 6 St. Luke's R
          Bayswater, W., (24 and 1 month), only son of Babu Seeta Ram, of Meerut, In
          sub-overseer, district board. Called 17 Nov., 1914.

     ,,   JAMES STANLEY RAE, barrister of the Bahamas, of Nassau, New Providence, Bahamas, (
          eldest son of James Maclure R., of Nassau, stipendiary and circuit magistrate. Ca
          27 Jan., 1919.

     ,,   SYED HASSAN SHAH, of Lahore, Punjab, India, and of 152 Holland Road, Kensington,
          (20), second son of S. Mohammad S., of Lahore, Punjab, India, pleader.

     ,,   SURENDRA NARAYAN RAY, of Calcutta, India, and of 28 South Hill Park, Hampstead, (
          second son of Babu Kali Narayan R., of Calcutta, Bengal, general manager of all
          zemindary estates under the Administrator General of Bengal. Called 4 June, 1913.

     ,,   PANNA LAL BHARGAVA, of Damoh, Central Provinces, India, and of 29 Poplar Grove, V
          Kensington Park, W., (19), fifth son of M. Badri Prasad B., of Damoh, Central Provin
          India, retired pleader. Called 17 Nov., 1913.

     ,, | VALLABHAI JAVERBHAI PATEL, pleader, of Gujrat, India, and of 23 Aldridge Vi
          | Bayswater, (34), fourth son of Javerbhai Galabhai, of Gujrat, India, landlord. Ca
          | 27 Jan., 1913.

     ,,   SYED MOHAMMAD, of Patna, India, and of 10 Lowther Mansions, Barnes, S.W., (18½),
          son of Syed Mohibbul Hakk, of Patna, Bengal, landholder. Called 17 Nov., 1913.

     ,,   SYED BASHIRUDDIN, of Neora, India, (25½), second son of the Hon. Syed Zahiruddin,
          Neora, Patna, Bengal, landholder. Called 4 June, 1913.

     15   SUNDAR DASS PAHWA, of Mofa, dist. Ferozepore, and of 26 Cromwell Road, S.W., (
          second son of L. Nanak Chand, of Mofa, Punjab, India, government servant.

     ,,   OSWALD PIROW, of Potchefstroom, Transvaal, Union of South Africa, (20), elder son of
          Ferdinand P., of Potchefstroom, Transvaal, Union of South Africa, doctor of medic
          Called 4 June, 1913.

     ,,   RAJ GOPAL REDY, of Hyderabad, Deccan, and of 198 Holland Road, W., (23), second so
          C. Krishna R., of Hyderabad, Deccan, India, zamindar. Called 17 May, 1916.

     ,,   HABIB ASHRAF, of Lucknow, and of 35 Westmoreland Road, Bayswater, W., (19 an
          months), first son of Md. Sultan A., of Lucknow, India, landed proprietor. Called 4 J
          1913.

     17   ALEC MICHAEL VAS, of Karachi, India, and of 82 Baron's Court Road, W., (21), third so
          A—— C—— V., of Karachi, India, government pensioner.

     ,,   DAVI DIAL SINGH, of Heshiarpur, Punjab, India, and of 70 West Side, Clapham Comn
          S.W., (27), eldest son of Lallu Heru Ram, of Heshiarpur, Punjab, pleader. Called 4 J
          1913.

     ,,   GOVIND PRASAD MATHUR, of Ajmer, Rajputana, and of 22 Leamington Road Villas, Lon
          W., (23), only son of L. Durga Prasada, of Ajmer, Rajputana, India, deputy magistr
          Beawar. Called 4 June, 1913.

MIDDLETEMPLE   ADMISSION   REGISTER
MENTIONING VALLABHAI PATEL 7

TO THE MIDDLE TEMPLE

Nov. 17   JAGAN NATH PURI, of Ghartal, Sialkot, India, and of 47 Linden Gardens, Chiswick, (11 7 months), first son of L. Ladha Mal P., of Ghartal, Sialkot, Punjab, India, landowner, banker. Called 17 Nov., 1913.

,,   SRISH CHANDER GOHO, of Calcutta, India, and of St. Peter's College, Cambridge, eldest son of Satya Charan G., of 66/1 Musjeed Baree Street, Calcutta. Called 26 Jan.,

,,   BISMA NATH MISRA, pleader, of Aska Ganjam District, Madras, (31), fourth son of Kula M., of Aska, India, landholder. Called 27 Jan., 1913.

18   SIDNEY HENRY WEST, clerk in H.M. Office of Works, of 148 Hermitage Road, Finsbury N., (25), second son of William W., of 148 Hermitage Road, Finsbury Park, gent.

,,   NAWAB DIN[1], of Armstrong College, Newcastle-on-Tyne, and of Sialkote, Punjab, I (22 and 7 months), eldest son of Sh. Pir Mahi, of Sialkote, Punjab, merchant and h proprietor. Called 4 June, 1913.

,,   MUHAMMAD ALI RAZA, of Madras, India, and of 11 Sutherland Avenue, Maida Vale, (19), second son of Khan Bahadur Muhammad Ghulam R., of Madras, superintende Government Post Office. Called 26 Jan., 1914.

,,   TYAB ALI AKBAR, of Bombay, and of 12 Lathbury Road, Oxford, (18), only son of Ali A Bombay, superintending engineer, P.W.D. Called 17 Nov., 1913.

,,   ROBERT STRUTHERS, of 30 Millar Crescent Morningside, Edinburgh, (24), only son o late Robert S., of Chapelton, Hamilton, Lanarks., Scotland. Called 17 Nov., 1914.

,,   RAMCHAND SAHIJRAM MALKANI, of Hyderabad, Sind, India, and of 21 Cromwell R South Kensington, (27), eldest son of Diwan Sahijram Tahibram, of Hyderabad, S zemindar.

,,   PRATAP SITARAM PANDIT, of Rajkot, India, and of 11 Uxbridge Road, Ealing, W., first son of Sitaram N;arayan; P., of Rajkot, India, barrister-at-law, Middle Temple. C in absence 14 May, 1919.

19   THOMAS WILLIAM DAVID, of Keble College, Oxford, and of 126 Newport Road, Car (19), third son of George D., of 126 Newport Road, Cardiff, Clam., solicitor.

,,   MAZHERUDDIN AHMED, of Paragalpur, Chittagong, and of 118 Shepherd's Bush Road, (21), fifth son of Moulvi Ashanullah C., of Paragalpur, Chittagong, Bengal, landhol Called 4 June, 1913.

,,   DEWAN NARINJAN DAS, of Sialkote, Punjab, India, and of 95 Iffley Road, Hammersmith, (20), only son of Dewan Charan D., of Sialkote, pleader. Called 16 April, 1913.

,,   SYED QADEER HASAN, of Fyzabad, United Provinces, India, and of the University Un Edinburgh, (18), eldest son of Syed Muneer H., of Fyzabad, United Provinces, In taluqdar. Called 24 June, 1914.

,,   HENRY BIRT LONGHURST, of Trinity College, Cambridge, (19), only son of Henry B— of 80 Seymour Street, W., London, and of the Middle Temple, barrister-at-law.

,,   LAL MOHUN VIVIAN BOSE, of Pembroke College, Cambridge, (19), only son of Lalit Mo B., of Bombay Presidency, India, Indian public works. Called 4 June, 1913.

,,   IQHAL SINGH UBERAI, of the University of Leeds, and of Sialkot City, India, (19), eldest of Jhanda Singh U., of Sialkot City, India, merchant.

,,   MOHAMED SARFRAZ ALI, of Fyzabab, Oudh, India, and of 151 Iffley Road, Oxford, (18 7 months), eldest son of M. Imtiar A., of Fyzabad, Oudh, India, pleader Called 24 N 1914.

,,   MOHAMED YUSUF, of Raj Nandgaon State, Central Provinces, India, and of Downing Colle Cambridge, (21 and 2 months), only son of Dawood Sheruf, of Raj Nandgaon, Cen Provinces, merchant. Called 4 June, 1913.

MIDDLETEMPLE   ADMISSION   REGISTER MENTIONING BARRISTER BISWANATH8

MIDDLE TEMPLE.

Declaration to be made by a Student Before Call to the Bar.

I, *Biswanath Misra*

being desirous of being called to the Bar by the Honourable Society of the MIDDLE TEMPLE, do hereby declare and undertake as follows:—

1.—That I am not a person in Holy Orders (or that I, being a person in Holy Orders, have not during the year next before the date of this declaration, held or performed any Clerical preferment or duty, or performed any Clerical functions, and do not intend any longer to act as a Clergyman].

2.—That I am not and have never since my admission as a Student of this Honourable Society been, and that I do no act and have never since my admission as aforesaid acted either directly or indirectly in the capacity of a Solicitor, Attorney-at-Law, Writer to the Signet, Writer of the Scotch Courts, Proctor, Notary Public, Clerk in Chancery, Parliamentary Agent, Agent in any Court original or appellate, Clerk to any Justice of the Peace, Registrar or High Bailiff of any Court, Official Provisional Assistant or Deputy Receiver or Liquidator under any Bankruptcy or Winding-up Act, Chartered or Incorporated or Professional Accountant, Land Agent, Surveyor, Patent Agent, Consulting Engineer, Clerk to any Judge, Barrister, Conveyancer, Special Pleader, or Equity Draftsman, Clerk of the Peace, or Clerk to any Officer in any Court of Justice.†

And that I do not act and have never since my admission as aforesaid acted either directly or indirectly in any capacity similar to any of those above enumerated ;

And that I have not and have never since my admission as aforesaid been and that I do not act and have never since my admission as aforesaid acted as a clerk to, nor am I, nor have I since my admission as aforesaid been in the service of any person acting in any of the above capacities or in any capacity similar thereto† (except as a Pupil of Mr. or Messrs.

of   from   19

to   19   ) : *

And that I do not hold and have never since my admission as aforesaid held any appointment which involves the performance of duties analogous to those of a Clerk to any Officer in any Court of Justice :†

And that I am not and have never since my admission as aforesaid been engaged in trade or an undischarged bankrupt.

3.—That if called to the Bar and so long as I remain a Barrister I will not in this country or elsewhere except so far as may be there permitted or recognised be or act directly or indirectly in the capacity of a Solicitor, Attorney-at-Law, Writer to the Signet, Writer of the Scotch Courts, Proctor, Notary Public, Clerk in Chancery, Parliamentary Agent, Agent in any Court original or appellate, Chartered Incorporated or Professional Accountant, Patent Agent, Clerk to any Judge Barrister Conveyancer Special Pleader or Equity Draftsman, Clerk to any Clerk of the Peace, or Clerk to any Officer in any Court of Justice, or in any similar capacity, or hold any appointment which involves the performance of Duties analogous to those of a Clerk to any Officer of any Court of Justice, and that so long as I am in practice as a Barrister I will not in this country or elsewhere except so far as may be there permitted or recognised be or act in the capacity of a Registrar or High Bailiff of any Court, Official Provisional Assistant, or Deputy Receiver, or Liquidator under any Bankruptcy or Winding-up Act, Land Agent, Surveyor, Consulting Engineer, Town Clerk, Clerk of the Peace, Clerk to any Justice of the Peace, Clerk to a Board of Guardians or Overseers, or Clerk in the Office of a County Council, nor will I hold any similar office, nor be nor act as a Clerk to, or in the service of any person acting in any of the capacities last above enumerated or in any capacity similar thereto.

Dated this   *7th* day of *January*   19*13*

(Signature)   *BNmisra*

* State name, address and profession or calling of the person or persons, firm or firms, whose pupil the Declarant was, and the period or periods for which he was such pupil.

† Where Regulation 3 has been held not to apply insert here " otherwise than as," &c.

PROPOSAL FOR THE BAR.

I have seen Mr. *Biswanath Misra* and have satisfied myself that he is a fit and proper person to be called to the Bar, and I intend to propose him for Call accordingly, in ______*Hilary*______ Term.

J Blake Odgers BENCHER.

This Form must be signed and sent to the Under Treasurer, Middle Temple, before the *14 Jan*

DECLARATION BEFORE CALL TO THE BAR9

For now, I can report that according to our admissions registered (available online at http://www.middletemple.org.uk/library-and-archive/archive-information-and-contacts/register-of-admissions) he was admitted on 17th November 1910, and Called to the Bar on 27th January 1913.

It may also be interesting to note that he was Called on the same day as Vallabhbhai Patel.

I hope these are interesting and useful, and wish you good luck with the celebrations tomorrow. Please let me know if you have any further questions about Misra.

BARNABY BRYAN

ASSISTANT ARCHIVIST

Ashley Building, Middle Temple Lane, London EC4Y 9BT

MAIL CORRESPONDENCE WITH MIDDLE TEMPLE ARCHIVE10

REFERENCES

1.   "Jati Prana Sindhura Aadya Taranga" – Late Sri Manmohan MIsra

2.   "Odisha Itihasara Banhi Purusha – Utkal Ratna Barrister Biswanath Misra" – Surjya Kumar Misra

3.   "Utkal Sammilani Prastab Sangraha" – Debendra Kumar Dash

4.   "Bichhinnanchalara Daradi Bandhu – Utkal Ratna Barrister Biswanath Misra" – Surjya kumar Misra

5.   "Orissa Review" August 2008, - Sridhar Charan Sahoo

6.   The Oriya Daily "ASHA"

7.   www.middletemple.org.uk

8.   Barnaby Bryan, Assistant Archivist, Ashley Building, Middle Temple Lane, London EC4Y 9BT

9.   Speeches in 1st, 3rd and 4th Central Legislative Assembly, Indian Parliament Library

www.ingramcontent.com/pod-product-compliance
Lightning Source LLC
LaVergne TN
LVHW041134180726
843490LV00005B/1405